The Joan Palevsky Imprint in Classical Literature

In honor of beloved Virgil—

"O degli altri poeti onore e lume . . ."

—Dante, *Inferno*

The publisher and the University of California Press Foundation gratefully acknowledge the generous support of the Joan Palevsky Endowment Fund in Literature in Translation.

Texts from the Middle

Texts from the Middle

Documents from the Mediterranean World, 650–1650

Edited by THOMAS E. BURMAN, BRIAN A. CATLOS,
and MARK D. MEYERSON

UNIVERSITY OF CALIFORNIA PRESS

University of California Press
Oakland, California

© 2022 by The Regents of the University of California

Library of Congress Cataloging-in-Publication Data

Names: Burman, Thomas E., editor. | Catlos, Brian A., editor. | Meyerson, Mark D., editor.
Title: Texts from the middle : documents from the Mediterranean world, 650–1650 / edited by
  Thomas E. Burman, Brian A. Catlos, and Mark D. Meyerson. Other titles: Documents from the
  Mediterranean world, 650–1650
Description: Oakland, California : University of California Press, [2022] | Includes bibliographical references
  and index.
Identifiers: LCCN 2021054526 (print) | LCCN 2021054527 (ebook) | ISBN 9780520296534 (paperback) |
  ISBN 9780520969018 (ebook)
Subjects: LCSH: Mediterranean Region—History—476–1517—Sources. | Mediterranean Region—
  History—1517–1789—Sources. | BISAC: HISTORY / Europe / Medieval | HISTORY / Europe / Great Britain /
  Middle Ages (449–1066)
Classification: LCC DE94 .T49 2022 (print) | LCC DE94 (ebook) | DDC 909/.09822—dc23/eng/20211202
LC record available at https://lccn.loc.gov/2021054526
LC ebook record available at https://lccn.loc.gov/2021054527

Manufactured in the United States of America

26 25 24 23 22
10 9 8 7 6 5 4 3 2 1

To the memory of J. N. Hillgarth (1929–2020)

On, si tu, fil, est amador de prudencia, ages saviea e sciencia, per la qual vules e sapies concordar prudencia e cautela, maestria, sens falsia e engan.

Therefore, son, if you are a lover of prudence, have wisdom and knowledge, through which you desire and know how to bring prudence and precaution, mastery, into concordance, without falseness and deceit.

—RAMON LLULL, *DOCTRINA PUERIL*

CONTENTS

TEXTS

ACKNOWLEDGMENTS

This textbook and reader project took shape over a long eight years of collaboration and we, the authors, received indispensable feedback, suggestions, and help from so many people that we have undoubtedly lost track of all of them. Apologies to those who contributed but have been overlooked in this list. You know who you are, and we want you to know we are grateful.

Thanks are due to the Mediterranean Seminar, notably, codirector Sharon Kinoshita (University of California, Santa Cruz) and the many participants of the seminar workshops who read and provided feedback on drafts of the textbook and accompanying document reader. Thanks particularly to the University of Colorado Boulder, the Medieval Institute at Notre Dame, the University of Toronto, and the Marco Institute at the University of Tennessee, Knoxville for funding workshops at which we discussed and refined the manuscript.

Individuals who we would like to thank include (in alphabetical order): Hussein Abdulsater (University of Notre Dame), Fred Astren (San Francisco State), Mohammad Ballan (SUNY Stony Brook), David Bocquelet, Remie Constable (of fond memory, late of the University of Notre Dame), John Dagenais (University of California, Los Angeles), Abigail Firey (University of Kentucky), Oren Falk (Cornell University), Alexandra Garnhart Bushakra (University of Tennessee, Knoxville), Claire Gilbert (Saint Louis University), William Granara (Harvard University), Dan Green (POM), Mayte Green-Mercado (Rutgers University), Daniel Gullo (Hill Museum and Manuscript Library), Harvey Hames (Ben Gurion University of the Negev), Demetrios Harper (Holy Trinity Orthodox Seminary), Peregrine Horden (Oxford University), Spencer Hunt (University of Notre Dame), Sharon Kinoshita (University of California, Santa Cruz), Sergio La Porta (Fresno State), Danny Lasker (Ben Gurion University of the Negev), Mahan Mirza (University of Notre Dame), Lee Mordichai (Hebrew University of Jerusalem), Stephen Ogden (University of Notre Dame), Karen Pinto (Loyola University, Maryland), Amy Remensnyder (Brown University), Gabriel Reynolds (University of Notre Dame), Denis Robichaud (University of Notre Dame), Teo Ruiz (University of California, Los Angeles), Cana Short (University of Notre Dame), Bogdan Smarandache

(University of Toronto), Stefan Statchev (Arizona State University), David Wacks (University of Oregon), Lydia Walker (University of Tennessee, Knoxville), Kenneth Baxter Wolf (Pomona College), Fariba Zarinebaf (University of California, Riverside), Nina Zhiri (University of California, San Diego).

It was Traci Crowell (then of Bedford/St. Martin's) who kickstarted this project, when she originally approached us to publish a Mediterranean textbook, at the precise moment that we had begun to discuss among ourselves. Several years later the University of California Press took on the project and brought it to completion, thanks to Lyn Uhl, who commissioned it, and Eric Schmidt and Cindy Fulton, who saw it through production. Kathy Borgogno did an excellent job tracking down images and coordinating cartography, as did Marian Rogers copy-editing.

To these must be added the anonymous readers who reviewed the manuscripts at various stages of development and production both for Bedford/St. Martin's and UC Press.

Alongside those named above, Thomas E. Burman would like to thank in particular his wife, Elizabeth Raney Burman, for her constant, indeed enthusiastic, support during the many years of work on this project. Though it has been nearly thirty years since he finished graduate school, he would like to thank his doctoral supervisors at the University of Toronto, the late J. N. Hillgarth and the late George Michael Wickens, both of whom energetically encouraged him to work on a project that brought the Latin-Christian and Arab-Muslim (and Arab-Christian) worlds together. The outside reader for that dissertation was Thomas F. Glick (Boston University), who, like Hillgarth, had long been thinking about medieval Spain from a broad Mediterranean point of view, and whose pathbreaking work—and congenial friendship—have been a constant inspiration. He would also like to thank the History Department and Marco Institute at the University of Tennessee, Knoxville, and the History Department and Medieval Institute at the University of Notre Dame for their institutional support along the way, and especially his graduate students in courses on the Mediterranean. Those in a joint University of Tennessee and University of Kentucky seminar a half decade ago (taught on Zoom with his dear friend Abigail Firey) read and gave valuable feedback on the first part of the book. More recently, graduate students at Notre Dame have read earlier drafts of the whole manuscript and have provided useful comments and insights. Notre Dame faculty and graduate participants in the Religion and Pluralism in the Medieval Mediterranean working group, supported by the Medieval Institute, have been and continue to be a source of collegial learning and discussion. He thanks that group in particular for reading and commenting on the portions of the book for which he was primary author. Collaborating with Brian Catlos and Mark Meyerson on this project has been one of the great pleasures of his academic life. They have been a constant source of deeply learned insight, helpful and good-natured criticism, and deep friendship.

In addition to those named above, Brian Catlos would like to thank Núria Silleras-Fernández (University of Colorado Boulder) both for the feedback she gave on this project and for her patience in surviving yet another book project. For deep and enduring inspiration thanks are due to Thomas F. Glick (Boston University), Andrew Watson (University of Toronto), and of course the link that joins him with his collaborators, the late J. N Hillgarth (University of Toronto), to whom this book is dedicated. He is grateful to the University of Colorado, Boulder and the University of California, Santa Cruz for their support, particularly his colleagues in Religious Studies and the departments and programs at CU Boulder that support the CU Mediterranean Studies Group. Thanks are also due to the many scholars and graduate students who have taken part in the activities of the Mediterranean Seminar since 2007—encounters that have transformed and enriched his scholarly life and understanding of the premodern Mediterranean, and made this project possible. The Institució Milà i Fontanals (Consejo Superior de Investigaciones Científicas) has provided a summer research home, and a venue in Barcelona for our seminar events. Finally, he thanks his coauthors, Thomas Burman and Mark Meyerson—exemplary scholars and model collaborators—for their constancy, generosity, and support.

Mark Meyerson would like to thank, in addition to those named above, Jill Ross, Benjamin Meyerson, and Samuel Meyerson for their support and encouragement. Inspiration has come from so many scholars working in this burgeoning field of Mediterranean studies, but special acknowledgment goes to our late, great teacher, J. N. Hillgarth, to the late Frank Talmage (University of Toronto), and to Thomas F. Glick, whose work has been such a great stimulus since the 1970s. He would also like to thank colleagues in the Department of History at the University of Notre Dame, and the Department of History and Centre for Medieval Studies at the University of Toronto for giving him the freedom and encouragement to teach Mediterranean-related courses, which were once regarded as novel. The Jackman Institute for the Humanities at the University of Toronto provided a congenial environment in which to write some chapters of this book. He would also like to thank his many students, undergraduate and graduate, whose enthusiasm and questions have spurred him to explore new (to him) corners of the Mediterranean and to consider interfaith relations from new perspectives. Finally, he would like to express his gratitude to his coauthors, Thomas Burman and Brian Catlos, for their immense learning, patience, and friendship, the best companions one could have for traveling through 1,000 years of Mediterranean history.

Introduction

Although casual readers may seldom encounter them, primary sources—the texts written by people at the time of the events themselves—are the principal foundations upon which our understanding of history is built. If most of the "artifacts" that are featured in the main textbook emphasize the physical or material evidence—objects and buildings—of the premodern Mediterranean, this collection of documents focuses exclusively on textual evidence.

The cultures and societies of the medieval and early Mediterranean were both literate and literary, and the peoples who lived along its shores produced volumes of material in a whole range of languages: not only the main "canonical" languages of Latin, Greek, Arabic, and Hebrew; but also regional languages such as Coptic, Armenian, Syriac, Slavonic, and Persian; local vernaculars, whether these were Romance, Germanic, Slavic, Turkic, Berber, or Arabic-based; and linguistic "hybrids," such as Aljamiado, Ladino, and Judaeo-Arabic, written using borrowed alphabets. Moreover, being relatively urbanized and commercialized, the societies of the premodern Mediterranean were impressively literate. Unlike medieval northern Europe, where writing and manuscript production were for many centuries almost entirely in the hands of narrow religious and secular elites, and the production of records was discouraged by the scarcity and expense of writing materials, here, many people of the middle social strata as well as many slaves could read and write (or have people read and write for them). In this connected world of long- and medium-distance communication and of commerce and exchange, people from all walks of life wanted to keep records of all sorts, and the increasing plentifulness and economy of paper encouraged and enabled them to do so.

Thus, the textual record for the times and places covered in the textbook is exceptionally rich and varied, and we have tried to reflect this in our selection of sources. These include scripture and works on theology, scientific texts, works of literature—stories, songs, and poems—chronicles and histories written at the time, letters and dispatches, biographies and memoirs, business contracts, receipts, account books, trial records, and so on. Together these provide a window onto not only the aspirations and agendas of the powerful but those of people from all walks of life and conditions. At times they give us—and this is exceptional for the history of the Middle Ages—an opportunity to hear ordinary people speaking to us across the centuries in their own languages (translated here) and often with their own voices.

THIS COLLECTION

The collection itself consists of a selection of readings corresponding to each of the fifteen chapters of the textbook, with between five and seven documentary units for each chapter. These vary in length from one to several pages; some consist of one primary source excerpt, but most include selections from two or more comparable texts written in different times and places and by members of different ethno-religious communities.

Reading primary sources is crucial to the study of history, particularly when one is faced with a narrative as complex as the one presented in *The Sea in the Middle*. In order to weave together a narrative that covered a thousand years and incorporated peoples and cultures from across Europe, Africa, and western Asia, we, the authors, were obliged to leave out many interesting details and to abbreviate many complicated episodes. The document collection has given us an opportunity to address some of the gaps in coverage that necessarily appear in the main narrative. Here, for example, in the primary source excerpts, we have tried to illuminate the role of women in the premodern Mediterranean—which has been largely obscured (as is typically the case with medieval history) both by contemporary observers and (until recently) by modern historians. Similarly, the documentary passages have given us a chance to highlight other groups that are generally left out of or glossed over in the historical narrative, be these peasants or members of the urban lower classes or ethnic and religious minorities.

We have also tried to maintain a balance in terms of the main religious cultures represented here, Islam, Christianity, and Judaism, as well as the many confessions and sectarian subgroups that characterize them. Part of the message of the book is that, for all they differed, the religious cultures of the Mediterranean shared much, not only in terms of heritage and theology, but in the way they approached social, economic, and political challenges. The same can be said for the geographic origin of the texts we have chosen and the people represented therein. We have tried to maintain a balance between the various regions discussed in the book, including the western European Mediterranean (Spain, France, and Italy), Anatolia and Balkans, the Levant and Middle East, and Egypt, North Africa, and sub-Saharan Africa.

All of this has involved hard choices. The documentary and textual record that survives varies markedly from region to region, over time, and from culture to culture. Sometimes this is a function of the types of texts that were produced and the types of records that were kept, and at others by the specific works that have survived—and the suitability for those surviving records to be excerpted in short digestible bites suitable for undergraduate students in a book such as this. As a result, the balance is necessarily imperfect, and this may lead some readers to suspect that certain themes, cultures, or regions have received preferential treatment or undue emphasis.

That has not been our intention, and indeed, we have deliberately worked to ensure that the greatest variety of genres, texts, linguistic traditions, and authors are represented here. After all, one of the main thrusts of the textbook is that the Western culture that emerged out of the premodern Mediterranean was not the product of a single tradition or a single line of transmission. Rather, it emerged out of a sustained process of dialogue, exchange, conflict, and competition that played out over the course of centuries and involved the continual introduction of new technologies, commodities, ideas, and strategies originating across the region and beyond.

A consequence of this is that we, the editors, have had to make difficult decisions, often passing up an "ideal" or "classic" text in favor of one perhaps less well-known or less evocative in the name of maintaining those balances. If despite our efforts, it may seem that some regions receive preferential treatment or undue emphasis, this is not a reflection of any scholarly prejudices on our part. The Iberian Peninsula and Italy or the Muslim Middle East may appear to have an outsized presence in this reader, but this only because of the uncharacteristic quantity and variety of primary sources that these regions produced and which survived. An impressive number have been translated into English and other modern European languages (and in some cases we have done the translations ourselves). Other regions at other times, such as the pre-Ottoman Balkans, non-Muslim and non-Byzantine Anatolia and the Levant, or northwest Africa, often produced less material of less variety or of which less has survived. As editors, we have had to balance representation and inclusivity with the objectives of clearly communicating the key themes of each chapter. Thus, the texts we have selected and those we have left out should not be construed as conveying any prejudices regarding the cultures that produced them or their importance in this history we have sketched out.

HOW TO USE IT

The readings here relate to themes explored in *The Sea in the Middle*—cross-references there are provided to the relevant reader unit—and this book follows the same chapter structure as the textbook. These primary source readings are intended to provide students with the raw material for discussions of those themes. By juxtaposing analogous or similar works we hoped to highlight both the similarities and differences in the approach of the various peoples of the Mediterranean to these subjects.

Each chapter of this book begins with a short preface highlighting the major themes to be explored and providing a chronological framework for the readings. The units within the chapters each begin with a short introduction, which provides a brief contextualization of the authors and the pieces, situating them in time and space, indicating the documents' original language, noting their genre, and providing clues to the authors' identities, objectives, biases, and intended audience. Instructors and students are expected and encouraged to flesh these out with their own research and readings. The three questions or points to consider that accompany each unit are intended to provide a starting point for in-class discussion but can also provide leads for potential essays or research assignments. As often as was possible we took these excerpts from texts that have already been published in English. Thus, those working on them in greater depth should have little trouble accessing the full texts or collections they are drawn from.

It should be noted that most of the selections are adapted rather than simply excerpted from their originally published translations. We have not changed the sense or substance of these passages, but merely brought them into line with the editorial and linguistic conventions of the textbook. In some cases, passages have had to be cropped considerably in order to fit them into this format. We have tried to make any such emendations clear, but in any case, readers who wish to delve deeper should consult the source texts as they were published.

And so, we hope that this little collection will help to breathe some life into the necessarily often rather abstract narrative of the main text. In these pages you will encounter travelers, pilgrims, merchants, pirates, warriors, queens, theologians, and missionaries. You will come to face-to-face with their fears, ambitions, agendas, and desires. It is our intention that in these pages you might gain a glimpse of the sorts of individuals who populated the cosmopolitan and dynamic world of the Mediterranean from the twilight of antiquity to the dawn of modernity—people no less fascinating, frustrating, intriguing, and complex than anyone you will meet today.

PART ONE

THE HELLENO-ISLAMIC MEDITERRANEAN (650–1050 CE)

ONE

The Legacy of Empire

The era from approximately 650 to 950 saw the irruption of Islam from the Arabian peninsula and the establishment of the Umayyad Caliphate with its capital at Damascus. The Persian Empire had crumbled, Byzantium was nearly conquered, and the Latin West had splintered into a clutch of "barbarian" kingdoms. By 750 the Islamic world stretched from almost the banks of the Indus to the shores of the Atlantic, into the South of France and down along the Nile. In that year a civil war brought down the Umayyads and established the 'Abbasid Caliphate of Baghdad, heralding the so-called Golden Age of Islam. But by the early 900s Baghdad was in crisis and two rival caliphates had emerged: a Shi'i Fatimid caliphate based in Egypt, and a new Umayyad caliphate of Córdoba. Islam was now entrenched on the southern shores of the Mediterranean, but Byzantium had recovered and reconstituted under the rule of the powerful Macedonian dynasty, while the Latin West had seen the tentative emergence of a new "Roman Empire," first under the rule of Charlemagne's Frankish Carolingian dynasty, and then under the German Ottonians.

The readings in this chapter examine various aspects of these campaigns of conquest and the internal stresses these imperial powers were subject to. We see the early fracture of the Muslim community into three opposing camps: Sunni, Shi'i, and Kharijite, the efforts of a Frankish ruler to stave off a Muslim attack in France, and contemporary and near-contemporary historians grappling with the underlying dynamics of Muslim conquest and Christian resistance in Spain. But not all was interreligious conflict: Christian and Muslim powers courted each other as allies, both on the ground in Spain and across the sea from Aachen to Baghdad, and—as we see in Byzantium—conflicts and intrigues within royal courts proved no less destabilizing than outside attacks.

1.1 THE BATTLE OF SIFFIN (657 CE)

In the aftermath of the murder of the third caliph, 'Uthman ibn 'Affan (644–656), the struggle for the caliphate was waged between 'Ali ibn Abi Talib, who had the support of Iraqi Muslims, the people of Medina, and many new converts, and Mu'awiya ibn Abi Sufyan, who represented the Meccan tribal elite.[1] This came to a head in 657 at the Battle of Siffin, which took place on July 26–28 on the banks of the Euphrates near Raqqa, Syria. Fearing defeat, Mu'awiya sought to sow dissent among 'Ali's forces by calling for Muslim unity and evoking the authority and sanctity of the Qur'an—ordering his troops to affix pages from it on the ends of their spears as they assembled on the battlefield. The gambit succeeded: 'Ali's forces split, with the Kharijites ("Splitters") refusing to fight and sparking a second revolt against 'Ali. Ultimately a Kharijite would assassinate 'Ali with a blow from a poisoned sword on January 29, 661, when he was at prayer in the mosque at Kufa, Iraq. The Battle of Siffin is an early milestone in the Sunni-Shi'i schism.

a. A Pious Ruse
Arabic • ca. 800 CE • Baghdad

The Book of the Combats of Siffin *is the earliest, fully extant account of the battle, written by the Shi'i historian and collector of* hadith, *Nasr ibn Muzahim al-Minqari (d. 827/8). This passage is from the eighth part of the book, which looks at the culmination of the battle.*

Tamim ibn Hudhaym said: When we saw the dawn after the night of clamor, suddenly, like banners among the ranks of the Syrians, from the center of the corps near to the position of Mu'awiya, we saw what appeared to be copies of the Qur'an tied to poles and lances. It was most of the pages of the Book of that army. Their lances were completely tied with the Qur'an, with three lances held aloft by each of ten units. Abu Ja'far and Abu al-Tufayl said that they faced 'Ali with one hundred copies of the Qur'an, and placed two hundred copies with each wing. All in all, there were five hundred copies of the Qur'an.

Abu Ja'far said that al-Tufayl ibn Adam came to 'Ali's cavalry, and Abu Shurayh al-Judhami came to the right flank, and Riqa' ibn al-Mu'ammar came to the left, and then they cried, —O you Arabs! God, God for your women and daughters, for who will defend them from Byzantium and the people of Persia tomorrow if you die? God, God for your faith! This is the Book of God between us.

And 'Ali said [to his army], —By God, you know they want nothing of the Book! Let you [warriors] judge between us, for indeed you are the true arbiters of the revealed truth! But 'Ali's companions were divided in their positions.

The people of Syria turned and yelled out in the darkness of the night, —O you people of Iraq! Who will care for our children if you kill us all, and who will care for yours if we kill

---

1. 'Ali, Muhammad's son-in-law and cousin, reigned as caliph from 656 to 661. Mu'awiya would be the first Umayyad caliph (661–680).

you? God, only God remains. The people of Syria changed their positions and raised the pages of the Book on the heads of their lances and adorned them on their horses, and the [Iraqis] craved for that [ceasefire] to which they were called. They raised the copies of the great Damascus Mosque Qur'an, carried by ten men, crying, —O you people of Iraq! The Book of God between us!

The account of 'Amar ibn Sa'd: When the people of Syria raised the pages of the Book aloft upon their lances, calling for the judgment of the Qur'an, 'Ali (may peace be upon him), said, —Servants of God! Truly, those who seek the judgment of the Qur'an are right, but Mu'awiya, 'Amr ibn al-'Aṣ, Ibn Abi Mu'ayt, Habib ibn Maslama, and Ibn Abi Sarh are no companions of the faith nor of the Qur'an. I know them better than you. I was their companion man and boy, and they were evil boys, and they are evil men. They may use the word —truth [to advance their interests], but that which they wish by its use is error. By God, they did not raise them without knowing what is in it; it is a stratagem, a deception, a trick!

Those who became [Kharijites] thereafter went to 'Ali with their swords upon their shoulders, called him by his name, but not —Commander of the Faithful, and said, —O 'Ali, command the people here to answer the Book of God when you are called to it, and if you do not we will kill you as we killed Ibn 'Affan. By God, we will do this if you do not answer.

'Ali said, —Woe unto you! I am the first one to call for obeisance to the Book of God, and the first to answer such a call. I am not free in my faith to refuse a call to the Book of God. But I am fighting them, and our hands are guided by the wisdom of the Qur'an. They have already disobeyed the command of God in this matter, rejected his unity, denied his Book. I have now told you that they intend to dupe you. They call you to deception.

To Consider

1. Why would Mu'awiya choose to place written pages of the Qur'an on his soldiers' spears?

2. For the author, who are the "good guys" and who are the "bad guys," and how does he distinguish them?

3. What does the passage reveal about the relationship between political authority and that of the Qur'an in the early caliphate?

Adapted from

a. Hagler, Aaron M. "The Echoes of Fitna: Developing Historiographical Interpretations of the Battle of Siffin." PhD diss., University of Pennsylvania, 2011. Pp. 70–71.

1.2 THE BATTLE OF TOURS (732 CE)

In 732 the ever-thinner Muslim forces that had subdued what is now Spain and southwestern France turned north to launch a raid on the rich church of St. Martin at Tours. About thirty miles southwest of the town Frankish forces under command of the palace mayor, Charles Martel ("the Hammer"), destroyed the raiding party, killing its leader, 'Abd al-Rahman al-Ghafiqi, the governor of al-Andalus.[2] In the aftermath, the Arab forces withdrew south, settling the frontier of their dominions just south of the Pyrenees in the decades that followed. In 737 Charles took control of the Frankish kingdom with the blessing of Pope Gregory III (731–741); his son, Pepin the Short (751–678), would rule it as king (768–814), succeeded by his son, Charles (Charlemagne), who took the title "Emperor of the Romans" in 800. Sporadic raiding continued into northern Europe from bases along the coast of southern France until the attack on St. Gall in Switzerland in 954.

The battle was mentioned in both Christian and Muslim sources. Arabic sources prior to the eleventh century neither name the battle nor provide a location.

a. A Latin Account of the Battle
Latin • ca. 754 CE • Toledo [?]

The Latin account here is from the so-called Chronicle of 754 *or* Mozarabic Chronicle, *which was written in al-Andalus by an anonymous cleric sometime after 754. Like earlier Visigothic chronicles, it follows events in Byzantium and Iberia. The author, well versed in Islamic history, avoids a polemical tone, perhaps in part because he is a Christian living under Muslim rule.*

Then 'Abd al-Rahman, seeing the land filled with the multitude of his army, cut through the rocky mountains of the Basques so that, crossing the plains, he might invade the lands of the Franks. . . . While 'Abd al-Rahman was pursuing the general Eudes, he decided to despoil the church of Tours by destroying its palaces and burning its churches.[3] There he confronted the consul of Austrasia[4] by the name of Charles [Martel], a man who had proved himself a warrior from his youth and an expert in things military, who had been summoned by Eudes. After each side had tormented the other for almost seven days with raids, they finally prepared their battle lines and fought fiercely. The northern peoples remained immobile like a wall, holding together like a glacier in the cold regions, and in the blink of an eye annihilated the Arabs with the sword. The people of Austrasia, greater in number of soldiers and formidably armed, killed the king 'Abd al-Rahman, when they found him, striking him on the chest. But suddenly, within sight of the countless tents of the Arabs, the Franks despicably put up their swords, saving themselves to fight the next day since night had fallen during the battle. Rising from their own camp at dawn, the Europeans saw the tents of the Arabs all arranged along with their canopies, just as the camp had been set up

---

2. The palace mayor was the head of the royal household. During the reign of a weak king, the palace mayor might wield the real power.

3. Eudes (or Odo), Duke of Aquitaine (d. 735), sometimes allied with the Frankish kingdom and sometimes with the Muslim forces against the Franks. In 721 he had defeated a Muslim army that was besieging his capital, Toulouse.

4. The name of the Merovingian Frankish kingdom.

before. . . .[5] They sent scouts to reconnoiter and discovered that all of the troops of the Ishmaelites had left. They had all fled silently by night in tight formation, returning to their own country. . . . Having no intention of pursuing the Saracens, they took the spoils and the booty—which they divided fairly amongst themselves—back to their country and were overjoyed.

b. A Muslim Account of the Battle
Arabic • mid-9th century • Fustat (Cairo)

The Conquest of Egypt and North Africa and al-Andalus, *a brief history written by the Egyptian jurist 'Abd al-Rahman ibn 'Abd al-Hakam (803–871), is the earliest surviving account of the Muslim conquest.*

Ubayda [had] appointed 'Abd al-Rahman 'Abd Allah al-'Akki as governor of al-Andalus. 'Abd al-Rahman was a virtuous man, and hence he undertook a military expedition to Ifranja.[6] [The Franks] are the most distant enemy of al-Andalus. 'Abd al-Rahman took a great deal of booty and he gained a victory over them. He obtained much gem-encrusted gold, covered with pearls, rubies and chrysolite, and he commanded that it be broken up.[7] He sent out one-fifth of it [to Ubayda] and divided [the rest] among the Muslims who were with him. . . . Then he led another military expedition against the Franks. He and all of his companions were martyred.

c. Edward Gibbon on the Significance of the Battle
English • 1776 CE • England

In his monumental The History of the Decline and Fall of the Roman Empire *(1776–1789), the British historian Edward Gibbon (1737–1794) looked back at the episode as a defining moment of European history, thus establishing the battle's modern academic and popular legacy, anticipating the twentieth-century notion of the "clash of civilizations."*

['Abd al-Rahman] passed without opposition the Garonne and Dordogne. . . . A victorious line of march had been prolonged above a thousand miles from the rock of Gibraltar to the banks of the Loire; the repetition of an equal space would have carried the Saracens to the confines of Poland and the Highlands of Scotland; the Rhine is not more impassable than the Nile or Euphrates, and the Arabian fleet might have sailed without a naval combat into the mouth of the Thames. Perhaps the interpretation of the Qur'an would now be taught in

---

5. In this period, "Europeans" (*Europenses*) was used to refer to the people of Latin Christendom. The word "Europe" derives from an ancient Near Eastern term referring to the geographic west.

6. Ifranja is "the land of the Ifranj"—the Franks.

7. Chrysolite is a generic term for green and yellow-green gems, including topaz.

the schools of Oxford, and her pulpits might demonstrate to a circumcised people the sanctity and truth of the revelation of Mahomet. . . .

From such calamities was Christendom delivered by the genius and fortune of one man. Charles. . . . In the onset of the seventh day [of the battle], the Orientals were oppressed by the strength and stature of the Germans, who, with stout hearts and iron hands, asserted the civil and religious freedom of their posterity. . . . After a bloody field, in which Abderame ('Abd al-Rahman) was slain, the Saracens, in the close of the evening, retired to their camp.

To Consider

1. How do the Arab and Latin accounts differ, and why might that be?

2. How does Gibbon's assessment relate to the contemporary sources?

3. What factors motivate the two sides?

Sources

a. *Chronicle of 754.* In *Conquerors and Chroniclers of Early Medieval Spain*, ed. and trans. Kenneth Baxter Wolf, 143–44. Liverpool: Liverpool University Press, 1999. Reproduced with permission of The Licensor through PLSclear.
b. Watson, William E. *Tricolor and Crescent: France and the Islamic World.* Westport, CT: Praeger, 2002. Pp. 152–53. Republished with permission of ABC-CLIO, LLC. Permission conveyed through Copyright Clearance Center, Inc.
c. Gibbon, Edward. *The History of the Decline and Fall of the Roman Empire.* 6 vols. 1796. London: Peter Fenelon Collier & Sons, 1901. Vol. 5, p. 389.

1.3 LEGENDS OF WOMEN AND THE CONQUEST OF AL-ANDALUS

Several legends quickly developed around the Arab conquest of Visigothic Hispania in 711. According to one, Julian, usually assumed to be the Byzantine governor of Septem (Ceuta, in Morocco), had sent his daughter to be educated at the court of the Visigothic king, Roderic. Here—according to the characterization of the time—the lustful king betrayed Julian's honor by raping her. When the Arab armies under Tariq ibn Ziyad arrived at his city, Julian saw an opportunity for revenge, lending them information, ships, and support for the invasion.

Some eleven years later, Pelagius or Pelayo, a local Christian strongman in the north of Spain, refused to pay tribute to the invaders, and defeated a punitive expedition sent after him. The small independent principality he founded became the Kingdom of Asturias, the forerunner of Castile-León. Eighth-century chroniclers also attributed his resistance to the dishonoring of his sister, Ermisenda, by a Berber governor, Munnuza, who had married her without Pelayo's consent.

The legend of Julian's daughter did not appear in any Andalusi-written accounts until the tenth century. By the eleventh century the tale was appearing in Christian chronicles, and Julian's daughter was called La Cava (roughly, "the Fallen"). The *Chronicle of Albelda*, written in the 880s, recounts Pelayo's victory, but makes no mention of her. By the late tenth century Arab chronicles mention the revolt of "Balay" (Pelayo) as the origin of Asturias, but no mention is made of a sister.

a. Julian's Daughter
Arabic • mid-9ᵗʰ century • Fustat (Cairo)

The Conquest of Egypt and North Africa and al-Andalus, a brief history written by the Egyptian jurist 'Abd al-Rahman ibn 'Abd al-Hakam (803–871) is the earliest surviving account of the Muslim conquest and the first to mention Julian's daughter.

There was a strait between [Tangiers] and the people of al-Andalus, and [ruling] over it was a non-Arab man called Julian [Yulyan], lord of Ceuta, and of a city on the passage to al-Andalus called Algeciras. Algeciras was one of the cities adjacent to Tangiers, and it was Julian's. He was accustomed to obey [the Visigothic king] Roderic, lord of al-Andalus, who lived in Toledo. Tariq wrote to Julian and flattered him and they exchanged presents. Now Julian sent his daughter to Roderic, lord of al-Andalus, for her education and instruction, and Roderic made her pregnant. When this news reached Julian he said, "I do not see how I can punish him or pay him back except by sending the Arabs against him." So he sent word to Tariq, saying, "It is I who will take you to al-Andalus." . . . Tariq answered, "I will not trust you until you send me a hostage," so Julian sent him his two daughters. He had no children other than these two. Tariq put them under secure guard in Tlemcen (in modern Algeria), and then he went out to Julian who was in Ceuta on the Straits (of Gibraltar). Julian rejoiced at his arrival and said to him, "I will take you over to al-Andalus."

b. Pelayo's Sister
Latin • early 10ᵗʰ century • Oviedo

The first mention of Pelagius's sister comes in the early tenth-century Chronicle of Alfonso III. *Written by an anonymous cleric in the court of the Alfonso the Great of Asturias, Galicia, and León (866–910), it was commissioned by the king to establish a link between the pre-Islamic Visigothic monarchy and his own line, and therefore his sovereignty over all of Iberia.*

The Arabs, after oppressing the region along with the kingdom, killed many with the sword and subjugated the rest to themselves by mollifying them with a covenant of peace. . . . They placed prefects throughout all of the provinces of Spain and paid tribute to the Babylonian king for many years until they elected their own king and established for themselves a kingdom in the patrician city of Córdoba. At almost the same time, in the region of the Asturians [in the north of Spain], there was in the city of Gijón a prefect by the name of Munnuza, a companion of Tariq. While he held the prefecture, a certain Pelayo, the swordbearer of the [former Visigothic] kings Witiza and Roderic, oppressed by the dominion of the Ishmaelites,[8]

---

8. The Arabs held that they were the descendants of Ishmael, who in their account was the son God ordered Abraham to sacrifice.

had come to Asturias along with his sister. On account of her, Munnuza sent Pelayo to Córdoba as his envoy. Before Pelayo returned, Munnuza married his sister through some stratagem. When Pelayo returned he by no means consented to it. Since he had already been thinking about the salvation of the church, he hastened to bring this about with all his courage. Then the evil Tariq sent soldiers to Munnuza, who were to apprehend Pelayo and lead him back to Córdoba, bound in chains. When they came to Asturias, seeking to apprehend him treacherously in a village called Brecce, the plan of the Chaldeans[9] was made known to Pelayo by a friend. Seeing that it would be impossible for him to resist the Saracens[10] because they were so numerous, Pelayo escaped from them. . . .

[Subsequently, Tariq sends an army of 187,000 to crush Pelagius and the rag-tag band of warriors he has gathered. After Bishop Oppa, a son of King Witiza, fails to convince Pelayo to surrender, they attack, at which point the Virgin Mary intercedes and the Muslim army is destroyed.][11]

To Consider

1. Do these legends seem believable?

2. Why would chroniclers attribute these political events to the mistreatment of women?

3. What role does religious identity play in these narratives of conquest, and what does that suggest?

Adapted from

a. Ibn 'Abd al-Hakam. *The History of the Conquests of Egypt, North Africa, and Spain.* In *Medieval Iberia: Readings from Christian, Muslim, and Jewish Sources,* ed. Olivia Remie Constable, 33. Philadelphia: University of Pennsylvania Press, 1997.

b. *The Chronicle of Alfonso III.* In *Conquerors and Chroniclers of Early Medieval Spain,* ed. and trans. Kenneth Baxter Wolf, 164–65. Liverpool: Liverpool University Press, 1999. Reproduced with permission of The Licensor through PLSclear.

1.4 TODA OF NAVARRE AND 'ABD AL-RAHMAN III

'Abd al-Rahman III (912–961), the first Umayyad caliph of al-Andalus, was constantly dealing with rebellious subordinates, both Muslim and Christian. In 934 he embarked on a campaign to subdue his rebellious governor of Zaragoza, the capital of the frontier province called the Upper March. Once in that region he decided to attack the neighboring Christian princes, some of whom had supported the rebel. This prompted Toda (d. 970), the

---

9. "Chaldeans," meaning "Persians," was another synonym for "Muslims."

10. "Saracen," from a Greek word referring to nomadic Arab raiders, became a synonym for "Muslim" in medieval Latin.

11. Oppa was the bishop of Seville, part of the Visigothic faction that aided the Muslims in 711 and helped to govern al-Andalus.

dowager queen and widow of King Sancho Garcés I (905–925) of Pamplona (or Navarre), to sue for peace. Toda's mother, Onneca—a daughter of King Fortún Garcés of Pamplona (870–905)—had been married to 'Abd al-Rahman's grandfather, the amir 'Abd Allah (888–912), making Toda the caliph's aunt. Toda was determined to secure 'Abd al-Rahman's support for the succession of her son, García Sánchez I (925–970), to the throne of Pamplona.

a. The Queen and the Caliph
Arabic • ca. 1050 CE • Córdoba

Abu Marwan Hayyan ibn Hayyan (d. 1075), who worked as a chancery secretary in the taifa kingdom of Córdoba in the decades after the fall of the caliphate is regarded as the greatest and most prolific historian of Islamic Spain. These passages are from the recently discovered fifth volume of his ten-volume Book for the Seeker of Knowledge of the History of al-Andalus (Al-Muqtabis), *an encyclopedic history that looked back to the glories of caliphal unity and synthesized many now-lost earlier chronicles.*

['Abd al-Rahman III] al-Nasir proposed to enter the enemy territory through the region of Guadalajara, but he was diverted from his path by the outright disobedience of the governor of Zaragoza, Muhammad ibn Hisham al-Tujibi, who did not join [al-Nasir], contrary to his orders, on account of which [al-Nasir] dispatched his cavalry through his territories. . . .

But, considering that holy war was better suited to fire up the volunteers who had joined his forces, [al-Nasir] prepared to invade the enemy territory of Pamplona, as the infidel area closest to his base in the Upper March. Then messengers arrived from the sly Toda, the daughter of Aznar, who pledged her obedience to him and invoked the links of her ancestors to those of the caliph, requesting that he grant her peace and withdraw his cavalry. In exchange, al-Nasir ordered that she come and visit him in his camp, as proof of her good intentions, granting her a safe conduct, forcing her to hastily gather her most important men, counts and bishops, arriving at his court in Calahorra, bearing a worthy gift. Al-Nasir ordered that, at her arrival, his army be waiting in formation in their ceremonial uniforms, a sight which overwhelmed her. Having been taken to his tent, where he was solemnly enthroned, and receiving her with some of his counts, she rendered him the appropriate honors, and humbly made her requests. Having been well received and honored by al-Nasir (he by which God had honored Islam), who made a treaty with her and her counts, which stipulated her complete submission and disengagement from the other Christian kings, allies, and relatives, and so on, such that she would cease to aid them and to harm the Muslims, opening her roads and aiding the Muslim frontier military commanders against any rebel, Toda was required [also] to free the hostages she had taken from the Banu Dhi al-Nun as a consequence of a tributary payment they had failed to give her. . . .[12] Concluding the

---

12. The Banu Dhi al-Nun were a Berber clan who served in the military. Later they would rule the *taifa* kingdom of Toledo.

treaty which he made the barbarians swear to, al-Nasir pledged his own good faith by [the strength of] his army and invested the son of the queen, Garcia son of Sancho, the Basque, [as ruler of] Pamplona and its region, giving her and her companions abundant gifts and clothing, which pleased them all. On the same day, she left for her own country, satisfied with the arrangement, and hastily freed the sons of the Banu Dhi'l-Nun, maintaining her strict obedience.

Toda's submission to al-Nasir was not pleasing to the barbarian Fortun, son of Garcia, known as Count Amat, commander of the fortress of Falces in the district of Pamplona, fifteen miles from Tudela, who, rising in opposition, unleashed his army. Truly, he was an ill-tempered person who bore a great enmity towards Muslims. Al-Nasir took his army against him, and fearing defeat, he hurried off in retreat, without requesting any safe conduct or truce. . . . Then al-Nasir ordered him to be seized and held captive, which sparked [Fortun's] anger and insolence with such rude words that the sultan was moved to kill him, thus saving the Muslims from his misdeeds. Thus, he was executed and quartered in [al-Nasir's] camp, to the great delight of the people of the frontier, who counted this deed as one of [al-Nasir's] great victories.

Isma'il ibn Badr, who had accompanied [the caliph] on campaign, mentions the visit of the barbarian Toda to al-Nasir in a panegyric he dedicated to him, saying:

> To him who led her highness,
>   Like the Queen of Sheba, surrounded by soldiers,
> Who upon seeing him saw only a bright star,
>   Which sparkled and flashed greatly.
> She hastened to prostrate herself before the light of his face,
>   For humility and prostration is what he is owed,
> Thus, he granted her the safe conduct of his own pardon
>   When she was at the very point of offering up her soul.
> So, continue to rule over us, just as he,
>   Who, while he walks the earth, follows the auspicious stars.

[Three years later, in 937, 'Abd al-Rahman was on campaign again, subduing Muslim rebels in Calatayud.]

After al-Nasir had dealt with Calatayud and its dependent fortresses, although he still faced constant threats from Zaragoza, he chose to offer to God the sacrifice of holy war to give thanks for the victory [God had] conceded. Thus, he prepared by cancelling his troops' leave, and used them to invade the territory of Pamplona, which was the closest enemy, and whose ruler, the barbarous Toda, daughter of Aznar, had broken her treaty, aiding the rebels against the loyalists. He devastated her territory far and wide, seizing both the plains and the highlands, and spending in those lands the fast of Ramadan and the Feast of the Fast-Breaking ('Id al-Fitr), meanwhile, destroying many of its fortresses and strongpoints.

To Consider

1. What role does religious identity play in relations between people across the frontier?

2. How does Toda's gender play into the account?

3. What does this episode suggest about 'Abd al-Rahman's approach to holy war?

Adapted from

a. Ibn Hayyan. *Crónica del califa Abderramán III an-Násir entre los años 912 y 942 = (Al-Muqtabis V)*. Trans. into Spanish Maria Jesús Viguera y Federico Corriente. Zaragoza: Anubar, 1981.

1.5 THE EMPEROR, THE CALIPH, AND THE ELEPHANT

The 'Abbasid Caliph Harun al-Rashid (of 1001 Arabian Nights' fame) and Charlemagne were on opposite sides of the Mediterranean. Envoys were exchanged, and in 802 and 807 the "Holy Roman Emperor" received an embassy bearing marvelous gifts including "Abu al-Abbas"—a live elephant, likely the first seen on European soil since Roman times. The elephant survived until 810, when it died suddenly while Charlemagne was campaigning against invading Danes.

The embassies and gifts are reported in two contemporary Frankish sources. No Arabic source mentions them.

a. An Embassy from Baghdad
Latin • ca. 817–830 CE • Aachen

The Frankish layman Einhard (d. 840), a scholar and builder, was a fixture in the court of Charlemagne and his son, Louis the Pious. His Life of Charlemagne *was modeled on classical biographies, such as Suetonius's* Lives of the Caesars *(121), and sought generally to present the emperor in the best light.*

He had such friendly relations with Aaron [Harun al-Rashid], the king of the Persians, who held almost the whole of the East except India, that he held him in favor more than all the kings and princes in the world and thought that he alone was worthy of his honor and generosity. Indeed, when Charles's ambassadors, whom he had sent with gifts to the [Church of] the Most Holy Sepulcher of our Lord and Savior and the place of His resurrection [in Jerusalem], came to him and told him of their lord's wishes, he not only allowed them to do what they requested but even granted him that holy and blessed place so it might be thought to be in his power. He sent his own legates back and sent magnificent gifts to Charlemagne, robes, spices, and other riches of the East, and a few years before he had sent an elephant, the only one he possessed, to Charlemagne, who had asked for one.

b. The Emperor's Elephant
Latin • ca. 807 CE • Aachen

The Annals of the Kingdom of the Franks *was an official chronicle produced by a series of anonymous authors at the Frankish court, beginning in 741 with the death of Charles Martel and into the reign of Louis the Pious with a strong focus on military affairs. The section from 796 to 807 is quite detailed and seems to have been written down contemporaneously.*

[In 801, in Pavia, the emperor] received news that envoys of Aaron, Amir al Mumminin, the king of the Persians, had arrived at the port of Pisa.[13] He sent messengers to meet them and had them presented at court between Vercelli and Ivrea (in northern Italy). One of them—for there were two—was a Persian from the East and the envoy of the Persian king, the other was a Muslim [*Sarracenus*] from Africa and the envoy of the *amir* Abraham, who ruled on the border of Africa in Fustat.[14] They reported that Isaac the Jew, whom the emperor four years earlier had dispatched with Lantfrid and Sigimund to the king of the Persians, was returning with large presents, but that Lantfrid and Sigimund had both died. Then the king sent Ecanbald, the notary, to Liguria to prepare a fleet on which the elephant and whatever else he brought along might be transported. . . .

In the month of October of the same year Isaac the Jew returned from Africa with the elephant and arrived in Port-Vendres (in southwest France). . . .

On July 20 of this same year [802] Isaac arrived with the elephant and the other presents sent by the Persian king, and he delivered them to the emperor at Aachen. The name of the elephant was Abul Abaz.

[In 807] Radbert, the emperor's emissary, died on his way back from the East. The envoy of the king of Persia by the name of Abdallah came to the emperor with monks from Jerusalem, who formed an embassy from the patriarch Timothy. Their names were George and Felix. This George is abbot of Mount Olivet, a native German, and called, by his real name, Egilbald. They came to the emperor and delivered presents which the king of Persia sent to him, that is, a tent and curtains for the canopy of different colors and of unbelievable size and beauty. They were all made of the best linen, the curtains as well as the strings, and dyed in different colors. The presents of the Persian king consisted besides of many precious silken robes, of perfumes, ointments, and balsam; also of a brass clock, a marvelous mechanical contraption, in which the course of the twelve hours moved according to a water clock, with as many little bronze balls, which fall down on the hour and through their fall made a cymbal ring underneath. On the clock there were twelve horsemen who at the end

---

13. 'Amir al-Mu'minin, "Prince of the Believers," was a caliphal title. "Aaron" is the translation of "Harun."

14. Referring to Ibrahim ibn 'Aghlab, the founder of the 'Aghlabid dynasty of Ifriqiya (Tunisia). Fustat, here, is a town near Kairouan.

of each hour stepped out of twelve windows, closing the previously open windows by their movements. There were many other things on this clock which are too numerous to describe now. Besides these presents there were two brass candlesticks of amazing size and height. All this was taken to the emperor in the palace at Aachen. . . .

. . . Leaving the palace without delay [in 810, Charlemagne] decided first to go and meet the fleet, then to cross the Rhine at Lippeham and wait for the troops that had not yet arrived. While he stayed there for a few days, the elephant which Aaron, the king of the Muslims [Sarracenorum], had sent him, suddenly died.

To Consider

1. Why would Charlemagne and these Muslim rulers form an alliance?
2. What is the significance of the gifts?
3. What are some of the challenges ambassadors would have faced, and why would a Jew be asked to serve in this role?

Adapted from

a. Einhard and Notker the Stammerer. *Two Lives of Charlemagne.* Trans. David Ganz. London: Penguin, 2008. Pp. 29–30.
b. Scholz, Bernhard Walther, and Barbara Rogers, eds. *Carolingian Chronicles: Royal Frankish Annals and Nithard's Histories.* Ann Arbor: University of Michigan Press, 1970. Pp. 81–82, 87, and 92. Republished with permission of University of Michigan Press. Permission conveyed through Copyright Clearance Center, Inc.

1.6 BASIL LAKAPENOS: A MIGHTY EUNUCH

Basil Lakapenos was undoubtedly the most powerful man in the Byzantine Empire from 945, when he was appointed *parakoinomenos* ("prime minister" or "first eunuch"). In 985 he was exiled by his ward, the young Basil II (976–1025), who charged him with embezzlement of royal lands. This may not have been unrelated to rumors that Lakapenos was behind the poisoning of the emperor's predecessor, John Tzimiskes (969–976). An illegitimate son of Emperor Romanus Lakapenos (920–944), Basil had survived the coup against his father and served five more emperors as an administrator and military commander, becoming fantastically wealthy in the process, at times running the empire all but single-handedly.

Eunuchs had long played a key role in Byzantine administration, serving as intimately trusted attendants, high-ranking officials, and generals. With their ethereal air and otherworldly appearance, members of this "third gender" had an angelic demeanor, suiting their role as mediators between the distant, divinely tinged imperial family and their subjects. Their role was somewhat analogous to the clergy of the Latin West, who also served in the administration and whose vows of celibacy prevented them too from establishing independent families and patrimonies that would challenge their lords.

a. John Skylitzes, *A Synopsis of Histories*
Greek • *late 11th century* • *Constantinople*

Little is known about the author John Skylitzes or Thrakesios (b. before 1050) other than that he rose to the highest echelons in the Byzantine civil service during the reign of Alexios Komnenos (1081–1118) and that he was a highly regarded historian in his time. The Synopsis is a synthetic secular political history covering events from 811 to 1057. One manuscript, the "Madrid Skylitzes," produced in Sicily in the twelfth century, contained 574 color illustrations, most of which have survived.

[After Constantine VII (913–959) seizes power he deals with the magnates and members of the royal family.]

The emperor castrated Romanos the son of Stephen (who would later become Sebasto-phoros[15]); and also [his half brother] Basil who was born to Romanos the elder,[16] by a slave woman. . . .[17]

[In 944 with the death of Romanos II (959–963) Basil helps the general Nikephoros Phokas (963–969) seize power.]

Many men were murdered in this lawless time, and while this was going on in the squares of the city, in the main thoroughfares, and marketplaces, and the back streets, they were acclaiming Nikephoros the conqueror. . . . The partisans of Basil the *parakoinomenos* prepared some ships, took the imperial galley and passed over to Chrysopolis with the entire fleet. There they brought Nikephoros on board and conveyed him to Hebdomon, from where they and all the city population bore him in procession through the golden gate into the capital, with cheering and applause, with trumpets and cymbals. When they arrived at the Great Church, they contrived to have the patriarch Polyeuktos place the imperial diadem on his brow.

[In 959 the Armenian general John Tzimiskes conspired to assassinate Nikephoros, with the support of Basil.]

After Nikephoros died, John Tzimiskes assumed responsibility for the Roman government. . . . John immediately summoned Basil the *parakoinomenos* by night and made him his associate in power. It was in no small measure owing to this man that the emperor Nikephoros gained the imperial throne, for which he was appointed president [of the Senate]—a position which did not exist before. . . . John [made (Basil) his associate in power) because he had been involved in affairs of state for many years. . . . Many times he had campaigned against the Hagarenes[18] and he was especially skilled in smoothly adapting himself

---

15. The Sebastophoros was an influential palace position held by eunuchs.

16. Romanos I Lakapenos, who served as regent for Constantine VII and later ruled (920–944), was born an Armenian peasant and rose through the ranks of the army under Basil I.

17. This likely occurred in 944. Basil was born sometime between 910 and 925.

18. "Hagarene," meaning a descendant of Abraham's concubine, Hagar, was one of the generic Christian terms for a Muslim.

to difficult situations. He quickly took matters into his own hands and expelled all those who remained in favor of Nikephoros. . . .

[Passing through Cilicia in 976, Tzimiskes asks who owns the rich estates he sees there.] [He] learnt from his interlocutors that it all belonged to Basil the *parakoinomenos*. . . . Yet of these acquisitions he saw nothing worthy of note which had been left to the public treasury. He was deeply troubled and heaved a great sigh, saying: "Oh, gentlemen, what a terrible thing it is if, when public funds are expended, the Roman armies are reduced to penury, the emperors endure hardships beyond the borders and the fruits of all this effort become the property of one—eunuch!" Thus, spoke the emperor, and one of those present reported what the emperor had said to Basil, which provoked him to wrath; so that, henceforth, he was looking for an opportunity to rid himself of the emperor. In due course he won over the emperor's usual wine pourer with flattery and bribed him with gifts. He prepared some poison, not the most deadly or one which speedily brings on ill effects, but one of those that gradually sap the strength of those who drink them. This toxin was served to the emperor in wine; he drank it and gradually fell ill, losing his energy. Finally, boils broke out on his shoulders and there was a copious haemorrhaging from the eyes. He returned to the capital and departed this life after reigning a little more than six years and as many months. . . .

. . .

John met his end in the way described; the right to rule now passed to Basil and Constantine, the sons of Romanos [II], in the month of September 6468 AM, fourth year of the indiction (947 CE), Basil being then in his twentieth year, Constantine three years younger.[19] But they only became emperors in appearance and name, for the administration of the affairs of state was undertaken by Basil the president, on account of the youth of the emperors, their immaturity and their as yet undeveloped aptitude.

To Consider

1. What effect does Basil's condition as a eunuch seem to have had on his career?

2. What does Basil's story disclose about the limits of Byzantine imperial power?

3. How does Basil's career relate to developments in the contemporary Islamic world?

Source

a. Skylitzes, John. *A Synopsis of Byzantine History, 811–1057*. Trans. John Wortley. Cambridge: Cambridge University Press, 2011. Pp. 230, 248–49, 271, 296, 299. Reproduced with permission of The Licensor through PLSclear.

---

19. Byzantines reckoned the years since creation (Anno Mundi), or by the indiction, a fifteen-year fiscal period.

TWO

Mediterranean Connections

In the famous "Pirenne Thesis," the Belgian historian Henri Pirenne (1862–1935) posited the expansion of Islam in the seventh and eighth centuries as marking the end of the Roman era and the fracturing of the Mediterranean trade system. The Frankish North, now poor and isolated, would remerge under the Carolingians as a distinct cultural and economic sphere, thus laying the groundwork for the European West. While appealing in its elegance, the thesis has not held up well under subsequent archaeological and historical research, which has shown that the decline of the Roman Mediterranean system preceded the Arabo-Islamic expansion and can be seen as not a consequence, but a cause. The interruption in trade and movement was less dramatic than assumed, and, in fact, the rise of the Islam served to reestablish and reinvigorate the Mediterranean commercial system. Nor were religious differences a barrier to collaboration and integration as previous historians have often assumed.

The readings in this chapter focus on movement within and beyond the Mediterranean world of the ninth through the eleventh century. We encounter Muslim Arabs, Persian pilgrims, Jewish merchants, and mercenary Vikings ranging as far afield as Central Asia, India, and Scandinavia. Traders faced challenges moving money and goods around the region, depending on the good graces of their patrons and the integrity of their partners. Thanks to the common linguistic, religious, and cultural elements that linked the peoples of the region, infidels and foreigners at times took on outsized roles in the domestic affairs of caliphates and empires—a situation that provided opportunities but could also lead to tension or provoke violence.

2.1 HARALD HARDRADI: A VIKING IN THE MEDITERRANEAN

The first Viking raids in the Mediterranean took place in 844, when longships attacked Muslim Seville. But the main point of contact was via the Black Sea and Volga Rivers, a highway for Norse traders and mercenaries. The most famous of these was Harald (or Haraldr) Sigurdarson, or Hardradi ("Tyrant" or "Stern Ruler"; ca. 1015–1066). By the 900s, many Norse were converting to Christianity, including Harald's father, Sigurd Syr, in 988. Exiled in 1030,[1] after a failed attempt to reinstall his half brother (later saint and king) Olaf II (1015–1028) on the throne of Norway, Harald headed south, first to the Kievan Rus and then on to Constantinople, then under the rule of the empress Zöe Porphyrogenita (1028–1050). Here, he joined the imperial Varangian guard, which he eventually led, and went on to serve in Serkland ("the land of the Muslims").[2] This involved an unsuccessful attempt to retake Sicily and to put down a Norman revolt on the Italian mainland, as well as fighting in the Balkans and the Holy Land, and battling Muslim corsairs around the Mediterranean. The sagas claim he went on pilgrimage to Jerusalem and bathed in the Jordan River.

Escaping from Byzantium in 1046 and the amorous advances of Zöe, he returned home and became king of Norway (1046–1066). In 1066 he invaded England but was killed by the Anglo-Saxon king Harold Godwinson (1066) at the Battle of Stamford Bridge. Godwinson was killed soon after by Duke William "the Conqueror" of Normandy at the Battle of Hastings.

a. Harald in Serkland
Old Icelandic • early 13ᵗʰ century • Reykholt, Iceland

Hardradi is the subject of an eponymous prose history, King Harald's Saga, *set down by the Icelander Snorri Sturluson (1178/79–1241) in the early thirteenth century, based on an earlier collection of royal sagas known as the* Morkinskinna *("Rotten Parchment"). In these passages, Harald leads the Varangians, and "Latin-speaking troops" (likely Normans), on a campaign against Muslim Africa and Sicily in the 1030s. In reality, Harald fought in Asia Minor and Palestine, but there is no record of an expedition to Ifriqiya.*

Harald now went with his army to Africa, to the parts which the Varangians called the Land of the Saracens.[3]

---

1. The Normans originated as Vikings, whose chieftain, Rollo, converted to Christianity in 911 and became the Count of Rouen, a vassal of Charles the Simple, king of West Frankia (911–923).

2. "Serk" is likely an adaptation of the Greek "Sarakenoi."

3. There is no record of an attack on Ifriqiya, so this likely refers to Harald's previous campaign in Palestine or Asia Minor. Sicily was under the rule of the Fatimid-supported Kalbid *amir*, Ahmad ibn Yusuf al-Akhal (1019–1036). Facing revolt from his Zirid-backed brother, Abu Hafs [?], al-Alkhal appealed to Byzantium. Michael VI (1034–1041) appointed him a *magistros* (a high court position), accepted his son as a hostage, and sent an army led by his general George Maniakes and including the Varangians to pacify the island.

There he increased the strength of his army considerably, and captured eighty towns; some of them surrendered and others were taken by storm.

From there he went to Sicily. . . . In the words of Illugi the Bryndale-Poet,[4]

Harald, you forced the Southern lands[5]
To submit to the great Emperor Michael.

Harald spent several years in Africa and garnered there an immense hoard of money, gold and treasure of all kinds. . . .

In this way Harald amassed a vast hoard of wealth—not surprisingly, considering that he had been plundering in the richest parts of the world where gold and treasure are the most plentiful. . . .

[Harald takes several strongly fortified towns in Sicily by using various stratagems and ruses.]

The fourth town Harald came to with his army was even bigger than all those which have been described already. It was so strongly fortified that there was no hope of taking it by storm. They laid siege to the town and blocked it so that no supplies could reach it.

[Harald held off the attack and spread rumors that he was ill and dying.]

The Varangians now went to parley with the townsmen, told them that their leader was dead, and asked the priests to grant him burial inside the town. Many of the townsmen present at this meeting were in charge of monasteries and other important establishments there, and each of them was eager to have his corpse for his own church, because they realized that precious offerings would accompany it. So all the clergy donned their robes and came out of the town in a splendid procession, bearing shrines and other holy relics. The Varangians, too, formed up a magnificent cortege, carrying the coffin on high under a canopy of precious cloth and many banners.

When the Varangians reached the gates they set the coffin down right across the entry, jamming open the gates. Then they sounded the call to arms with all their trumpets and drew their swords; the rest of the Varangian army came bursting out of the camp fully armed and rushed on the town shouting their war-cries. The monks and other priests in the procession who had been competing to be the first to receive the offerings were now twice as anxious to be as far away as possible from the Varangians; the Varangians killed anyone they could lay their hands on, priests and laymen alike, rampaged through the whole town, killing all the inhabitants and plundering everything they could find.

They took an enormous amount of booty there.

---

4. Illugi Bryndœlaskáld was an obscure poet apparently from southwestern Iceland.

5. Magnusson and Pálsson translate this as "Mediterranean lands," which is often the sense in which the Norse used the word "Sunnlǫnd."

b. Harald in Verse
Old Norse • ca. 1060 CE • Norway

The Norse often communicated in verse. Passages from two poems, the first by Harald's court bard and companion in arms, Thjódólfr Arnórsson (d. 1066?), and the second by the king himself, recount his fighting in Sicily.

> The African lord did fail
> The hail-freckled land to shield,
> And his people's lives protect
> Against such a mighty prince.

> One time, before, when far away
> On foreign shores I reddened blades,
> In sultan's court the sabre loud[6]
> Did sing—but that was then.

c. A Byzantine View
Greek • ca. 1178 CE • Constantinople

Harald is mentioned in Byzantine sources, including the Strategikon, *a military manual by a Georgian-Armenian author known as Kekaumenos (fl. 1070s), who apparently fought alongside Harald in Bulgaria, and to whom a short essay known as "Advice to an Emperor" (excerpted here) is attributed.*

Araltes [Harald], who was young and admired the might of the Romans, left the country and desired to enter our service and show respect to the blessed Lord Emperor Michael [VI] the Paphlygonian and see with his own eyes Roman customs and government. He brought with him a company of five hundred brave men, and entered the service of the Emperor, who received him in a seemly manner, and sent him to Sicily because the Roman army was there, making war in the island. Araltes went there and did many notable things, and when the war was over he returned to the Emperor, who gave him the title *Manglavites* ("ceremonial bodyguard").

To Consider

1. What impression do the Norse have of the Mediterranean and its inhabitants?
2. What role does religious or ethnic identity play in the narrative?
3. Does Harald's ruse seem believable, or is it likely a fable? Why?

---

6. Literally "Saracen's" fortress, town, domain, or court.

Sources

a. Sturluson, Snorri. *King Harald's Saga: Harald Hardradi of Norway; From Snorri Sturluson's Heimskringla*. Trans. M. Magnusson and H. Pálsson. London: Penguin, 1966. Pp. 51–60.
b. Unpublished translations by Oren Falk (Cornell University, Department of History). Used with his permission. See also *Morkinskinna: The Earliest Icelandic Chronicle of the Norwegian Kings (1030–1157)*, trans. Theodore M. Andersson and Kari Ellen Gade (Ithaca: Cornell University Press, 2012), 253.
c. Blöndal, Sigfús. *The Varangians of Byzantium*. Cambridge: Cambridge University Press, 2007. Pp. 57–58. Reproduced with permission of The Licensor through PLSclear.

2.2 RELIGIOUS RELATIONS IN FATIMID CAIRO

Under the Fatimids, greater Cairo was a bustling metropolis—a center for domestic and international trade, manufacturing, service industries, and, of course, the royal administration. It was also home to a very diverse population, including Egyptians, Arabs, Berbers, and sub-Saharan Africans, as well as Armenians and some Greeks and Persians. The majority of the population was Coptic Christian, but there were also Melkites (Byzantine Orthodox) and Syriac, Ethiopian, and Armenian congregations. Most Jews were Rabbanite, but there were also Karaites and Samaritans. Of the Muslims, the majority were Sunni, but the ruling family together with a small minority were Shi'i Isma'ilis.

In this cosmopolitan and diverse environment, all of these peoples rubbed shoulders— as neighbors, customers, tenants, colleagues, competitors, and friends, and many felt a strong identity as Cairenes that often overrode communal differences. Sectarian violence was rare. However, as part of a divide-and-rule policy, the Fatimids cultivated communal differences, and often employed non-Muslims in key positions of the administration, and this could aggravate tensions.

a. A Satirical Poem
Arabic • late 10th century • Cairo

This barbed verse criticized the Fatimid caliph al-'Aziz (975–996) for the diversity of his court, referring to his wazir, *Ya'qub b. Killis (a former Jew), and Fadl, his military commander (a Coptic Christian).*

Become Christian, for Christianity is the true religion!
Our times demonstrate this. So, recite the Trinity!
[The Christians] are strengthened and exalted,
Whereas that which is not theirs is neglected, and so it is ruined.
Don't worry about anything else:
Ya'qub, the *wazir*, is the Father, and this 'Aziz is the Son, and the Holy Spirit is Fadl.

b. A Wealthy Christian
Persian • mid-11th century • Yagavan, Badakshan ([?] modern Tajikistan)

The Persian traveler Nasir Khusraw describes the prodigious wealth of Fatimid Cairo, which he visited in the 1040s, and recounts an anecdote.

The people are so secure under the sultan's reign that no one fears his agents, and they rely on him neither to inflict injustice nor have designs on anyone's property. I saw such personal wealth that were I to describe it, the people of Persia would not believe it. . . .

I saw one man, a Christian and one of the most propertied men of all Egypt, who was said to possess untold ships, wealth, and property. In short, one year the Nile failed and the price of grain rose so high that the sultan's grand *wazir* summoned the Christian and said, "It has not been a good year. The sultan is burdened with the care of his subjects. How much grain can you give, either for sale or as a loan?" The Christian replied, "For the happiness of the sultan and the *wazir,* I have enough grain in readiness to guarantee Egypt's bread for six years." At that time there were easily five times the population of Nishapur in Cairo, so that anyone who knows how to estimate can figure out just how much grain he must have had. . . . What wealth must there be for the ruler not to inflict injustice and for the peasantry not to hide anything!

c. Repression and Restoration
Arabic • 11th century • Cairo

The History of the Patriarchs of the Egyptian Church *was a chronicle compiled in Arabic over the course of the Middle Ages by a series of Coptic Christian clerics. These passages recount the repression of Christians (and Jews) under the messianic caliph al-Hakim (996–1021), and the restoration of Christians' rights under his successor, al-Zahir (1021–1036), during the regency of al-Hakim's sister, Sitt al-Mulk. Al-Hakim had forced caliphal bureaucrats to convert to Islam, applied a rigorous interpretation of the "Pact of 'Umar," and imposed drastic public morality laws on Muslims. In the wake of his assassination/disappearance in 1021, the religion of the Druze (Duruz) developed, recognizing him as Mahdi ("the Guided One" who heralds the end-time).*

Another among [the ten chiefs of state] was known as the chief Fahd ibn Ibrahim [a Christian]. [Al-Hakim] set him above all the secretaries and chiefs of the departments. He caused him to be brought into his presence and said to him, "You know I have chosen you and set you above all those who are in my state. Listen to me and join me in my religion, and I will raise you even higher, and you shall be to me as a brother." But he did not answer [al-Hakim's] words. He ordered that he should be beheaded and his body burned with fire. The fire remained alight on him for three days but he was not burned. . . . This was a miracle of God—praise be to Him!—for he was a pious man in whom there was great compassion. . . .

. . . Then [al-Hakim] ordered the *nakus* should not be struck in the lands of Misr, and after a little, he ordered the crosses which were upon the domes of the churches should be pulled down, and that the crosses which were [tattooed] on the hands of the people should be erased.[7] Then he ordered that the Christians should have a belt fastened around their waists and that they should wear black turbans on their heads and that they should ride with wooden stirrups and that none of them should ride with iron stirrups, and they should wear crosses a span in length, then he ordered again to make [the crosses] a cubit and a half. [He ordered] the Jews to dye the borders of their turbans and that they should wear belts, and they should make a wooden ball in the form of the calf they worshiped in the deserts, and that none of the Christians and Jews should enter a bath with Muslims.

[Al-Zahir] did not interfere in anything of the affairs of his father, and there was in his days great tranquility and peace, and he remained king for sixteen years. The religion of the Christians was in a good state and its people respected.

In his days the churches were rebuilt till they returned to the state [in which] they had been and [were even] better.

To Consider

1. What may have been some of the sources of tension between Muslims and non-Muslims in Fatimid Egypt?

2. Why did official policy regarding Christians and Jews vary over time?

3. To what extent can the minorities in Fatimid Egypt be described as repressed? If so, how?

Sources

a. Catlos, Brian A. "To Catch a Spy: The Case of Zayn Al-Dîn and Ibn Dukhân." *Medieval Encounters* 2 (1996): 112–36. Republished with permission of Brill. Permission conveyed through Copyright Clearance Center, Inc.

b. Nāṣir-i Khusraw. *Nāṣer-e Khosraw's Book of Travels (Safarnāma)*. Trans. W. M. Thackston. Albany: Bibliotheca Persica, 1986. Pp. 55–56.

c. Ibn al-Muqaffaʻ, Sāwīrus. *History of the Patriarchs of the Egyptian Church: Known as the History of the Holy Church, Volume 2, Part 2, Khaël III–Šenouti II (A.D. 880–1066)*. Ed. and trans. Aziz Atiyah and Yassa ʻAbd al-Masih. Cairo: Institut Français d'Archéologie Orientale, 1948. Pp. 185–86, 188–89, 208–9. Reproduced with permission of The Licensor through PLSclear.

2.3 THE CALENDAR OF CÓRDOBA

The Book on the Division of Seasons and Benefits of Bodies is an almanac written in Islamic Córdoba in or shortly after 973. It is usually attributed to the Muslim physician and scholar ʻArib ibn Saʻid (d. 980/1), with material contributed by or taken from his contemporary Reccemund, or Rabiʻ ibn Ziyad, a Christian who served the caliph ʻAbd al-Rahman III

---

7. The *nakus* is a wooden clapper used by churches in the Near East in place of bells. "Misr" can refer to greater Cairo, or to Egypt as a whole.

(912–961) as a bureaucrat, diplomat, and eventually, bishop. A Latin version may have been composed by Reccemund, or translated by Gerard of Cremona (d. 1187).

The book follows the format of a traditional Arabic almanac, which includes astrological data, and information relating the times of year to health and agricultural production, noting major holidays as well as other practical details.

a. The Calendar of Córdoba
Arabic and Latin • after 973 CE and mid-10th–mid-12th century •
Córdoba and possibly Toledo

The text below is a translation of the Arabic and the Latin texts. The Arabic text translated here was written in Hebrew characters in the manuscript. Underlined passages do not appear in the Latin version. Brackets indicate editor's additions.

Month of September
In Syriac: *alul*; in Coptic: *tut*
Number of days: 30
Zodiac sign: Virgo
Lunar stations: 3: al-Sarfa, al 'Awwa', and al-Simak[8]

The beginning of the month appears in the summer season, and its regimen is the same as that of the preceding months. It is in the course of this month that winter begins. Nature: cold and dry.

Element: earth. Nature: cold and dry.

The best food and drinks to consume, the best movements to make, and the best places to live are those which moisten the body, with a warming tendency, but which do not permit superfluous elements to accumulate.

This season is contrary to all ages and to all temperaments throughout all the lands. Less harm is sustained by those who are by nature hot and wet; it best suits children and adolescents, whose constitutions are naturally moist.

1st Duration of the day: 12 and 2/3 hours. Duration of the night: 11 and 1/3 hours. Height of the sun at midday: 55 1/4°. Shadows are equal to 7/12 of the height of the object. Among the Christians, the Feast of (Saint) Terentianus, the bishop, and his fellow martyrs.[9] It is said to be the day of death of Joshua, son of Nun—prayers be upon him.[10]

5th Dusk comes 1.5 hours after the sun sets; dawn begins 1.5 hours before it rises.

8th Among Christians, the Feast of (the Virgin) Mary.

---

8. Each "lunar station" corresponds to one of the twenty-eight groups of stars the moon moves through in one year. These three refer to stars in the constellations of Leo (al-Sarfa) and Virgo (al-'Awwa' and al-Simak).

9. There were several saints by this name. This may have been the first-century bishop of Iconium (Konya) or a victim of the persecutions under Diocletian (284–305).

10. In the Old Testament, Joshua was the Israelite leader—the first "judge"—selected by God to succeed Moses.

9th The star Spica rises at dawn; this is its shape: O. *Al-Fargh al-Muqaddam* sets at dawn; this is its shape: OO.[11] The station of the moon is *al-Fargh al-Muqaddam*, which lasts 3 nights. It is a favorable station. Spica rises <u>opposite</u>.[12] The Nile is good. Heat decreases. This is the last station of summer. Its rain is called *hamim* or *ramadi*.

14th Among Christians, the Feast of Cyprian the Wise, bishop of Carthage, put to death in Africa. <u>His feast is celebrated in the Church of St. Cyprian in Córdoba.</u>[13]

15th Duration of the day: 12 and 1/5 hours. Duration of the night: 11 and 4/5 hours. Height of the sun at midday: 54 1/4°. Shadows are equal to a third of the height of the object. <u>Feast of (Saint) Emilia.</u>[14]

. . .

24th Among Christians, the Feast of the beheading of John, son of Zachary—prayers be upon him.[15]

25th In Egypt. Ostriches begin to lay. It is said that each lays between thirty and forty eggs over forty days, which they lay in a straight line, all of which crack open bearing chicks, except for six or seven, which are called "the abandoned ones."[16]

. . .

30th Among the events of this month which are not usually featured in the tables and which do not correspond with particular days, I would point out the following: Peaches, jujubes, pomegranates, and quinces are ripe. Sugar cane and bananas begin; some olives darken; new oil makes its appearance, as do acorns and chestnuts; the ash trees mature. Field work and sowing begin in the hills of Córdoba. <u>The first asparaguses appear in the hills.</u> Vultures of the type called of Niebla leave the ocean and are hunted up to the beginning of spring. The swallows return to the seaside. At the end of the month, the heads of the gulls whiten—these are the seabirds whose heads turn black in spring. It is during this month that letters of assessment (these are addressed to provincial revenue agents to proceed with their requisitions) are sent.

---

11. Al-Fargh al-Muqaddam is the lunar station comprising the stars Alpha Pegasi and Beta Pegasi.

12. Spica, or Alpha virginis, is the brightest star in the constellation of Virgo, and one of the brightest in the night sky.

13. Cyprian, a theologian and "Father of the Church," was martyred in 285 under Emperor Valerian (253–260).

14. Probably Emilia of Caesarea (d. 375), the wife of Saint Basil the Elder and mother of Saints Basil the Great, Macrina, Gregory of Nyssa, and Naucratius.

15. John the Baptist, also venerated as a prophet by Muslims.

16. Ostrich eggs, valued as exotica and used in religious ritual, were traded across the Islamic and Christian Mediterranean.

To Consider

1. Who was likely the intended audience of this Arabic text?

2. Which calendar (Christian or Islamic) is used, and why?

3. What are the principal themes, and why are they important?

4. What are the various intellectual and religious traditions the text draws on? Why?

Adapted from

a. *Le Calendrier de Cordoue*. Ed. and trans. Charles Pellat and Reinhart Dozy. Leiden: Brill, 1961. Pp. 134–45. Reproduced with permission of The Licensor through PLSclear.

2.4 JEWISH TRADERS' LETTERS FROM THE CAIRO *GENIZA*

Traditionally Jewish documents that feature the word "God" are typically disposed of in a storage space (*geniza*) before they are eventually buried. An immense *geniza* was discovered at the Ben Ezra Synagogue in Babylon-in-Egypt (Old Cairo) in the mid-eighteenth century. It held hundreds of thousands of crumbling letters, contracts, and judicial and commercial documents, most dating to the late ninth to the mid-thirteenth century. Scholars working with these fragments—most written in Arabic, Aramaic, or Hebrew, some in Hebrew, some in Arabic script (the latter referred to as Judeo-Arabic)—have been able to reconstruct in detail the social, economic, legal, and religious life of the Cairene Jewish communities. Many of the documents preserved in the Cairo *geniza* are copies of correspondence between the Jewish merchants whose trade networks radiated out of al-Fustat (Old Cairo).

The following readings are from letters dating from the first half of the eleventh century.

a. Pirates
Arabic • early 11th century • Alexandria

A pepper trader from Alexandria writes to his associate in Mahdia (Ifriqiya), from Amalfi (Italy), where he was to trade with a Christian merchant Yuhanna ("John"), but had been pursued by a pirate.

We suffered hardship and . . . came near to the capital Constantinople. After we cruised on the sea for eighteen days he attacked us again. Then it became evident they were on their way to one of the coasts of the Muslims. So we returned to Crete. We did not cease to gulp our blood until we arrived in Amalfi after more than seventy days. This was not enough: We came to a town whose property had been confiscated, and we did not find anyone to buy any goods from us, be it pepper or frankincense, or anything else, not even one *dirham*'s worth. We put our goods in warehouses and are now waiting for God's help. I do not worry for my own things. I worry for you and your goods that I am unable to sell. I really regret this very much.

b. An Unhappy Partner
Arabic • early 11th century • Kairouan

Ibn al-Siqili of Kairouan (Ifriqiya) writes to the "merchant-prince" Joseph ibn 'Awkal in Fustat, complaining of bad treatment.[17]

My elder and master, you say that I took the brazilwood and sent it to Spain, I did not take it for myself, nor have I made any profit from it. Rather, it caused me losses, I acted thus because I relied upon you and your high rank on the matter of the goods sent by me to you on my account. I was sure you would write to me exactly the opposite of what you have written, which offended me so much, and for which I do not know any reason. . . .

. . . Then you sent those pearls and I worked hard collecting their price. For how long shall this go on?! Should I not have taken one quarter of the profit? Through me you have made a profit of close to one dinar per dinar, and all of this was of no advantage to me. . . .

. . . What disturbed me most was your failure to pay Ibn Yazdad[18] . . . the sum that I asked you to pay them or to give them the equivalent in goods. . . . You have withheld payment, while this is a debt upon me. And this, at a time when your merchandise was in Spain! Their letters insulting me have now come to everyone and my honor has been disgraced.

c. Urgent Business
Arabic • early 11th century • Kairouan

Two brothers of the Taherti clan of Kairouan write to their associates, three brothers of the powerful Tustari clan of Fustat, with various requests regarding their trade of luxury textiles.[19]

I have another wish, my lord. Should a caravan set out in which trustworthy Muslims, who have given you sureties, will travel, let the merchandise of my brothers be sent with them as if it were yours. They would profit from this in many respects.

---

17. In the late tenth and early eleventh centuries Abu Ya'qub Abu'l-Faraj Yusuf ibn 'Awkal was the head of a Mediterranean-wide trading enterprise, and a leader of the Jewish community who served as an intermediary between Jews in the Maghrib and in Palestine and Iraq. The family business had been founded by his father, Ya'qub; among its niches was importing gems from India for the elite and exporting flax for cloth around the Mediterranean. Yusuf was not a traveling merchant, but worked through agents and intermediaries, including his four sons.

18. Ibn Yazdad was a Jewish merchant, perhaps a Karaite of Persian origin.

19. The Tustari family were Persian Karaite Jews who emigrated to Fustat in the late tenth century, establishing a major trading enterprise that lasted for four generations. Family members became leaders of the Jewish community there and fixtures at the Fatimid court. Originating in Kairouan, the Tahertis, another important trading family, also established an office in Fustat. They spanned three generations in the eleventh century and were politically influential in Zirid Ifriqiya.

The balance for the garments ordered will be sent to you with the pilgrims' caravan in a purse of gold *dinars*.

d. A Deadbeat

Arabic • early 11ᵗʰ century • Alexandria

Yeshu'a ibn Isma'il, a trader originally from the Maghrib but now based in Alexandria, explains his difficulties to a partner regarding the sale of some wax.

When Jacob arrived in Fustat I was in a very serious condition, and he tried to take advantage of me. Our friends extricated the wax from him with difficulty. . . . When I arrived in Alexandria, I met him, and he said, "Yes," but put me off from day to day, until he was about to leave. . . .

This is what happened to me with him. Please when he arrives, take from him what he still owes me. And when he says: "I have paid the expenses for the wax," our friends here are witness that he did not pay a penny for it. Only you can save me from him. You have entrusted him with the shipment, so you must save me from him.

To Consider

1. What were the challenges of carrying out international commerce in this era, and how were they overcome?

2. What qualities made a "good" merchant? Why might Jewish merchants prefer to trade with other Jewish merchants?

3. What sorts of commodities are being traded, and over what distances? What does this tell us?

Source

a–d. Goitein, S. D. *Letters of Medieval Jewish Traders.* Princeton: Princeton University Press, 1972. Pp. 44–45 (1), 29–32 (2), 78 (3), and 126–27 (4). Republished with permission of Princeton University Press. Permission conveyed through Copyright Clearance Center, Inc.

2.5 IBN FADLAN AT THE FRONTIERS OF THE MEDITERRANEAN WORLD

Ahmad ibn Fadlan was apparently a courtier in Baghdad during the reign of the 'Abbasid caliph al-Muqtadir (908–932). Falling afoul of the powerful eunuch Nadhir al-Harami, he was ordered to lead a mission to the land of the Bulghars (in the middle Volga) in 921. The embassy came at the request of the Bulghar king, who asked that members of the *'ulama'* be sent so he might be instructed in Islam, together with funds to support him against his rivals, particularly the Khazar kingdom. According to his own account (uncorroborated by other evidence), Ibn Fadlan encountered a whole array of Central Asian and Caucasian peoples, as well as Vikings. Scholars in the past accepted Ibn Fadlan's account largely uncritically; recently, doubts have been raised as to whether any such mission took place.

a. The Kingdom of the Khazars
Arabic • 10th century • Baghdad

In these passages Ibn Fadlan recounts his impressions of the kingdom of the Khazars, a Turkic people who lived between and to the north of the Black and Caspian Seas.

The king of the Khazars, whose title is *khaqan*, only appears in public once every four months. He is called the Great Khaqan, whereas his lieutenant is known as *khaqan bey*.[20] It is he who leads the armies, directs the affairs of the kingdom, appears in public, and receives the allegiance of neighboring kings. . . .

It is the custom of the Great King never to give public audience and never to speak to the people. No one, except for those whom we have mentioned, has access to him. It is up to his lieutenant, the *khaqan bey*, to nominate officers for all positions of authority, to inflict punishments, and to take charge of the government. . . .

. . .

When the Great King dies, it is customary to build him a house of twenty chambers and in each chamber to hollow out a tomb for him. They break up stones until they become like powdered antimony.[21] They spread a layer of this powder and then throw quicklime on top of the body. Beneath this house is a river, a great river that flows rapidly, which they divert over the tomb.

They say: "This is so that no devil, or man, or maggot, or reptile, can reach it."

Once the king has been buried, they cut off the heads of those buried with him so that no one knows in which of the chambers he lies. They call his tomb paradise and they say:

"He has entered Paradise."

All the chambers are decorated with silk brocade woven with gold.

. . .

It is the custom of the king of the Khazars to have twenty-five wives, each of whom is the daughter of a king of a neighboring country. He is given them freely or he takes them by force. He also has slave girls as concubines for his bed, sixty in number, every one of them extremely beautiful. All these women, whether free or slave, are kept in an isolated castle, where each of them has her own alcove roofed with teak, and each alcove is surrounded by a pavilion. Each of them has a eunuch who protects her from all eyes. . . .

When the Great King goes riding, all the troops set out with him as an escort, keeping the distance of a mile between him and them. None of his subjects sees him without prostrating themselves face to the ground, and they only lift their heads after he has gone.

. . .

---

20. *Bey* or *beğ* is a Turkic word meaning "prince." *Khaqan*, also Turkic, means "ruler over other rulers."

21. A metal, usually found in mineral form, which was used for dyeing, as well as cosmetic and medicinal purposes.

The king of the Khazars has a great city on the River Itil [modern Volga], on both banks of the river. The Muslims live on one bank and the king and his followers on the other. The head of the Muslim community is one of the king's officers and is known as *khaz*, and he is a Muslim. All legal decisions concerning Muslims living in the lands of the Khazars, or visiting the country on business are referred to this Muslim officer. He is the only person with the authority to examine their affairs or judge their quarrels.

. . .

The Muslims in this town have a congregational mosque where they perform the Friday prayer. It has a tall minaret and certain number of muezzins. When the king of the Khazars learned in the year 310/921 that the Muslims had destroyed the synagogue that was in Nar al-Babunaj,[22] he ordered the minaret to be destroyed and the muezzins put to death.

"If I did not fear that not a synagogue would be left standing through the lands of Islam," he said, "I would have destroyed the mosque."

The Khazars and their king are all Jews. The *Saqaliba* and all the neighboring peoples are subject to him and he speaks to them as if they were slaves and they obey him most humbly.[23]

To Consider

1. Is this account believable?

2. Who would this information be useful to?

3. Does Khazaria seem like a Jewish kingdom?

Source

a. Ibn Fadlan, Ahmad. *Ibn Fadlan and the Land of Darkness*. Trans. P. Lunde and C. Stone. London: Penguin, 2012. Pp. 55–58.

---

22. Likely Darband, in Dagestan, but perhaps, Pumbedita, home to the Gaonic Academy.
23. The Saqaliba were pagan "Slavs," traded as slaves to the Islamic world in great numbers.

THREE

Conversion and the Consolidation
of Identities

The period from 650 to 1050 saw adherents and leaders of the older faiths of Judaism and Christianity reacting and adjusting to the political, social, and religious changes set in motion by the rise of the new, Islamic faith. Christians and Jews living under Muslim dominion grappled with the challenges that the faith, culture, and Arabic language of their rulers presented to their communal cohesion and religious identity. Within the borders of the shrunken Byzantine Empire, emperors and leaders of the Orthodox Church endeavored to grasp the full implications of Islam's rise for the sacred status of the emperor and the primacy of their church while making what they thought were necessary changes to the spiritual practices of Orthodox believers. The popes in Rome, meanwhile, adapted to the new circumstances and opportunities created by the reduced power of Byzantine emperors in Italy and the Christianization of northern Europe, which resulted not only in many more Christians coming under the authority of the Roman Church but also in the emergence of monarchs, such as the Frankish Carolingians, who were keen to support and defend the church.

The readings examine Christians addressing the religious implications of their Arabization under Muslim rule; the complex relationship between Jewish minorities and Muslim rulers; and the response of Carolingian rulers and church leaders to the influx and activities of Jews in Europe partly facilitated by Islam's Mediterranean dominance. Also explored are the Byzantine emperors' controversial institution of iconoclasm, partly in reaction to Islam's stance against religious images; and the papacy's efforts to legitimize its incorporation of Byzantine territories in Italy into the Papal States and to navigate its crucial relationship with the new power in Europe, the Carolingian empire.

3.1 CHRISTIAN ARABIZATION IN MUSLIM LANDS

As Christians throughout the Muslim world gradually adopted the Arabic language for purposes of speaking, reading, and writing, concerned church leaders and laypersons warned their coreligionists about the threat that they believed Arabization presented to the Christian community and the faith of its members, who were losing knowledge of their own scriptural and liturgical languages. The first reading comes from a Latin treatise, the *Indiculus luminosus* ("Letter of the Enlightened") of Paul Alvarus (d. ca. 861), a Spanish Catholic layman who, along with his friend the priest Eulogius, was a principal supporter of the "martyrs" of Córdoba. The two also worked to preserve Latin as the language of high culture and learning among Christians in Umayyad Córdoba. Alvarus wrote the *Indiculus luminosus* to defend the actions of Christians who were publicly attacking the Islamic faith, as well as to demonstrate through biblical exegesis that the Prophet Muhammad was the Antichrist. The second reading, written by the Coptic theologian and bishop of al-Ashmunayn, Egypt, Sawirus ibn al-Muqaffaʾ (ca. 905–987), is from his Arabic summary of the main doctrines and practices of the Coptic Church, the *Kitab al-Idah* ("Book of the Elucidation"). Prior to becoming a bishop in the early 950s, Sawirus had served as an Arabic scribe in the Fatimid government, and, after a few years there, retired to a monastery near Cairo to devote himself to theological study. Because of his growing fame as a scholar, the leaders of al-Ashmunayn selected him as bishop. Sawirus wrote numerous theological, liturgical, and apologetic works in Arabic, one of the first Coptic authors to do so.

a. Paul Alvarus
Latin • 854 CE • Córdoba

What trained person, I ask, can be found today among our laity who with a knowledge of Holy Scripture looks into the Latin volumes of any of the doctors? . . . Do not all Christian youths, handsome in appearance, fluent of tongue, conspicuous in their dress and action, distinguished for their knowledge of Gentile [Muslim] lore, highly regarded for their ability to speak Arabic, do they not all eagerly use the volumes of the Chaldeans [Arabs], read them with the greatest interest, discuss them ardently, and, collecting them with great trouble, make them known with every praise of their tongue, the while they are ignorant of the beauty of the Church and look with disdain upon the Church's rivers of paradise as something vile. Alas! Christians do not know their own law, and Latins do not use their own tongue, so that in all the college of Christ there will hardly be found one man in a thousand who can send correct letters of greeting to a brother [in Latin]. And a manifold crowd without number will be found who give out learnedly long sentences of Chaldean rhetoric.

b. Sawirus ibn al-Muqaffaʾ
Arabic • late 10ᵗʰ century • al-Ashmunayn

In these times differing statements about the Orthodox Faith abound among the Copts. Every one of them has an opinion which is at variance with the opinion of every other one, and he calls him an infidel. . . . The reason for this ignorance of theirs involves their language, because the Arabic language has overcome them. There is no one of them left who knows what he is reading about in church in the Coptic language. They have come to the point of hearing but not understanding. And for this reason there has disappeared from among them that knowledge of the Christian creed. . . .

. . . And due to the loss of their original Coptic language . . . they have come to the point of not hearing any mention of the Trinity among themselves except rarely, nor is there any mention of the "Son of God" among them except in the way of a figure of speech. Rather, most of what they hear is that God is singular, everlasting, and the rest of that kind of language which the others [the Muslims] speak. The believers [Christians] have become accustomed to it and they are brought up on it, with the result that the very mention of "the Son of God" has come to the point of being difficult for them, and they are not aware that it has any explanation or meaning.

To Consider

1. What social and political factors account for Christians' adoption of Arabic?

2. What impact did Arabization potentially have on the religious faith of Christians, and how did Arabization create division within the Christian community?

3. Why did Paul Alvarus write in Latin, and Sawirus ibn al-Muqaffa' in Arabic?

Sources

a. Colbert, Edward P. *The Martyrs of Córdoba, 850–859: A Study of the Sources.* Washington, DC: Catholic University Press of America, 1961. P. 301. Republished with permission of Catholic University of America Press. Permission conveyed through Copyright Clearance Center, Inc.
b. Griffith, Sidney. "The *Kitab Misbah al-'Aql* of Severus ibn al-Muqaffa: A Profile of the Christian Creed in Arabic in Tenth-Century Egypt." *Medieval Encounters* 2 (1995): 25, 29. Republished with permission of Brill. Permission conveyed through Copyright Clearance Center, Inc.

3.2 BYZANTINE ICONOCLASM

The iconoclastic policies of Byzantine emperors excited great controversy, because they attacked the icons—painted or mosaic images of Christ, Mary, and the saints—to which so many clerics and laypersons were devoted. The following readings were all written by critics of iconoclasm. The author of the first reading, the monk Theophanes (ca. 758/60–818), took up the religious life after serving in the court of Leo IV (775–780) and became the abbot of a monastery. In 787 he attended the Second Council of Nicaea, which restored the veneration of icons. The passage from his *Chronicle* below offers an account of the origins of iconoclasm. Theophanes later opposed the "second iconoclasm" initiated by Leo V (813–820), which resulted in his imprisonment and death. The second reading comes from the Council of Nicaea's defense of icons. John Skylitzes (ca. 1050–1110), a judge in the imperial service, wrote the third reading, the *Synopsis of Histories,* long after the end of iconoclasm.[1] In the reading below he describes the resistance of Empress Theodora (830–856) and her mother to the iconoclasm of her husband, Theophilos (829–842). After Theophilos's death, Theodora was regent for her son Michael III until 856. She convoked the synod in 843 that put an end to iconoclastic policies once and for all.

a. Theophanes
Greek • 810–815 CE • Western Anatolia

A Jewish wizard . . . came to Yazid [Yazid II (720–724)]. He told him he would rule the Arab state for forty years if he would condemn the honored and revered icons in the Christians' churches throughout the entire empire. . . .

But the Emperor Leo [III (717–741)] caused us many evils, because he shared this malignant, illegal, and evil doctrine. He found a partisan for his stupidity: a man named Beser, who had been a Christian prisoner in Syria and had apostatized from his faith in Christ and converted to the Arabs' doctrine. . . . Leo favored him . . . because he agreed with Leo's wicked doctrine. . . .

Leo deduced that God was angry at him [because of Muslim attacks and plague in Syria], but still more shamelessly incited battle against the august, holy icons. He had as an ally Beser. . . .

The masses of the imperial city, dismayed at their newfangled teachings, intended to attack Leo. They killed some of the Emperor's men who had destroyed the icon of the Lord on the Bronze Gate, with the result that Leo caused many of them (especially those distinguished by noble birth or rhetorical skill) to be punished for their piety by mutilation, lashes, exile, and fines. This brought an end to the schools and pious education which had prevailed since the time of Constantine the Great. . . . The Saracen-minded Leo condemned them and many other fine things.

b. The Second Council of Nicaea
Greek • 787 CE • Nicaea

We all, therefore, see and understand that the painting of icons is something that has been handed down to the Church before the holy councils, as well as after them, like the traditions of the gospel. Thus, as when we receive the sound of reading with our ears, we transmit it to our mind, so by looking with our eyes at the painted icons, we are enlightened in our mind. . . . By reading and also by seeing the reproduction of the painting, we learn the same thing, this is, how to recall what has taken place. . . .

With a tongue pointed like a knife and sharpened with falsehood, they [the iconoclasts] think that the immaculate faith of us Christians has changed into one of icon-adoration. To this they add insult, calling it a 'base and material worship of creatures'. Not one Christian who has ever lived under the sky has worshipped an icon. . . . This is something that has

---

1. For more on this work, see the introduction to "Basil Lakapenos: A Mighty Eunuch" in the readings for chapter 1, p. 19.

been vanquished by the coming of Christ. . . . The Church possesses various things dedicated to God, which are placed there for the remembrance of God and of his saints: the making of icons is one of these.

c. John Skylitzes
Greek • late 11ᵗʰ century • Constantinople

When Theodora was crowned with the diadem, her mother, Theoktiste . . . had her own house close by the monastery of Gastria and there she would receive Theodora's children, of which there were five [daughters]. . . . She [Theoktiste] gave them various gifts which were attractive to the female sex. Then, taking them aside, she would earnestly entreat them not to be feeble nor to remain the women they were, but to play the man and to think the kind of thoughts which were worthy of and appropriate to their mother's breast. They were to hold in abomination their father's heresy and to do homage to the outward form of the holy icons. Whereupon she would thrust some of the icons (which she kept in a chest) into their hands, setting them against their faces and lips, to sanctify the girls and to stir up in them a devotion to the icons. Now it did not escape Theophilos' attention that she was habitually behaving in this manner. . . . This put the emperor into a rage, but such was the respect and devotion he had for his wife that he was restrained from dealing very severely with his mother-in-law.

To Consider

1. Why does Theophanes associate the origins of iconoclasm with Jews, Muslims, and Christian converts to Islam?

2. How does the Second Council of Nicaea argue for the restoration and use of icons, and why is it so concerned in its statement to assert that Christians do not "worship" icons?

3. Why might women have been especially devoted to the use of icons, and how does the episode of Theodora and Theokiste help explain the bitterness of the iconoclast controversy in Byzantium?

Sources

a. Theophanes the Confessor. *The Chronicle of Theophanes*. Trans. Harry Turtledove. Philadelphia: University of Pennsylvania Press, 1982. Pp. 93–94, 97.

b. Sahas, Daniel J. *Icon and Logos: Sources in Eighth-Century Iconoclasm*. Toronto: University of Toronto Press, 1986, © Daniel J. Sahas. Pp. 61, 69.

c. Skylitzes, John. *A Synopsis of Byzantine History, 811–1057*. Trans. John Wortley. Cambridge: Cambridge University Press, 2011. Pp. 54–55. Reproduced with permission of The Licensor through PLSclear.

3.3 THE *DONATION OF CONSTANTINE*

Sometime in the 750s or 760s a cleric in papal circles in Rome forged a document known to history as the *Donation of Constantine*. Supposedly written on March 30, 315, the *Donation* begins with a fictitious account of Pope Sylvester I's (314–335) baptism and miraculous cure from leprosy of the first Christian Roman emperor, Constantine I (306–337), and then records the concessions the grateful emperor made to the pope and his successors. The papacy's use of a forgery may strike modern readers as odd. Yet in an age in which documentary evidence was sparse, it was not unusual to draw up "documents" or to fashion "histories" that articulated ideas and claims that were consonant with the authors' deeply held beliefs, beliefs they regarded as "true." Still, the timing of the forgery was significant, for in it the author (or authors) made a statement of papal ideology that responded to or legitimized changes in the mid-eighth-century world that the popes inhabited. The most momentous change was the widening gap between the papacy and the Byzantine Empire and the papacy's new relationship with the Frankish Carolingian dynasty. The popes had condemned the iconoclastic policies of the Eastern emperors, and when the latter proved unable to protect papal Rome from the Lombards, the Carolingian Peppin III (751–768) defeated the Lombards and granted the papacy lordship over Byzantine lands that the Lombards had earlier seized, territory integral to the emerging papal state. In its assertions about papal primacy in the wider Christian world and the superiority of spiritual authority to secular authority, the *Donation* would become part of the papacy's arsenal in its conflicts with Eastern Churches over theological and jurisdictional issues, and in its struggles with monarchs in the Latin West over the proper relationship between papal and royal power—that is, until 1439–1440, when the Italian humanist Lorenzo Valla proved it to be a forgery.

a. The *Donation*
Latin • 750-767 CE • Rome

And when, with the blessed Sylvester as my teacher, I [Constantine] had learned that I had been restored to full health through the kindness of St. Peter himself, we [Constantine], together with all the people of Rome who are subject to the glory of our rule, considered it appropriate that just as Peter seems to have been constituted as the vicar of the Son of God on earth, in the same way the pontiffs, who represent the prince of the apostles, should obtain a greater power of supremacy than that which the earthly beneficence of our serenity is seen to have. We thought that this should be conceded to him [Sylvester] from us and from our empire. . . . We decreed that his sacrosanct Roman church should be honored with veneration to the extent of our power, and that the most sacred seat of St. Peter is gloriously exalted above our empire and earthly throne. . . .

We ordain and decree that he [the pope] should have dominion over the four principal dioceses of Antioch, Alexandria, Constantinople, and Jerusalem, as well as over all the churches of God in the world. And the pontiff who, for the time being, is head of the sacrosanct Roman church is more exalted than and chief of all the priests in the whole world. All those things which pertain to the worship of God or the stability of the Christian faith are to be administered according to his judgment. It is just indeed that the holy law should have the source of its dominion where the founder of the holy laws, our Savior, ordered St. Peter to build the cathedral of the apostles. . . .

We do concede and by this gift confer our imperial Lateran Palace, which excels all other palaces in the world, . . . upon the blessed Sylvester, our father, and upon all the succeeding popes, who shall ever sit upon the throne of Peter even until the end of the world. We give them next a diadem, that is the crown of our head; a miter; a shoulder band, that is, the collar which usually surrounds our imperial head; a purple mantle, a scarlet tunic, and all the other imperial garments. . . . We give them also the imperial sceptre, spears, standards, banners . . ., all the advantage of our high imperial rank, and the glory of our power. . . .

We have also decreed that our most venerable father Sylvester, supreme pontiff, and all his successors, ought to wear the diadem, that is, the crown of purest gold and jewels, which we have given him off of our own head, for the glory of God and the honor of St. Peter. The most holy pope, however, did not at all wish to use the golden crown above the clerical crown which he wore for the glory of St. Peter. But we, with our own hands, placed a miter of gleaming splendor on his head in token of the glorious resurrection of our Lord. Then, holding the bridle of his horse, we did him the office of groom out of reverence for St. Peter. . . .

Behold, in imitation of our power, in order that the supreme pontificate should not deteriorate, but should rather be adorned with more power and glory than the earthly empire, we do give and relinquish to the power and dominion of the oft-mentioned most blessed pontiff, our father Sylvester, the universal pope, and to his successors, our palace, as we have said before, the city of Rome, all the provinces, districts, and cities of Italy and the western regions. We make this inviolable gift, through this our sacred imperial charter, and decree that all these things shall permanently remain within the holy Roman church.

Therefore have we deemed it fitting to have our empire and the power of our kingdom transferred to the eastern regions; to have a city erected in our name in the most suitable spot of Byzantium; and to have our empire established there. For it is not right that the earthly ruler should have his power in that place where the supreme priest and head of the Christian religion has been established by the heavenly Ruler.

To Consider

1. What political and religious conditions in the eighth century lent the author of the *Donation of Constantine* the confidence to make such assertions about papal supremacy in the Christian world and the origins of this supremacy?

2. In the ongoing debate in the Latin West between church and state over their relative powers, why might the *Donation* have been a useful piece of evidence for the supporters of the papacy?

3. What does the *Donation* reveal about the power of "history" and religious symbolism in a world governed mostly by those who wielded a sword?

Source

a. Cantor, Norman, ed. *The Medieval World 300–1300.* 2nd ed. New York: Macmillan, 1963.
    Pp. 132–39.

3.4 JEWS IN EARLY MEDIEVAL EUROPE

The existence of Jews in early medieval Europe and the conditions of Jewish life hinged on the policies of Christian monarchs and the Catholic Church. Neither in this pre-1050 period nor later did kings and clergy always agree on what was the appropriate status for Jews in Christian society. The writings of the Church Fathers shaped clerical views, and none more than those of Saint Augustine of Hippo (354–430), which were fundamental to the formulation of papal Jewish policy. The first reading comes from Augustine's theological masterpiece, *The City of God*. In it, Augustine offers reasons for the Jews' continuing existence in Christian society. While monarchs were well aware of the church's view of the Jews' proper place in Christendom, other interests guided their treatment of the Jews, as seen in the second reading, a charter of protection that the Carolingian emperor Louis the Pious (814–840) issued to two Jews. The charter is addressed to royal officials throughout the empire, instructing them to execute it. Officials at Louis's court copied this charter into a formulary, which included exemplars of documents that officials would have issued to other individuals—Jews in this case—at the emperor's request. Louis's policies were generally favorable to Jews, and Archbishop Agobard of Lyon (816–840) was a strident critic of them. The third reading, from Agobard's *On the Insolence of the Jews*, was addressed to Louis. The title reflects Agobard's perspective.

a. Saint Augustine
Latin • after 410 CE • Hippo (modern Annaba, Algeria)

Yet the Jews who slew him [Jesus Christ] and chose not to believe him . . ., having been vanquished rather pathetically by the Romans, completely deprived of their kingdom . . . and scattered throughout the world (so that they are not lacking anywhere), are testimony for us through their own scriptures [the Hebrew Bible] that we have not contrived the prophecies concerning Christ. . . . Hence, when they do not believe our scriptures [the New Testament], their own, which they read blindly, are thus fulfilled in them. . . . For we realize that on account of this testimony, which they unwillingly provide for us by having and preserving these books [the Hebrew Bible], they are scattered among all the nations, wherever the church of Christ extends itself. . . .

For there is a prophecy given previously in the Psalms (which they still read) concerning this, where it is written . . . : "Slay them not, lest at any time they forget your law; scatter them in your might" [Psalm 59:12]. God thus demonstrated to the church the grace of his mercy upon his enemies the Jews, because, as the Apostle says, "Their offense is the salvation of the Gentiles." Therefore, he did not kill them . . . lest, having forgotten the law of God, they not be able to provide testimony on our behalf in this matter of our present concern.

b. Charter of Louis the Pious
Latin • ca. 814–824 CE • Aachen

May all people know that we have taken under our protection the following Hebrews, Rabbi Domatus and his nephew Samuel. Accordingly, neither you nor your subordinates nor your successors should presume to disturb these Jews illegally or to cause them physical harm. Nor should you at any time presume to seize from them any of their private property. . . . Do not presume to exact from the above Hebrews taxes, horse fees, residence fees, and road tolls. In addition, we permit them to trade and travel freely to sell their possessions to whomever they will. They have the right of living by their own laws. And they may hire Christian [men] to work for them, except on Christian feast days and Sundays. They are also free to acquire foreign slaves and to sell them within our borders. If a Christian has a dispute or litigation with them, he must bring in his behalf three acceptable Christian witnesses, in addition to three acceptable Hebrew ones, and thus argue his case. If Jews have a dispute or litigation with a Christian, they must produce Christian witnesses in their behalf.

c. Agobard of Lyon
Latin • ca. 827 CE • Lyon

Lying, [the Jews] boast to simple Christians that they are dear to you [Emperor Louis] on account of their ancestors; that they honorably come and go in your presence; that most esteemed [Christian] people seek their prayers and their blessings, admitting that they wished to have a lawgiver of the sort that the Jews had. They say that your advisers have been incited against us on their account, because we prohibit Christians from drinking their wine. As they haughtily proclaim this, they brag that they received large amounts of silver from them [Louis's advisers] for the purchase of the wine, and that, in reviewing the laws of the Church, no reason can be found why Christians must abstain from their food and drink. They present edicts in your name, sealed with golden seals, whose contents we think are untrue. . . . They expound the glory of their ancestors. They are permitted to build new synagogues in violation of the law. It has reached the point that simple Christians say that Jews preach better to them than do our own elders. Worst of all, the aforementioned royal officials ordered that market days, which used to be on Saturdays, be changed, so that their [Jewish] Sabbath not be violated, and they gave them [the Jews] the choice of days on which they should be held henceforth.

To Consider

1. According to Augustine, what do the subjection and scattering of the Jews symbolize, and why is Jewish survival useful for Christians?

2. What are Emperor Louis's motives in issuing such a charter on behalf of Jews? Does the charter seem to be in accord with Augustine's view of the Jews' status?

3. Why is Agobard so upset about the Jews, and how do Jews seem to challenge clerical ideals of a proper Christian society?

Sources

a. Cohen, Jeremy. *Living Letters of the Law: Ideas of the Jew in Medieval Christianity.* Berkeley: University of California Press, 1999. Pp. 32–33.

b. Stow, Kenneth R. *Alienated Minority: The Jews of Medieval Latin Europe*. Cambridge, MA: Harvard University Press, 1992. P. 60. Copyright © 1992 by the President and Fellows of Harvard College. Used by permission. All rights reserved.

c. Cohen. *Living Letters*. P. 127.

3.5 JEWISH COMMUNITIES AND MUSLIM AUTHORITIES IN THE CAIRO *GENIZA*

The Cairo *geniza* is an unparalleled source for the history of the Jews of the Muslim world between 1000 and 1250.[2] The *geniza* documents included here shed light on relations between Jews and the Fatimid government in the first half of the eleventh century. The first reading finds an unnamed Fatimid caliph refereeing a dispute between the Rabbanite and Karaite communities. The latter rejected the authority of the Talmud and its rabbinic interpreters. The second reading is a petition from the Rabbanite community of Tripoli (Lebanon) directed to a Karaite government minister, Abu Nasr Fadl al-Tustari, seeking his help in getting a royal license to build a synagogue, since theirs was lost during Caliph al-Hakim's (996–1021) persecution of religious minorities. The Tustaris, both Abu Nasr and his more powerful brother Abu Sa'd Ibrahim, often ignored sectarian differences and assisted Rabbanite Jews. In the third reading, an individual Jew beseeches another Jewish official to assist him in dealing with Muslim collectors of the poll tax (*jizya*). The fourth reading is a letter written by the head of a religious academy (*yeshiva*) in Jerusalem on behalf of the local Rabbanite community to a counterpart in Fustat regarding the efforts of the Jews of Fustat to provide aid to their coreligionists in Jerusalem.

a. Rabbanites versus Karaites
Arabic • 11th century • Egypt

A petition was submitted by the Rabbanite Jewish Community to the Court of the Commander of the Faithful [the caliph] in which they requested that they be treated in accordance with the exalted document which had been issued on their behalf, to the effect that their rabbis should be enabled to fulfill the commandments of their faith and the customary usages of their ancestors in their houses of worship, and that they be free to serve their communities in Jerusalem, Ramleh, and other cities. . . .

Therefore, the Commander of the Faithful has commanded that an open decree be issued, in which it is stated that neither of the two Jewish communities, namely the Rabbanites and the Karaites, are to be allowed to interfere with each other. . . . The Karaites cannot be allowed to obstruct the way of Rabbanite communal leaders by keeping them away from the districts of Jerusalem and Ramleh. Businessmen of both communities should be allowed to follow their own customary usages, as they wish, with regard to the conduct of business or abstention therefrom on their holidays.

---

2. For more on the Cairo *geniza*, see the introduction to "Jewish Traders' Letters from the Cairo *Geniza*" in the readings for chapter 2, p. 31.

b. License to Build a Synagogue
Hebrew • early 11th century • Tripoli (Lebanon)

We the entire congregation of Tripoli . . . wish to inform your excellency [al-Tustari] that we are in great distress because we have no place to pray. Everywhere else, the synagogues have been returned to the House of Israel—except in our town. The reason for this is that our synagogue was converted into a mosque. We are, therefore, petitioning our master to show us kindness with an edict from the government permitting us to build for ourselves a synagogue—as has been done everywhere else—on one of our ruined properties on which servants of the ruler dwell without paying any rent. We may point out to our lord [al-Tustari] that this very year the congregation in Jubayl rebuilt their synagogue, and no Muslim said anything. We also wish to inform our lord that we will pay an annual rent for the place to the Gentiles [Muslims].

c. Escaping a Tax Collector
Arabic • 11th century • Egypt

O master [a Jewish courtier named Abu Nasr], do not ask about my condition, which is one of sickness, infirmity, want, and excessive fear because of the search for me by the tax officer who is bearing down upon me. He is issuing warrants for my arrest. . . .

Now I seek refuge in God—praised be He—and in you. Protect me! . . . You can accomplish this for me by asking Shams al-Din [the chief tax officer in Cairo] to write a letter to the authorities in al-Mahalla that they should register us as missing, for everyone says that my only chance of salvation is in being registered as missing.

Then, if God should ordain that some money will be found to pay my poll tax, let it be said that it is for the fugitives, since it is not for myself alone, but for me and my sons, as I am held responsible for their poll tax as well.

d. Aid for the Jews of Jerusalem
Hebrew • early 11th century • Jerusalem

A letter from our envoy has arrived relating how you helped and aided him; how you encouraged the people to help their poor brethren time after time; and you informed them with touching words of their misery, their helplessness, and this heavy burden which has weighed like a yoke upon its inhabitants.

. . . the Arabs sit here as an imposition on the city [Jerusalem], imposing officials and fixed payments upon its men, in return for which they [the Arabs] do not molest those of the House of Israel who come to seek atonement among its stones, . . . who come to circumambulate the gates of the Temple to pray over them with upraised voices, . . . and who come to ascend the Mount of Olives with song and to stand there on holidays facing the Shrine of the Lord, the place of the Divine Presence. . . . Now the heavy tax is a fixed levy, and we are but few in number. We have only enough to pay a small part of it. The remainder we have to borrow at interest so that the pilgrims to the Holy City will not be threatened with tax notices. Thus, it is a duty for all Israel to support those who live in Jerusalem.

To Consider

1. Why was it so important for the Jewish community to have Jews who either served as officials in the Muslim government or had connections with Muslim officials?

2. How could the Muslim government act as a positive force in helping Jewish communities maintain their religious life and traditions?

3. What do these sources reveal about socioeconomic differences among the Jews and the effects of the Muslim government's taxation on individual Jews and their communities?

Source

a–d. Stillman, Norman A. *The Jews of Arab Lands: A History and Source Book.* Philadelphia: Jewish Publication Society of America, 1979. Pp. 192–94, 198–99, 204.

FOUR

Peoples of the Book Reading
Their Books

While the medieval Mediterranean was peopled overwhelmingly by believers in three different religions who tended to play up the differences among themselves, they actually had a great deal in common. Most notably they were all monotheistic, and each believed that the one God had spoken to them in a holy book that informed them about what they needed to know and do to achieve salvation and eternal life. These holy books—the Hebrew Bible, the Christian Bible, and the Qur'an—were rather difficult to understand in many ways (and of course most people could not read), so around each holy book a highly educated class of scholars developed who were capable of understanding them and teaching what they meant. For this reason elaborate educational institutions developed within each religious community, and a whole set of other books such as commentaries sprang up to help make the sacred texts more accessible. Intriguingly, ancient Greco-Roman thought was nevertheless deeply influential among medieval intellectuals as well, especially a strand of ancient philosophy called Neoplatonism. Since the holy books of these religions were not always clear, finally, there were disputes within each religion about what their meaning was. For this reason they all needed mechanisms to define right belief and right practice.

The readings in this chapter illustrate many of these dynamics—the similarities and differences among the sacred texts; the issue of the authority of translated holy books, which was particularly pressing for Greek and Latin Christians; the nature of schools and education; the character of some of the ancillary books that Mediterranean monotheists used to help interpret their holy books; what Neoplatonists taught; and the great range of interests that Mediterranean intellectuals could display despite what seem like narrow educational systems.

4.1 WHICH IS THE BIBLE? WHICH IS THE QUR'AN?

Though some portions of the Hebrew Bible were written more than a millennium before the Qur'an, both books, as well as the texts that Christians added to the Hebrew Bible to form what they call the New Testament, speak about humans, God, and nature in very similar terms. God is one; He is a just judge and merciful ruler. In all three books, time is conceived of as moving in a straight line from creation to a moment sometime in the future when all humans who ever lived will be judged and an eternal kingdom of peace will be established. Moreover, the books mention many of the same people: Abraham, Moses, Elijah, for example, are mentioned in all three, while Jesus, Mary, and the Jesus's disciples play substantial roles in both the Christian Bible and Qur'an. As a result it is often difficult to tell on first reading of a passage which one of these books it comes from. Below are two passages, one from the Qur'an and one from the Bible.

One is Psalm 8 from the Hebrew Bible.

Hebrew • first millennium BCE • Ancient Israel or Judah

The other is the first sura of the Qur'an

Arabic • early 7th century • Arabia

1. O Lord, our Sovereign,
        how majestic is your name in all the earth!
   You have set your glory above the heavens.
        Out of the mouths of babes and infants
   you have founded a bulwark because of your foes,
        to silence the enemy and the avenger.
   When I look at your heavens, the work of your fingers,
        the moon and the stars that you have established;
   what are human beings that you are mindful of them,
        mortals that you care for them?
   Yet you have made them a little lower than God,
        and crowned them with glory and honor.
   You have given them dominion over the works of your hands;
        you have put all things under their feet,
   all sheep and oxen,
        and also the beasts of the field,
   the birds of the air, and the fish of the sea,
        whatever passes along the paths of the seas.
   O Lord, our Sovereign,
        how majestic is your name in all the earth!
   In the name of God, Merciful to all, Compassionate to each!

2. Praises be to God, Lord of the Worlds:

Merciful to all,
Compassionate to each!
Lord of the Day of Judgement.
It is you we worship, and upon You we call for help.
Guide us to the straight path,
The path of those upon whom Your grace abounds,
Not those upon whom anger falls,
Nor those who are lost.

To Consider

1. Which passage is from the Bible? Which from the Qur'an?

2. How do you know?

Sources

Khalidi, Tarif, trans. *The Qur'an: A New Translation.* New York: Viking Penguin, 2008. P. 3.
Psalm 8, NRSV. Used by permission of Viking Books, an imprint of Penguin Publishing Group, a division of Penguin Random House LLC. All rights reserved.

4.2 THE PROBLEM OF SCRIPTURAL TRANSLATION

While all three major religious groups of the medieval Mediterranean had their holy book—the Hebrew Bible for Jews, the Christian Bible for Christians, and the Qur'an for Muslims—each major religious group's holy book was in a different language. The Christian Bible for the Latin Church was in Latin (this was Saint Jerome's translation, called the Vulgate, which he produced in the late fourth and early fifth centuries), while the Qur'an was in Arabic for all Muslims. The Bible that medieval Greek Christians read and studied was—not surprisingly—entirely in Greek: the Greek New Testament plus a Greek translation of the Hebrew Bible called the Septuagint (i.e., "the Seventy"), originally made by Greek-speaking Jews between the third century BCE and the second century CE (this was actually one of several Greek versions translated by late antique Jews). As always with translations, there was anxiety: Did the Greek version of the Bible accurately communicate the meaning of the Hebrew original? A widely retold story among both Jews and Christians about how the Septuagint came into being addressed that anxiety. Scholars today refer to the various versions of this story as the "Myth of the Septuagint." The version that follows is from an anonymous, late antique, Christian writer often referred to as Pseudo-Justin. The passage is drawn from his *Cohortatio ad Graecos* ("Exhortation to the Greeks").

a. Myth of the Septuagint
Greek • 260–300 CE • Western Mediterranean

Ptolemy, king of Egypt, formed a library in Alexandria and collected books from every quarter and filled it. Then, learning that certain ancient histories written in Hebrew characters had been preserved with scrupulous care, and being desirous to know what was written therein, he sent to Jerusalem for seventy wise men, who were familiar with the speech of both Greeks and Hebrews, and bade them translate the books. And, in order that they should be free from all disturbance and the sooner complete their task, he gave orders . . . that little cells, in number as many as the translators, should be erected there, to the end that every man should execute his translation apart by himself. . . . When he found that the seventy men had not merely expressed the same ideas but had employed the very same phraseology, and had not so much as in a single word failed to agree with each other, but had written on the same themes in the same language, he was amazed, and, believing that the translation had been written by divine power, he recognized that they merited every honour, as men beloved of God.

To Consider

1. Why would this story appeal to Greek-speaking Jews in antiquity? Why would it appeal to Christians, especially Greek Christians?

2. What claims about the authority of the Septuagint does this story implicitly assert?

Source

a. Wasserstein, Abraham, and David Wasserstein. *The Legend of the Septuagint from Classical Antiquity to Today.* Cambridge: Cambridge University Press, 2006. Pp. 106–7. Reproduced with permission of The Licensor through PLSclear.

4.3 STUDYING IN ELEVENTH-CENTURY IRAQ AND FRANCE

Each of the major Mediterranean monotheistic religions had its own revered holy text in its own language. The Hebrew Bible and Talmud (in Hebrew and Aramaic) for Jews, the Vulgate Latin Bible for Latin Christians, the Greek Bible for Greek Christians, and the Arabic Qur'an for Muslims. Both lower and higher education within all three of these communities was conducted overwhelmingly in the language of the holy text in schools exclusive to each community. This meant that there were obvious differences between the education one received in each community. For example, while the pagan works of Greco-Roman antiquity played virtually no role in the standard curriculum of Jewish and Muslim schools, their impact was substantial among both Greek and Latin Christians (though each community read only those classical works that were in their own language). There were many similarities as well. At the advanced level all students were taught to focus intently on the minute details of the holy texts, in many cases, especially among Jews and Muslims, memorizing them entirely, and they all learned that each passage could have more than one level of meaning—a literal or historical meaning, a legal meaning, a moral meaning, and others depending on their community. The passages below give us windows into what education was like in two very different parts of the Mediterranean cultural sphere: Iraq and northwestern France.

a. Education in Twelfth-Century Baghdad
Arabic • ca. 12th century • Baghdad [?]

In this passage a student by the name of Abu Ali al-Fariqi (d. 1134) about whom we know little describes his student days. He came to Baghdad in 1064 to study law with a great scholar named Abu Ishaq al-Shirazi (1003–1083),[1] who was then teaching at a mosque adjacent to which a khan or inn had been built to house students such as al-Fariqi. Although not technically a fully formed madrasa, this mosque-inn complex, as one scholar has referred to such institutions, was the direct ancestor of the great madrasas that would begin to be founded about the time al-Fariqi came to Baghdad.

I took up residence in a *khan* [inn] facing the mosque of Abu Ishaq in the quarter of Bab al-Maratib where the colleagues of the Master and the law students studying under his direction resided. When we were many, there were about twenty of us; when we were few, there were about ten. Master Abu Ishaq was teaching us the [Islamic] law course in a period of four years; so that when the law student had learned his course during this period of time, it was no longer necessary for him to study anywhere else. He used to give us a lesson following the morning-prayer, and another following the prayer of nightfall. In the year 460 [i.e., 1068], I crossed over to the West Side [of Baghdad] to Master Abu Nasr ibn al-Sabbagh[2] and studied his [legal] work *al-Shamil* under his direction; then I returned to Abu Ishaq and became his colleague until he died.

b. Education at the Monastery of Bec in Northwestern France
Latin • late 11th century • France

This passage is from a letter by Saint Anselm of Canterbury (1033–1109). Also known as Anselm of Bec (after the name of the monastery where he was long a monk, prior, and abbot) or Anselm of Aosta (the name of his Italian hometown), he was a brilliant theologian, often considered the founder of the Latin scholastic movement. During his long career as monk, Saint Anselm was intimately involved in education. This letter gives us insight into what learning in a Latin-Christian monastery was like at about the same time.

I have learned that Dom[3] Arnoul is giving you lessons. If this is so, I am delighted; as you may have noticed, I always wanted to see you make progress, and I now desire it more than ever. I have also heard that he excels in declensions; now, as you know, it has always been a

---

1. Al-Shirazi was a major figure in the development of the Shafi'i school of Islamic jurisprudence, one of the four schools that have survived to the present.

2. Al-Sabbagh was one of al-Shirazi's intellectual rivals in Baghdad.

3. "Dom," short for "Dominus," which means "lord" in Latin, was an honorific title of address for monks in some parts of the Latin-Christian world.

hard chore for me to decline[4] with children, and I am aware that in this science you made less progress with me than you should have. I send you, as to my dearest son, this word of advice, this plea, in fact, this order: everything you may read with him, or in any other way, apply yourself to declining it with care. And don't be in the least ashamed to study in this way, even if you think you don't need to, as if you were just a beginner. For, with him, you are consolidating in yourself, as you hear them, the things you already know, so as to remember them the more firmly; and under his instruction, if you do make an error, you will correct it and learn what you do not as yet know.

If he is not reading with you, and this through any negligence on your part, I am grieved; I want this done, and wish you to work at it as much as you can, particularly with regard to Virgil and the other authors whom you didn't read with me, avoiding those who contain any obscenity. If for some reason you are prevented from attending his classes, make every effort to decline, as I have told you to do, completely from the beginning to the end with the utmost concentration, and whenever you can, the greatest possible number of books you have already read. Also, show this letter to my dear friend in which, as well as asking you in a few words to give him all your affection, I ask him to prove that I can rely on his true friendship, and I assure him that whatever he does for you, it is for my own heart that he will be doing it. It is a long time since we pledged our mutual friendship; I shall never forget it; may he also be kind enough to remember it.

With all the respect in your power, extend our greetings to him and also to Prior Dom Gondulphus, and the other fathers and brothers who are with you. God be with you, my dearest child; and above all, do not disdain the advice of one who loves you with all his fatherly affection.

To Consider

1. According to the first passage, what was more important in Muslim education in the Middle Ages, the prestige of the educational institution or the renown of the scholar? What does this say about the nature of medieval Islamic education?

2. What levels of education does Saint Anselm's letter describe or allude to? Is there any reference in it to specifically religious learning?

3. What similarities and differences are there between the systems of education described in the two passages?

---

4. Much of the meaning of a Latin sentence is communicated by a series of special endings called declensions that clarify the relationships between words in a sentence. By "declining," Anselm means teaching students to recognize and understand these five different kinds of endings so that they are able to understand the meaning of each sentence.

Sources

a. Adapted from George Makdisi, *The Rise of Colleges: Institutions of Learning in Islam and the West* (Edinburgh: Edinburgh University Press, 1981). P. 30. Reproduced with permission of The Licensor through PLSclear.

b. Leclercq, Jean, OSB. *The Love of Learning and the Desire for God: A Study of Monastic Culture.* Trans. Catherine Misrahi. New York: Fordham University Press, 1981. Pp. 120–21. Republished with permission of Fordham University Press. Permission conveyed through Copyright Clearance Center, Inc.

4.4 *HADITHS* ON FASTING, CHARITY, AND THE *HAJJ*

From a very early point in Islamic history scholars supplemented the Qur'an with a large body of other sources called *hadiths*[5]—traditions of the Prophet Muhammad and of other early Muslims—when it came to explaining Islamic belief, practice, and law. Originally these circulated orally, but large, semicanonical collections of them began to be written down in the ninth century, and from then on when scholars cited *hadiths* they typically did so from one of the six most authoritative collections. The three *hadiths* that follow concern basic aspects of Islamic piety and are typical of the genre. Notice that each one begins with a chain (called an *isnad*) of early Muslims going back usually to an early follower of Muhammad—in the first two cases to Abu Hurayrah (d. ca. 678), in the third case to A'isha (d. 678), wife of the Prophet—and then to the Prophet himself testifying to its authenticity. These *isnad*s were carefully studied by Muslim scholars, and were one of the ways of determining which traditions could be considered authentic and which not. In most Islamic works on law, theology, or spirituality, *hadiths* are cited nearly as often as the Qur'an itself.

a. A *Hadith* on Fasting
Arabic • 9th century • Bukhara

'Abd Allah ibn Maslamah related to us, from Malik, from Abu al-Zinadi, from al-A'raji, that Abu Hurayrah—may God be pleased with him—reported that the Messenger of God (i.e., Muhammad) . . . said: "Fasting is an armor with which one protects oneself; so let not him (who fasts) utter immodest (or foul) speech, nor let him act in an ignorant manner; and if a man quarrels with him or abuses him, he should say twice, 'I am fasting.' And by Him in Whose hand is my soul, the odor of the mouth of one fasting is sweeter in the estimation of God than the odor of musk. He gives up his food and his drink and his (sexual) desire for My sake; fasting is for Me and I will grant its reward; and a virtue brings reward ten times like it."

b. A *Hadith* on Charity
Arabic • 9th century • Bukhara

Ishaq ibn Nasr related to me, that 'Abd al-Razzaq related to us [i.e., Ishaq], from Ma'mar, from Hammam, from Abu Hurayrah—may God be pleased with him—that the Prophet . . .

---

5. The Arabic word *hadith* means "account" or "report" in this usage.

said: "On every bone of the fingers charity is incumbent every day: One assists a man in riding his beast or in lifting his provisions to the back of the animal, this is charity; and a good word and every step which one takes in walking over to prayer is charity; and showing the way (to another) is charity."

c. A *Hadith* on the *Hajj* (Pilgrimage)
Arabic • 9th century • Bukhara

'Ali ibn 'Abd Allah related to us, when he said, "Sufyan related to us [i.e., 'Ali] when he said, I heard 'Abd al-Rahman ibn al-Qasim who said, I heard al-Qasim when he said, I heard A'ishah saying, We went out with nothing in view but the hajj, and when we reached Sarif, I menstruated. The Messenger of Allah . . . entered upon me and I was weeping. He said, What is the matter with thee? Hast thou menstruated? I said, Yes. He said: This is a matter that Allah has ordained for daughters of Adam, so do what the pilgrims do, except that thou shalt not make circuits round the House."

To Consider

1. All authentic *hadith*s have a chain of witnesses affixed at the beginning, just as here. What do you suppose is the purpose of this?

2. What would Christians and Jews likely think of the sentiments expressed here?

3. How would you paraphrase the meaning of the third tradition?

Adapted from

a–c. 'Ali, Maulana Muhammad, ed. and trans. *A Manual of Hadith.* Lahore: Ahmadiyya anjuman ishaati-Islam, 1944. Pp. 223–24, 210, 244. (*Isnad*s for these passages have been added from the Arabic original by Spencer Hunt.)

4.5 A CHRISTIAN AND A MUSLIM INTERPRET THEIR SCRIPTURES

Writing commentaries explaining a civilization's important books is a practice that goes back at least to Greco-Roman antiquity, with works such Virgil's *Aeneid*[6] and Aristotle's many treatises[7] receiving such treatment well before 650. This practice continued unabated throughout the medieval and early modern Mediterranean. Indeed commentaries, especially on holy books, were one of the most important genres of writing in this period. Two passages, one from a Latin-Christian commentary on the Bible, the other from a Muslim commentary on the Qur'an, follow.

---

6. Virgil (70–19 BCE) is generally considered Rome's greatest poet. His epic poem, the *Aeneid*, describes the founding of the city of Rome by Aeneas, a warrior fleeing the fall of Troy.

7. Plato (ca. 427–347 BCE) and his student, Aristotle (384–322 BCE), are considered the two greatest philosophers of Greco-Roman antiquity.

a. From Bede's Commentary on the Acts of the Apostles
Latin • late 7ᵗʰ or early 8ᵗʰ century • Wearmouth (Northern England)

A monk from the monastery of Wearmouth in far northern England, Bede (673–735) has often been called the most learned man in the Latin West in his lifetime. Among his many works are several commentaries on books of the Bible, including the Acts of the Apostles,[8] from which this passage is taken. The portions in italics are direct quotations from the relevant scriptural text; the rest is Bede's commentary.

3:1 *Now Peter and John[9] were going up into the temple, and so forth.*
At the ninth hour, when the apostles were about to enter the temple, they first cured a lame man who had been enfeebled for a long time. Then, laboring continuously until evening, they imbued many thousands of people with the word of faith, because the teachers of the church, coming at the end of the world, also preach first to ailing Israel[10] and afterwards to the gentile[11] world. For they are the laborers whom the householder brought into the vineyard at the ninth and the eleventh hour.

3:2a *And a certain man, who had been lame from his mother's womb, was being carried.*
Because the people of Israel were found rebellious, not only after the Lord's incarnation, but even from the earliest times when the law was given, they were as if lame from the mother's womb. This was well prefigured by Jacob's being blessed, indeed, but lame when he wrestled with the angel [see Gn 32:24–29], for this same people, when they prevailed over the Lord in his passion, was in some of [its members] blessed through faith, but in others lame through infidelity.

3:2b *Whom every day they put at the temple[12] gate called the beautiful.*
The beautiful gate of the temple is the Lord. Whoever enters through him will be saved. Enfeebled Israel, being unable to walk to this gate, was brought there by the word of the law and the prophets, so that she might request help from those who were entering into the interior places of the wisdom of the faith which she was to hear. Those who place the prophecies of things to come as it were at the gate are the hearers, but Peter is the guide into the temple. To him, in virtue of his strong profession of faith, the epithet of "rock" and the keys of heaven were given.

---

8. A book in the Christian New Testament.
9. Peter and John were two of Jesus's disciples.
10. I.e., the Jews
11. I.e., not Jewish.
12. I.e., the great Jewish Temple that once stood on the Temple Mount in Jerusalem.

b. From al-Tabari's Commentary on the Qur'an
Arabic • late 9th or early 10th century • Baghdad

This passage is from the famous (and immense) commentary on the Qur'an by Abu Ja'far Muhammad ibn Jarir al-Tabari (839–923), an Iranian Muslim who was also an important historian of early Islam. Here he discusses a single Qur'anic verse recounting a key moment in God's dealings with Satan. Once again the portions in italics are quotations from the Qur'an; the rest is the scholar's commentary.

2:34 And when We[13] said to the angels: "Prostrate before Adam"; so they prostrated, save Satan; he refused and waxed proud, and so he became one of the unbelievers.

His words[14] "And when We said . . ." are connected with his words "And when your Lord said to the angels . . ." (Qur'an 2:30). It is as if He were saying to the Jews of the Children of Israel who inhabited the place of the Messenger's emigration [i.e., Medina], while enumerating his blessings to them and reminding them of His favors, as we have previously described: "Recall what I did for you when I bestowed my blessing on you. I created all that is in the earth for you. And [recall] when I said to the angels that I was placing a vicegerent on earth, and honoured your forefather Adam with My knowledge, and My [marks of] favour and generosity. . . . And [recall] when I made the angels prostrate before him, and they did."

Then He made Satan an exception from all the [angels], and showed, by doing this, that he was [in fact] one of them, and that he had been commanded to prostrate with them, as He says: "save Satan"—he was not of those who prostrated. He [God] said: "What prevented you from prostrating when I commanded you?" (Qur'an 7:11–12). So God stated that He commanded Satan to prostrate before Adam, among the angels whom He had commanded. Then He excepted him from what He stated about their having prostrated before Adam, disqualified him from his description of them as obedient to His command, and negated of him the [act of] prostration before His servant, Adam, which He had affirmed of his angels.

To Consider

1. Does Bede explain the passages mostly by paraphrasing them, or by referring to other parts of the Bible? What does he mean by "enfeebled Israel"?

2. What aspects of the Qur'anic text does al-Tabari believe his readers will not understand without explanation? Is there anything in the verse that al-Tabari does not explain?

3. What are the differences and similarities between Bede's commentary on the Acts of the Apostles and al-Tabari's commentary on the Qur'an?

---

13. When God speaks in the Qur'an—which happens frequently—it is often in the first person plural.

14. I.e., God's words in the passage just quoted.

Sources

a. Bede. *Commentary on the Acts of the Apostles*. Trans. Lawrence T. Martin. Pp. 43–44. Copyright 1989 by Cistercian Publications, Inc. © 2008 by Order of Saint Benedict, Collegeville, Minnesota. Used with permission.
b. Adapted from al-Tabari, *The Commentary on the Qur'ān*, trans. J. Cooper, Wilferd Madelung, and Alan Jones (New York: Oxford University Press, 1987–), vol. 1, pp. 238–39. Reproduced with permission of The Licensor through PLSclear.

4.6 PLOTINUS ON BEAUTY AND THE ONE

While many schools of philosophy had flourished at different times in antiquity—Platonism, Aristotelianism, Stoicism—by the last few centuries of the Roman Empire the most influential one was something of a mixture of Platonism with Aristotelianism referred to by modern scholars as Neoplatonism. This philosophical system began to influence Jewish thinkers by the first century CE, and influenced Christian scholars almost from the beginning of the church. It continued to predominate in the Mediterranean throughout the early Middle Ages, including among Islamic intellectuals who knew the important Neoplatonic works after their translation into Arabic in the period from the late eighth to early tenth century. Though not all Jewish, Christian, and Muslim thinkers believed these pagan works could help elucidate their faiths, a very large number did, and so we find Peoples of the Book all around the Mediterranean studying Neoplatonic works.

a. Plotinus on Beauty
Greek • 3rd century • Rome

One of the most influential Neoplatonist philosophers was Plotinus (204–270), whose Enneads—*a huge collection of short essays—covered the full range of Neoplatonist thought, and who, directly or indirectly, influenced theologians and philosophers from all three religions. In this passage from the* Enneads *Plotinus elaborates on how the human perception of beauty might relate to an eternal Principle of beauty that exists in the realm of being well above humanity.*

Let us, then, go back to the source, and indicate at once the Principle that bestows beauty on material things. Undoubtedly this Principle exists; it is something that is perceived at the first glance, something which the Soul names as from an ancient knowledge and, recognizing, welcomes it, enters into unison with it. But let the [human] Soul fall in with the Ugly and at once it shrinks within itself, denies the thing, turns away from it, not accordant, resenting it. Our interpretation is that the [human] Soul—by the very truth of its nature, by its affiliation to the noblest Existents in the hierarchy of Being—when it sees anything of that kin, or any trace of that kinship, thrills with an immediate delight, takes its own to itself, and thus stirs anew to the sense of its nature and of all its affinity. But, is there any such likeness between the loveliness of this world and the splendours in the Supreme? Such a likeness in the particulars would make the two orders alike: but what is there in common between beauty here and beauty There? We hold that all the loveliness of this world comes by communion in Ideal-Form.

b. Plotinus on the One
Greek • 3ʳᵈ century • Rome

In this second passage Plotinus speaks directly about the divine One, the very origin of all things at the top of the hierarchy of being.

We are in search of unity: we are come to know the principle of all, the Good and First; therefore we may not stand away from the realm of the Firsts and lie prostrate with the lasts: we must strike out for those Firsts, rising from things of sense which are the lasts. Cleared of all evil in our intention toward the Good, we must ascend to the Principle within ourselves . . . ; only so do we attain to knowledge of that which is Principle and Unity. We shape ourselves into Intellectual-Principle; we make over our soul in trust to Intellectual-Principle so that we have this vision of the One. . . . The One, then, is not Intellectual-Principle but something higher still: Intellectual-Principle is still a being but that First is no being but precedes all Being. . . . Generative of all, the One is none of all; neither thing nor quantity nor quality nor intellect nor soul . . . : it is self-defined, unique in form or, better, formless, existing before Form was, or Movement or Rest.

To Consider

1. Why might such philosophizing, which refers to none of the scriptural texts of Jews, Christians, or Muslims, have appealed nevertheless to them?

2. What is the goal of Plotinus: to know the One, or to be changed into the One?

3. What about Plotinus's goal(s) would appeal to scriptural monotheists?

Source

a–b. Plotinus. *Enneads* 1.6.2 and 6.9.3. Adapted from Stephen MacKenna's translation, as reprinted in Algis Uzdavinys, *The Heart of Plotinus* (Bloomington, IN: World Wisdom, 2006), pp. 57, 210–11.

4.7 IBN HAZM CRITIQUES THE CHRISTIAN GOSPELS AND EXPLORES THE NATURE OF LOVE

One of the greatest thinkers of medieval Islam, Ibn Hazm of Córdoba (d. 1064) was both famously contentious and extremely productive as a scholar and intellectual, writing extensively on Islamic law in particular. He was, quite unusually, a Zahirite—a member of a school of Islamic jurisprudence that no longer exists that emphasized that the only sources of Islamic law were the Qurʹan and the Hadith, with no recourse to reasoning by analogy or the consensus of the faithful, as the other schools allowed. But he wrote on many other topics as well and was a poet too. The two passages below derive from his non-legal works.

a. From Ibn Hazm's *Detailed Examination*
Arabic • 11ᵗʰ century • al-Andalus

Ibn Hazm wrote an extensive encyclopedia about all the sects and religions that he was familiar with entitled Detailed Examination in Regard to Religions, Heresies, and Sects—*one of the first works in what would become an important genre in Islamic literature. In his treatment of Christianity in that work he offers a good example of the thinking of many Muslim scholars about the Christian Gospels: that they were collectively riddled with contradictions and logical errors, as the first passage below indicates.*

And in [Matthew 11:18–19] the Messiah said . . . : "John [the Baptist] came to you and he did not eat or drink, and you said, 'He is possessed.' Then the Son of Man came and you said, 'This man is a glutton and imbiber of wine, a wanton friend of tax collectors and sinners.'" In this passage there is lying and contradiction to Christian teaching. The lying occurs when [the Messiah] says that "John did not eat or drink" . . . [but in] the first chapter of the Gospel of Mark it says that the food of John [the Baptist] . . . was locusts and wild honey. . . . One of the two [Gospel] accounts is a lie without doubt. The contradiction to Christian teaching occurs when the passage relates that John did not eat and drink while the Messiah did eat and drink. Now the one whom God makes able to do without food and drink He has doubtlessly distinguished and raised in status above anyone who cannot do without food and drink. So John [the Baptist], therefore, must have been more virtuous than the Messiah.

b. From Ibn Hazm's *Collar of the Dove*
Arabic • 11ᵗʰ century • al-Andalus

*Quite strikingly, Ibn Hazm was also a superb observer of the psychology of erotic love, as this second passage from his equally famous treatise on this topic—*The Collar of the Dove—*makes clear. He is thus an excellent example of how wide-ranging Mediterranean scholars could be in their interests.*

After verbal allusion, when once the lover's advance has been accepted and an accord established, the next step consists in hinting with the glances of the eyes. Glances play an honourable part in this phase, and achieve remarkable results. By means of a glance the lover can be dismissed, admitted, promised, threatened, upbraided, cheered, commanded, forbidden. . . . Only a small fraction of the entire repertory is capable of being sketched out and described, and I will therefore attempt to describe here no more than the most elementary of these forms of expression.

To make a signal with the corner of the eye is to forbid the lover something; to droop the eye is an indication of consent; to prolong the gaze is a sign of suffering and distress; to break off the gaze is a mark of relief; to make signs of closing the eyes is an indicated threat. To turn the pupil of the eye in a certain direction and then to turn it back swiftly, calls attention to the presence of a person so indicated. A clandestine signal with the corner of both eyes is a question. . . .

The next scene in the love-play, now that confidence prevails and complete sympathy has been established, is the introduction of the Messenger. He needs to be sought and chosen with great care, so that he shall be both a good and energetic man; he is the proof of the lover's intelligence, for in his hands (under God's Providence) rests the life and death of the lover, his honour and his disgrace.

The Messenger should be presentable, quick-witted, able to take a hint and to read between the lines, possessed of initiative and the ability to supply out of his own understanding things which may have been overlooked by his principal; he must also convey to his employer all that he observes with complete accuracy; he ought to be able to keep secrets and preserve trusts; he must be loyal, cheerful and a sincere well-wisher. Should he be wanting in these qualities, the harm he will do to the lover for whom he is acting will be in strict proportion to his own shortcomings.

To Consider

1. What does the first passage tell us about what Ibn Hazm believed about the proper nature of a revealed scripture?

2. How would you explain the fact that one intellectual could be the author of both these works?

3. Does the passage on "hinting with the eyes" undermine Ibn Hazm's reputation as a very serious, argumentative religious thinker?

Sources

a. Ibn Hazm. *Al-Faṣl fī al-Milal.* Trans. Thomas E. Burman. In *Medieval Iberia: Readings from Christian, Muslim, and Jewish Sources,* ed. Olivia Remie Constable, 2nd. ed., 107–9. Philadelphia: University of Pennsylvania Press, 2012.
b. Ibn Hazm. *Ring of the Dove: A Treatise on the Art and Practice of Arab Love.* Trans. A. J. Arberry. London: Luzac and Company, 1953. Pp. 68, 73.

PART TWO

AN AGE OF CONFLICT AND COLLABORATION (1050–1350 CE)

FIVE

Holy and Unholy War

The decline of the imperial powers of the early medieval Mediterranean—the Byzantine Empire, the Ottonian "Roman" Empire, and the Abbasid, Fatimid, and Umayyad Caliphates—around the year 1000 CE was caused in part by climatic changes that undermined the economic and social fabric and institutional structures of these societies, and set into motion new waves of migration and movement into the Mediterranean from its African, West and Central Asian, and European hinterlands. The Mediterranean became an arena of conflict for warrior and mercantile powers, none of which were large enough to exert regional hegemony and which were consequently and out of necessity drawn into relationships of collaboration even as they competed against each other. Rulers made treaties with infidel princes and—if anything—the role of minority individuals and communities in the apparatus of state increased. Although the causes of conflict and competition may have been primarily economic, religious identity continued to serve as the ideological foundation for the legitimacy of rulers and as a conceptual framework for "international relations."

The readings here highlight these themes—from declarations of Crusade and *jihad* at the turn of the eleventh century to the Almohads' apparent abrogation of the *dhimma*, the "pact of protection," accorded to non-Muslims in the Qur'an. The readings show how members of religious minorities could rise to the pinnacles of power yet remained vulnerable to violent retaliation. The imperial papacy is seen caught between its commitment to fight the Infidel and defend Christendom and the compromises demanded by the exercise of imperial power, while hostile relations between Byzantines and Latins show that a common faith was not necessarily a recipe for collaboration, and hint at the role of ethnicity in shaping individual identity and communal relations.

5.1 THE FALL OF YUSUF IBN NAGHRILLA

In the mid-eleventh-century *taifa* kingdom of Granada, a population of Jews, Mozarab Christians, Andalusi Muslims, and Berbers of various nations was ruled over by the Zirids, a dynasty of Sanhaja warriors from Tunisia. From the 1030s to 1056, the power behind the throne was the rabbi, poet, statesman, and ha-Nagid ("prince of the Jews") Isma'il (Shmuel; Samuel) ibn Naghrilla of Córdoba. He was much admired by Muslim Andalusis and, despite his status as a *dhimmi*, served as *wazir*, tax collector, and general, skillfully navigating the intrigues of court, and serving as confidant to the king, Badis ibn Habus al-Muzaffar (1038–1073). His son, Yusuf (Yehosef; Joseph), endeavored to continue his father's work, but his clumsy machinations, including his rumored assassination of the heir apparent, provoked opposition within the royal family, among foreign Muslims, and within the Jewish community. In a desperate gambit to maintain power, in 1066 he secretly colluded with the Ibn Sumadih, king of neighboring Almería, promising to open the gates of the city in exchange for being crowned king of Granada and becoming a client of the rival kingdom. On the night of the planned attack, Yusuf was preemptively toasting his success, unaware that Ibn Sumadih had lost his nerve and turned his army back. When the plot was revealed, the populace rose up and killed Yusuf and his supporters, including many among the city's Jews, although both the kingdom and the city would retain a robust community.

a. The Fall of Yusuf and the Attack on the Jews of Granada
Arabic • 1094/5 CE • Aghmat, Morocco

'Abd Allah ibn Buluqqin, the last Zirid king of Granada (1073–1090), was deposed and imprisoned by the Almoravids at Agmat in Morocco, where he composed an exculpatory memoir and history of his family's rule in al-Andalus—in part to fend off charges the Zirids had collaborated with Christians and Jews. He hated Yusuf, who he believed had poisoned his father, Buluqqin. Here, in his book, The Explanation of the Situation That Prevailed under the Zirid Dynasty in Granada *(in Arabic,* Al-Tibyan) *he recounts the moment the plot was exposed.*

In accordance with God's decree that they should perish on Saturday 10 Safar [March 27], the Jew [Yusuf] decided to carouse that night with some of al-Muzaffar's leading slaves who had agreed to act in concert with him, although some of them secretly detested him.[1] The Jew then told them about Ibn Sumadih and assured them the latter would be coming to their

---

1. Al-Muzaffar was the throne name of 'Abd Allah's grandfather Badis ibn Habbus (1038–1073). The author always refers to Yusuf disparagingly as "the Jew"—because he believed Yusuf had murdered his father, Buluqqin, by poison. By contrast he often speaks highly of Isma'il, referring to him by the honorific "Abu Ibrahim."

aid and formally assign to them the rights of this and that village in the Vega of Granada.[2] One of these slaves who secretly hated him went up to him and said, "We know all about this. Now tell us about the way you've assigned these rights. Is our master [al-Muzaffar] alive or dead?" One of the Jew's entourage gave him an answer and rebuked him for his impudence. The slave immediately took umbrage and ran out blind drunk, shouting, "Hey folks! Have any of you heard about al-Muzaffar being betrayed by the Jew and that Ibn Sumadih's about to enter the city?" Everyone, high or low, heard of it from each other, and dashed in with the intention of killing the Jew. The latter managed to talk al-Muzaffar into coming out and then declared, "Here's your Prince alive and well!" The Prince tried to calm the mob, but all in vain. It was too late. The Jew turned and fled for his life inside the palace pursued by the populace, who finally ran him down and did him to death. They then turned their swords on every Jew in the city and seized vast quantities of their goods and chattels.

b. A Poem against Badis ibn Habus and the Jews of Granada
Arabic • before 1066 CE • Elvira, Kingdom of Granada

Abu Ishaq al-Ilbiri (d. 1067) was a jurist and bureaucrat in Zirid Granada who fell out of favor and was exiled to nearby Elvira, perhaps as a result of Yusuf's machinations. A stickler for the application of Islamic law, he wrote poems against Muslim jurists who he felt did not observe the law with sufficient rigor. At some point before 1066 he circulated a lengthy poem shaming the Zirid king and enjoining him to purge the Jewish dhimmis from his administration, given that in principle non-Muslims should not exercise authority over Muslims.

Go, tell all the Sanhaja
    the full moons of our time, the lions in their lair
The words of one who bears them love, and is concerned
    and counts it a religious duty to give advice.
Your chief has made a mistake
    which delights malicious gloaters
He has chosen an infidel as his secretary
    when he could, had he wished, have chosen a Believer.
Through him, the Jews have become great and proud
    and arrogant—they, who were among the most abject
And have gained their desires and attained the utmost
    and this happened suddenly, before they even realized it.
And how many a worthy Muslim humbly obeys
    the vilest ape among these miscreants.

---

2. Ma'n ibn Sumadih was ruler of the *taifa* kingdom of Almería (1041/42–1052). During the mandate of Isma'il ibn Naghrilla, Almería sent an army to conquer Granada, but it was crushed by Granadan forces under Isma'il's command (by his account).

And this did not happen through their own efforts
  but through one of our own people who rose as their accomplice.
Oh why did he not deal with them, following
  the example set by worthy and pious leaders?
Put them back where they belong
  and reduce them to the lowest of the low. . . .

  . . .

Their chief ape has marbled his house[3]
  and led the finest spring water to it.
Our affairs are now in his hands
  and we stand at his door.
He laughs at us and at our religion
  and we return to our God.
If I said that his wealth is as great
  as yours, I would speak the truth.
Hasten to slaughter him as an offering,
  sacrifice him, for he is a fat ram
And do not spare his people
  for they have amassed every precious thing.
Break loose their grip and take their money
  for you have a better right to what they collect.
Do not consider it a breach of faith to kill them
  —the breach of faith would be to let them carry on.
They have violated our covenant with them
  so how can you be held guilty against violators?

c. A Jewish View of Yusuf's Fall
Hebrew • ca. 1160/61 CE • Toledo, Castile

The philosopher and scientist Abrahim ibn Daud (ca. 1110–1180) was born in Córdoba and emigrated to Christian Castile after the arrival of the Almohads. It is suggested he participated in the "school of translation" at Toledo, and was put to death on account of his religious beliefs. His Book of Tradition *presents a history of the Jews of al-Andalus since the foundation of the community in Roman times, focusing on the Rabbanite elite and their struggle against Karaism.*

[Shmu'el's (Isma'il's)] son, Rabbi Jehoseph [Yusuf] ha-Levi the *Nagid*, succeeded to his post. Of all the fine qualities which his father possessed, he lacked but one. Having been reared in wealth and never having had to bear a burden [of responsibility] in his youth, he lacked

---

3. A reference to the first Alhambra palace, built by Yusuf.

his father's humility. Indeed, he grew haughty—to his own destruction. The Berber princes became so jealous of him that he was killed on the Sabbath day, the ninth of Tebet [4]827, along with the community of Granada and all those who had come from distant lands to see his learning and power. He was mourned in every city and in every town.

To Consider

1. Why would the kings of Granada empower Jewish officials?

2. Was the reaction against Yusuf religious or political?

3. How does this episode reflect the status of Jews in al-Andalus and the Islamic Mediterranean?

Adapted from

a. Ibn Buluggin, 'Abd Allah. *The Tibyān: Memoirs of 'Abd Allah B. Buluggīn, Last Zīrid Amīr of Granada.* Trans. Amin T. Tibi. Leiden: E. J. Brill, 1986. P. 75. Reproduced with permission of The Licensor through PLSclear.

b. Lewis, Bernard. "An Anti-Jewish Ode: The Qasida of Abu Ishaq against Joseph ibn Nagrella." In *Salo Wittmeier Baron Jubilee Volume on the Occasion of His Eightieth Birthday,* ed. Saul Lieberman, 657–68. Jerusalem: American Academy for Jewish Research, 1975. Pp. 659, 660, 662.

c. Cohen, Gerson D. *A Critical Edition, with a Translation and Notes, of the Book of Tradition (Sefer ha-Qabbalah).* London: Routledge & K. Paul, 1969. Pp. 75–76.

5.2 THE TRIAL OF PHILIP OF MAHDIA

Roger II of Sicily (count, 1105–1130; king, 1130–1154) ruled over a population of Muslims, and Latin and Greek Christians. Modeling his administration on that of the Arabic chancery of Fatimid Egypt, he entrusted much of the administration of his kingdom to the "Palace Saracens"—former Muslim slaves (including many eunuchs) from North and Central Africa, who had ostensibly converted to Christianity. One of these, his chamberlain and admiral, Philip of Mahdia, helped complete Roger's conquest of "Africa" in 1153, when he captured Bône ('Annaba, in modern Algeria). Recalled to the capital, Philip was put on trial and executed. In the succeeding decades the Sicilian kings continued to confide in the "Palace Saracens."

a. The Trial of Philip of Mahdia
Latin • ca. 1160 CE (with additions from the 1260s?) • Salerno

Romuald of Salerno, a cleric and courtier of Roger's successors, is credited as author of the Chronicon, *or* Annals, *a history of the Sicilian kingdom. The anecdote appears in the margin of the twelfth-century manuscript and was almost certainly added by an editor, perhaps as late as the 1260s. There is little doubt, however, that it is based on contemporary written and/or oral sources. Philip had just returned from conquering 'Annaba, thus completing Roger's "Kingdom of Africa."*

So that everyone in the world may know plainly how King Roger was Catholic with all his effort, and how he burned with fervor and zeal for the Christian faith, the testimony of the following deeds will make plain.

King Roger had a certain eunuch by the name of Philip who by his honest service became greatly favored and pleasing to him. And because he found him to be faithful in his affairs and a suitable executor of his business, he placed him in charge of the whole palace and established him as master of his entire household. Since, in this manner, as time went by [Philip] grew in his esteem and affection, he was appointed admiral of [Roger's] fleet and sent with it to 'Annaba, which he captured and plundered by the edge of the sword, and returned to Sicily in triumph and glory.[4]

But because he was revealed as ungrateful to the author of all of his blessings, and repaid the Celestial King with evil for good, he deservedly incurred the anger and indignation of the terrestrial king. Indeed, beneath of the cloak of a Christian name he acted like a secret soldier of the devil, and as a sort of trap he gave out the appearance of a Christian, while he was completely a Muslim in thought and deed. He hated Christians, and esteemed pagans greatly. He entered churches unwillingly, but often visited the synagogues of the evil ones and provided them with oil for filling their lamps and whatever else was needed. He deeply spurned Christian traditions and did not cease from eating meat on Fridays and in Lent, but sent his envoys with offerings to the tomb of Muhammad, and commended himself to the priests of that place with many prayers.[5]

When, then, this and other wicked deeds, which he obscured with the shadow of a Christian name, came to the ears of King Roger, moved by the zeal of God but according to his own wisdom, he had [Philip] summoned to his court for the aforementioned crimes. But since [Philip] was confident in the grace and esteem of the king, he responded manfully to his accusers and what had been said against him, and denied them as if they had been completely false. But by the working of divine justice, his accusers proved that which they said was true by the testimony of honorable men.

Philip, then, believing himself to have been discovered, and fearing the king's sentence, began to beg forgiveness and seek the mercy of the king, and pledged that from then on in future he would be a Catholic Christian.

Then, the king fired up by the flame of faith, bursting into tears, said, "May you know by your faith, dear subjects, that my soul has been pierced by the greatest pain, and goaded by great stabs of anger, because this, my minister, whom, once his sins had been cleansed, I raised from a boy to be catholic, has been revealed as a Muslim, and this Muslim carried out works of faithlessness under the name of faith. Yet, had he offended our majesty in other ways: had he carried off even the greater part of our treasury, he would have certainly found forgiveness before us, and would have obtained mercy in recollection of all of his good service.

---

4. 'Annaba or Bône is on the coast of modern Algeria.

5. In fact, the Tomb of the Prophet in Medina had an honor guard made up of African eunuchs. Philip could well have been in contact with these via slaves and functionaries in the Fatimid court.

But, because by his deeds he has principally offended God, and he provided others with the opportunity and example to sin, I should not remit such injury to Our faith and offense to the Christian religion even to my own son, nor should I pardon any other kin. By this deed, let the whole world know that I love the Christian faith with all my will, and will not cease from avenging injury to it even from my own ministers. It is for this that laws are established, and our laws are girded by the Sword of Impartiality that they might wound the enemy of the faith with the Sword of Justice, and they might, thus, lead the faithless into the Snare of Dread."

Then the counts, magistrates, barons and judges who were present, attentive to the just soul of the king, set themselves apart, and having taken counsel for a long time, said, giving sentence: "We order Philip, a derider of the Christian name and agent of the works of faithlessness under the guise of faith, to be burned by vengeful flames, so that he who rejected the fire of charity, may know the fire of combustion, and that no relic of this most evil man might remain, but that, having been converted into ashes by temporal fire, he may go on to be burned in perpetuity by the eternal fire."

Then, with the magistrates having spoken, having been tied to the hooves of wild horses, he was violently dragged to the lime-kiln which was in front of the palace, where he was loosed from the feet of the horses, thrown into the midst of the flames, and was quickly burned up. Moreover, the other accomplices and collaborators in his iniquity were also given the death sentence.

Thus, by this deed, it was made most manifest that king Roger was a most Christian and catholic prince, who in order to avenge an injury of the faith did not spare even his chamberlain and own protégé, but handed him over to the flames, to [Roger's] honor and glory.

b. From *The Complete History* (ca. 1180–1231) of 'Izz al- Din 'Ali ibn al-Athir
Arabic • ca. 1180–1231 CE • Damascus

'Izz al- Din 'Ali ibn al-Athir (1130–1263) was one of the great historians of medieval Islam. His encyclopedic The Complete History *began with the biblical creation and continued to his own day. His source for Philip of Mahdia's story was likely the refugee Zirid prince 'Abd al-'Aziz ibn Shaddad (d. after 1186), who, having been dispossessed of his lands by the Almohad invaders, visited the Norman court at Palermo in 1156–1157 en route to Damascus, where he likely met the historian.*

In this year the fleet of Roger, king of the Franks in Sicily, sailed to the city of 'Annaba, and in command over them was his eunuch Philip of Mahdia. Then, [Philip] besieged the town, gathered Arab troops [to use] against it, and captured it in the month of Rajab [September/October 1153]. He took the inhabitants prisoner and seized their property, but connived with certain scholars (*'ulama'*) and pious men so that they could flee to the countryside with their families and possessions.[6] Thereafter, he remained for ten days, and then returned to

---

6. Such negotiations were not uncommon in the Islamicate and Christian Mediterranean in order to achieve a conquest with minimal resistance.

Mahdia along with some prisoners, and [then] returned to Sicily. Thereafter, Roger arrested him on account of the kindness with which he had favored the Muslims of 'Annaba.

And then Philip and all of his eunuchs were said to be Muslims and to have concealed this. And there were witnesses against him that he did not fast with the king and that he was a Muslim. Next, Roger gathered [his] bishops, priests and knights and they sentenced [Philip] to be burned [to death], and he was burned in Ramadan [November/December 1153]. And this was the first debilitation which befell the Muslims in Sicily.

To Consider

1. Why would Roger model his palace administration on the Fatimid court?
2. Which of the two accounts seems plausible, and why?
3. What makes this episode quintessentially "Mediterranean"?

Adapted from

a–b. Catlos, Brian. "Who Was Philip of Mahdia and Why Did He Have to Die?" *Mediterranean Chronicle* 1 (2011): 100–102.

5.3 FRANKS AND MUSLIMS IN CRUSADE-ERA PALESTINE AND SYRIA

Frankish noblemen, clergy, and commoners settled in Crusader-ruled Syria and Palestine in the wake of the conquest of Jerusalem in December 1099. After Salah al-Din's (1174–1193) reconquest of Jerusalem in 1187 the area of Frankish settlement was reduced to the ports of Tyre, Acre, and Antioch, a strip of Syrian coastline, and a few inland enclaves. The conquest of Tyre in 1261 and Antioch in 1268 brought an end to the Frankish presence here. The Frankish principalities traded and carried out diplomacy with local Muslim princes; and although there was much hostility, native Muslims and Franks lived side by side, and often interacted peacefully.

a. The Chronicle of Fulcher of Chartres
Latin • 1101–late 1120s CE • Jerusalem/Chartres, France

Fulcher of Chartres (d. after 1128) was a priest who was present at Clermont, accompanied the armies of the First Crusade, and went on to serve as royal chaplain to Baldwin I of Jerusalem (1100–1118). As early as 1101 he began to write a chronicle of the Crusade, which he completed in the late 1120s. Here he reflects on the Frankish settlers' new sense of homeland.

Consider, I pray, and reflect how in our time God has extended the West into the East. For we who were Westerners now have been made Easterners. He who was a Roman or a Frank has been made in this land a Galilean or Palestinian.[7] He who was of Rheims or Chartres, has become of Tyre or Antioch. We have already forgotten our birthplaces; to many of us they

---

7. "Roman" meaning here an Italian.

have become either unknown or are unspoken of. Here, one already possesses one's own homes and servants as if he had inherited these from his father, and they have taken as wives not only a fellow countrywoman, but a Syrian, or Armenian, or even a Muslim who has received the grace of baptism.[8] Some have in their homes their father-in-law, or daughter-in-law, or son-in-law, or stepson, or stepfather. One grows vines, while another tills the field. Different languages, now made common, become known to both nations, and faith unites those whose forefathers were unknown to each other. Whereby, it is written, "and the lion will eat straw like the ox" [Isaiah 65:25]. He who was a foreigner is now almost a native, and he who was a tenant has now been made a dweller.

b. The Franks through Arab Eyes
Arabic • 1180s CE • Damascus

'Usamah ibn Munqidh (1098–1188) was a Syrian nobleman, poet, warrior, and diplomat, who was born the same year as Clermont and died a year after Salah al-Din's conquest of Jerusalem. He traveled extensively in Syria, Egypt, and the Latin East, and came to know the Franks, some of whom he befriended very well. His memoir, The Book of Contemplation, *written in his last years, includes candid reflections on many subjects, including the Christian newcomers.*

Anyone who is recently arrived from the Frankish lands is rougher in character than those who have become acclimated and have frequented the company of Muslims. Here is an instance of their rough character (may God abominate them!): Whenever I went to visit the holy sites in Jerusalem, I would go in and make my way up to the al-'Aqsa Mosque, beside which stood a small mosque that the Franks had converted into a church.[9] When I went into the al-Aqsa Mosque—where the Templars, who are my friends, were—they would clear out that little mosque so that I could pray in it.[10] One day, I went into the little mosque, recited the opening formula "God is great!" and stood up in prayer. At this, one of the Franks rushed at me and grabbed me and turned my face towards the east, saying, "Pray like *this!*"

A group of Templars hurried towards him, took hold of the Frank and took him away from me. I then returned to my prayers. The Frank, that very same one, took advantage of their inattention and returned, rushing upon me and turning my face to the east, saying, "Pray like *this!*"

So the Templars came in again, grabbed him and threw him out. They apologized to me, saying, "This man is a stranger, just arrived from the Frankish lands sometime in the past few days. He has never before seen anyone who did not pray towards the east."

---

8. "Syrian" refers to a Syriac Christian.

9. The al-Aqsa Mosque is on the Temple Mount in Jerusalem, and is often characterized as the third most important mosque in the Islamic world.

10. The Templars were one of the monastic military orders dedicated to the protection of the Holy Land and Christian pilgrims; the Temple Mount was their headquarters.

"I think I've prayed quite enough," I said and left. I used to marvel at that devil, the change of his expression, the way he trembled and what he must have made of seeing someone praying towards Mecca.

On another occasion, one of 'Usamah's agents recounted having been invited to dine in the home of a Frank in Antioch.

I went along with him and we came to the home of one of the old knights who came out in one of the first expeditions of the Franks. He was since removed from the stipend-registry and dismissed from service, but he had some property in Antioch off which he lived. He presented a very fine table, with food that was extremely clean and delicious. But seeing me holding back from eating, he said, "Eat and be of good cheer! For I don't eat Frankish food: I have Egyptian cooking-women and never eat anything except what they cook. And pork never enters my house." So I ate, though guardedly, and we left.

To Consider

1. Why would Franks be so eager to culturally assimilate in the Near East?

2. Why would Knights Templar protect a Muslim who was praying in their church?

3. If 'Usamah had many friends who were Franks, why would he say, "May God abominate them"?

Adapted from

a. Hagenmeyer, Heinrich. *Fulcheri Carnotensis Historia Hierosolymitana: 1095–1127.* Heidelberg: Winter, 1913. Pp. 748–49. For an English translation, see Edward Peters, *The First Crusade: The Chronicle of Fulcher of Chartres and Other Source Materials* (Philadelphia: University of Pennsylvania Press, 1998).
b. Cobb, Paul M. *The Book of Contemplation: Islam and the Crusades.* New York: Penguin Books, 2008. Pp. 147, 153.

5.4 LATIN-BYZANTINE RELATIONS

Relations between the Latin lands and Byzantium had long been rocky—a simmering distrust aggravated by religious divisions, cultural differences, Latin military aggression against the Byzantine Empire, and the empire's intrigues against the Crusaders. Latins coveted the wealth and prestige of the empire, while from the 1100s Byzantium became increasingly dependent on Latin warriors and Italian traders, the former infiltrating the court through marriage and service, and the latter aggressively acquiring and undercutting Byzantine naval power. This relationship led to social and political integration, but also to tensions, which occasionally flared up as sectarian violence, sometimes officially sanctioned. Tensions were aggravated when the widow of Manuel Komnenos (1143–1180), the Latin princess Maria of Antioch (1161–1180), came to power as regent for their son Alexios (1180–1183). In 1182 the populist usurper Andronikos Komnenos (1183–1185) unleashed the fury of the Constantinople mob on the city's Italians, who had opposed his seizure of power. Ultimately, the Venetians would take their revenge first with the torture and execution of the deposed Andronikos, and later with the 1204 sack of Constantinople and the partition of the empire.[11]

a. The Expulsion of the Venetians
Greek • 1180s CE • Constantinople

John Kinnamos (d. ca. 1185) was an imperial secretary to Manuel I (1143–1180) who wrote The Deeds of John and Michael Comnenus, *a history of the reign of Manuel and his predecessor John II (1118–1143). Here he recounts official reprisals taken against the Venetians in 1171.*

At that time [Manuel] committed the Venetians who lived in Byzantion and anywhere else in the Romans' land to public prisons and caused their property to be registered in the state treasury. . . .[12] The nation is corrupt in character, jesting and rude more than any other, because it is filled with sailors' vulgarity. As they formerly offered an allied force to emperor Alexios [Komnenos; 1081–1118] when . . . Robert crossed from Italy to Durrës and besieged that place, they received various recompense, and in particular a confined space in Byzantion was assigned to them, which the commonality call the "Embolon" [Quarter].[13] Also on this account they alone [of all the merchants] . . . pay tithes on commerce to none of the Romans. . . . . . . Their immoderate enrichment from that source quickly elevated them to boastfulness. They used to treat the citizen like a slave. . . .

Angered thereat, emperor John [II Komnenos; 1118–1143] expelled them from the Roman state [in 1122]. They were eager to take vengeance on the Romans. Having readied a fleet of their ships, they assailed the land; they took Chios and ravaged the celebrated islands of Rhodes and Lesbos. Landing in the Palestinians' territory they besieged and took Tyre along with them; the wretches pursued a course of piracy by sea and had no mercy on mankind. Therefore, the emperor admitted them on the previous terms and raised them to still more bragging and pride.

b. Anti-Latin Violence
Latin • 1180s CE • Tyre

William of Tyre (ca. 1130–1186) was a second-generation eastern Frank, who was educated in Europe and returned to serve the kings of Jerusalem as an ambassador, royal tutor, chancellor, and

---

11. For contrasting accounts of the sack of Constantinople in 1204, see Harry J. Magoulias, *O City of Byzantium: Annals of Niketas Choniatēs* (Detroit: Wayne State University Press, 1984), 315–18; and Margaret R. B. Shaw, *Chronicles of the Crusades* (Baltimore: Penguin, 1985), 249.

12. Byzantion is Constantinople; the "Romans" here means Byzantines.

13. In 1081 the Norman Duke of Apulia, Robert Guiscard, attacked Durrës (modern Albania) in Byzantine Dalmatia, and the Venetians provided naval support to the empire.

archbishop of Tyre (1175–1186). He wrote several histories, including a detailed account of the Frankish kingdoms, The History of Deeds Done beyond the Sea. *Here, he recounts the anti-Latin violence sponsored by Andronikos in 1182.*

The conspiracy [of Andronikos Komnenos] continued to gain strength [and] . . . this change of affairs led to consternation among the Latins, for they feared that the citizens would make a sudden attack on them. . . . Those who were able to, therefore, fled from the wiles of the Greeks and the death which threatened them. . . .

The aged and infirm, however, with those who were unable to flee, were left in their homes and on them fell the wicked rage which the others had escaped. For Andronikos, who had secretly caused ships to be prepared, led his entire force into the city. As soon as they entered the gates these troops, aided by the citizens, rushed to that quarter of the city occupied by the Latins and put to the sword the little remnant who had been either unwilling or unable to flee with the others. . . .

Regardless of treaties and the many services which our people had rendered to the empire, the Greeks seized all those who appeared capable of resistance, set fire to their houses, and speedily reduced the entire quarter to ashes. Women and children, the aged and the sick, all alike perished in the flames. . . . They also set fire to churches, and venerated places of every description, and burned, together with the sacred edifices, those who had fled there for refuge. . . . Monks and priests were the special victims of their madness and were put to death under excruciating torture. . . .

. . . It is said that more than four thousand Latins of various age, sex and condition were delivered to barbarous [Muslim] nations for a price.

In such fashion did the perfidious Greek nation, a brood of vipers, like a serpent in the bosom or a mouse in the wardrobe evilly requite their guests—those who had not deserved such treatment and were far from anticipating anything of the kind; those to whom they had given their daughters, nieces, and sisters as wives and who, by long living together, had become their friends.

To Consider

1. Which account seems more credible, and why?

2. If the Greeks disliked the Latins so much, why were so many Latins living in Constantinople?

3. What do these passages suggest about the intensity of hostility between members of the same religion?

Adapted from

a. Kinnamos, Ioannes. *Deeds of John and Manuel Comnenus.* Trans. Charles Macy Brand. New York: Columbia University Press, 1976. Pp. 209–10.
b. William of Tyre. *A History of Deeds Done beyond the Sea.* Trans. and ed. Emily Atwater Babcock and August C. Krey. New York: Columbia University Press, 1943. Vol. 2, pp. 464–65.

5.5 PAPACY AND POWER

With the eleventh-century Gregorian reforms the papacy began to emerge as a centralized, interregional institution that claimed a monopoly on the interpretation and dissemination of the faith, and authority over the entire church and the rulers of Christendom. This brought the bishops of Rome into conflict with Latin kings and nobility in the Investiture Controversy, and with the Byzantine Empire, resulting in the Great Schism of 1054. As part of its charge the papacy sought to regulate trade with the enemies of Christendom, particularly Muslim lands.

a. A Papal Embargo
Latin • 1179 CE • Rome

The Third Lateran Council was convened by Alexander III (1159–1181). The canons (laws) promulgated dealt with various aspects of church reform, but also included a prohibition against trading certain goods with Muslims. This general prohibition was refined and re-promulgated regularly through the sixteenth century.

[Canon] 24. Cruel avarice has so seized the hearts of some that though they glory in the name of Christians they provide the Muslims with arms and wood for helmets, and become their equals or even their superiors in wickedness and supply them with arms and necessaries to attack Christians. There are even some who for gain act as captains or pilots in galleys or Muslim pirate vessels. Therefore, we declare that such persons should be cut off from the communion of the church and be excommunicated for their wickedness, that Catholic princes and civil magistrates should confiscate their possessions, and that if they are captured they should become the slaves of their captors. We order that throughout the churches of maritime cities frequent and solemn excommunication should be pronounced against them. Let those also be under excommunication who dare to rob Romans or other Christians who sail for trade or other honorable purposes. Let those also who in the vilest avarice presume to rob shipwrecked Christians, whom by the rule of faith they are bound to help, know that they are excommunicated unless they return the stolen property.

b. Permission to Trade
Latin • 1198 CE • Rome

The papacy sometimes collected fines on those who broke the embargo, but at times it granted exemptions, including this one, by Innocent III (1198–1216) to the city of Venice.

Besides the indulgence we have promised to those going at their own expense to the East, and besides the favor of apostolic protection granted to those helping that country, we have renewed the decree of the Lateran Council which excommunicated those who presume to give arms, iron, or wood to the Saracens for their galleys and dhows, and which excommunicated those who act as helmsmen on their galleys and dhows, and which at the same time decreed that they should be deprived of their property for their transgressions by the secular arm and by the consuls of the cities, and that, if caught, they become the slaves of their captors. Following the example of Pope Gregory (VII; 1073–1085), our predecessor of pious memory, we have placed under sentence of excommunication all those who in future consort with the Muslims, directly or indirectly, or who attempt to give or send aid to them by sea, as long as the war between them and us shall last.

But our beloved sons, Andreas Donatus and Benedict Grilion, your messengers, recently came to the Apostolic See and were at pains to explain to us that by this decree your city was suffering no small loss, for she is not devoted to agriculture but rather to shipping and to commerce. We, therefore, induced by the paternal affection we have for you, and commanding you under pain of anathema not to aid the Muslims by selling or giving to them or exchanging with them iron, flax, pitch, pointed stakes, ropes, arms, helmets, ships, and boards, or unfinished wood, do permit for the present, until we issue further orders, the taking of goods, other than those mentioned, to Egypt and Babylon, whenever necessary. We hope that in consideration of this kindness you will bear in mind the aiding of Jerusalem, taking care not to abuse the apostolic decree, for there is no doubt that whosoever violates his conscience in evading this order will incur the anger of God.

c. A Request for Protection
Latin • 1246 CE • Rome

In 1246 Innocent IV (1243–1254) wrote to Abu Zakariyya Yahya (1229–1249), the sultan of Tunis, seeking protection for the clergy and Christian merchants in the Hafsid realms. Identical letters were sent to the Muslim rulers of Bougie and Ceuta.

Innocent, the servant of the servants of God, fearing of and close to the Lord, to the illustrious king of Tunis.

. . . Since, therefore, as We understand, many Christians live under the rule of your magnificent scepter, and go there in order to exercise commerce . . . We most attentively request and advise your royal highness, that you allow our venerable brother . . . the Bishop of Morocco, and those worthy Friars Minor who that bishop has dispatched there for the great benefit and glory of your realm, to freely sojourn there, together with those Christians, just as has been the case for some time, so that you might receive the divine reverence of the Apostolic See with merciful piety.[14]

To Consider

1. What sorts of commodities would the papacy try to limit, and why?
2. How would merchants likely have reacted to these restrictions?

---

14. "Friars Minor" refers to members of the Franciscan Order. The Franciscan Lope Fernández Daín had been ordained bishop of Morocco in Marrakesh in October 1246.

3. What do these sources suggest regarding the willingness and ability of the papacy to control trade?

Adapted from

a. Tanner, Norman P., ed. *Decrees of the Ecumenical Councils*. Washington, DC: Georgetown University Press, 1990. P. 223. © Tanner, Norman P., Burns & Oates, an imprint of Bloomsbury Publishing Plc.
b. Cave, Roy C., and Herbert H. Coulson. *A Source Book for Medieval Economic History*. Milwaukee: Bruce, 1936. Pp. 104–5.
c. Mas Latrie, Louis de. *Traités de paix et de commerce et documents divers concernant les relations des Chrétiens avec les Arabes de l'Afrique septentrionale au moyen-âge*. Paris: Plon, 1866. Vol. 2, p. 13 (Document XVI, in Latin). Reproduced with permission of The Licensor through PLSclear.

5.6 THE ALMOHAD REVOLUTION

The Almohads have often been portrayed as reactionary "fundamentalists" who violently persecuted Christians and Jews. In fact, the Almohad ideology, crystallized in *tawhid*—their doctrine of divine unity—represented an Islamic "reformation," synthesizing various strands of Islamic thought, including mysticism, and was grounded in the rigorous application of logic, which led them to view all non-Almohads, including Sunni Muslims, as illegitimate unbelievers. Both the Almohad expansion in the Islamic West and the resistance against it were characterized by extreme violence, although their persecution of non-Muslims has clearly been exaggerated. Some have suggested Almohadism constituted effectively a new monotheistic religion. It exercised a profound influence on Christian thought, helping lay the foundations of European rationalism and the scientific revolution. Beginning as a movement among newly Islamicized Berbers led by the prophetic figure Ibn Tumart (d. ca. 1030), it was quickly converted into a dynastic project by Ibn Tumart's disciple, 'Abd al-Mu'min, who overthrew the Almoravids and conquered much of North Africa and al-Andalus, claiming the title of caliph (1147–1163).

a. From the Almohad Manifesto
Arabic • 1171 or 1183 CE • Morocco

The Most Precious Thing Desired, *a collection of teachings attributed to Ibn Tumart but heavily edited, lays out the fundamentals of Almohadism, including the definition of* tawhid.

Tawhid is affirmation of the One and rejection of gods, associates, masters and idols other than Him. It is necessary to reject and disbelieve in all things that are worshipped other than Him and to disavow them. The Prophet himself made clear and explained *tawhid* when he said: He who proclaims the oneness of God and disbelieves in any object of worship lower than God, his wealth and blood are protected, and his account lies with God.

b. The Logic of Almohadism
Arabic • 1183 CE • Córdoba [?]

The 'Aqida, or Creed of the Almohads, was intended to show the irrefutable logic of tawhid. It was commissioned by the second caliph, Abu Yaqub Yusuf (1163–1184), and was likely composed by the great Aristotelian philosopher Muhammad ibn Rushd (or "Averroës"; 1126–1198). The passage below is from the second chapter.

It is by the necessity of reason that the existence of God, Praise to Him, is known. Necessity is what is not open to doubt and what no reasonable man can deny. And this necessity is of three kinds: what is necessarily true, what is necessarily possible, and what is necessarily impossible. And what is necessarily true is that for which there is no way out of its existing, as, for example, the needs for an action to have a doer.... This necessity is independently present in the minds of all who are endowed with reason.... And for that reason, God, may he be Blessed and Exalted, calls attention to this in His Book, saying, "And there is no doubt as to God, the Creator of the Heavens and the Earth?" [Qur'an 14:11].... Thus, we have proved by this that the Creator, Praise to Him, is known by the necessity of Reason.

c. The Economics of Faith
Arabic • early 14th century • Damascus [?]

Shams al-Din al-Dhahabi (1274–1348) was a prolific historian and religious scholar of Turkman origin based in Syria. His account of the Almohad policies is unreliable but reflects preconceptions regarding the movement among Sunni Muslims.

After the conquest of Marrakesh (1147), Abd al-Mu'min summoned the Jews and the Christians and said to them, "Did you and your forefathers not deny the mission of the Prophet! Did you not refuse to believe that he was the messenger that your sacred texts had prophesied? ...'" And they said, "Yes." ... "Therefore, we must not leave you in this situation, in which you insist upon your heresy. We do not need your taxes. Islam or death!" Then he set a date for them, so they had some time to dispose of the property which they could not carry, i.e. that they should sell their immobile assets before leaving the country. The majority of Jews immediately decided to observe the Islamic religion verbally and externally. This is how they protected their assets. As for the Christians, they moved to Spain, and only a minority converted to Islam. Synagogues and monasteries were destroyed across the kingdom.

To Consider

1. What are the political, social, and cultural consequences of regarding one's religious doctrine as logically self-evident?

2. What does al-Dhahabi's account suggest is the underlying motivation for toleration of minority communities?

3. Can Almohad ideology be seen to prefigure later European attitudes to "outsiders"?

Adapted from

a. Bennison, Amira K. "Almohad Tawḥīd and Its Implications for Religious Difference." *Journal of Medieval Iberian Studies* 2 (2010): 195–216. P. 204. Reprinted by permission of the publisher (Taylor & Francis Ltd, http://www.tandfonline.com).

b. Constable, Olivia Remie. *Medieval Iberia: Readings from Christian, Muslim, and Jewish Sources.* 2nd ed. Philadelphia: University of Pennsylvania Press, 2012. P. 192.

c. Corcos, David. "The Nature of the Almohad Rulers' Treatment of the Jews." *Journal of Medieval Iberian Studies* 2 (2010): 264–65, 285.

SIX

A Connected Sea

The collapse of the caliphal/imperial order in the mid-eleventh century ushered in an age of conflict and competition, as both outsiders and previously marginalized principalities and peoples struggled to stake their claim in the prosperous and populated Mediterranean world. On a formal level this competition was often framed as religious or ethnic struggles, and the rhetoric of conflict suggested that the region had splintered into unremittingly hostile factions, particularly along the Christian-Muslim divide. Paradoxically, however, competition in the highly interdependent Mediterranean economy was a catalyst also for integration and collaboration, in the realms of both trade and politics. The Islamicate, Latin, and Byzantine spheres became both suppliers and markets for each others' goods, and conduits for resources that lay far into their hinterlands and beyond. The demands of *realpolitik* prompted alliances between Christian and Muslim powers against their coreligionists. And Christians, Muslims, and Jews of varying backgrounds and orientations found themselves as fellow citizens, fellow travelers, and fellow adherents to the same broad cultural and religious traditions.

The documents here demonstrate these ambiguities of ethno-religious relations in this period. The Crusader Crown of Aragon courts Muslim subjects at home and Muslim clients abroad. Travelers, traders, missionaries and clergy confront the complexities of a world far wider and more diverse that they had previously imagined. Pilgrims move through sacred geographies that resonate with and reflect the traditions of the various "Peoples of the Book," and are confronted with a lived diversity that often runs counter to their presumptions and prejudices. And in the end, then, as today, money it seems is the great equalizer, as merchants and travelers of various faiths put aside their differences and develop strategies of coexistence and collaboration in order to pursue their own very earthly agendas.

6.1 THE POWER OF NEGOTIATION

The transregional dynasties of the Mediterranean faced particular problems, involving ruling over populations of different ethnic, linguistic, and religious identities, and exercising power over long distances, together with the usual challenges of premodern rulership, such as the problem of perennially rebellious nobility and family members. Conflict was often violent, but negotiation and the skillful use of treaties were a key strategy. For example, as the Crown of Aragon expanded into the Islamic Mediterranean both via conquest and through diplomacy, its rulers grappled with the challenges of ruling over infidel populations and forging alliances with non-Christian rulers, even as they cast themselves as Crusaders and defenders of the church.

a. The Surrender of Murcia
Catalan • before 1276 CE • Crown of Aragon

Jaume (James) I of Aragon (1213–1276), known as "the Conqueror," laid the foundations for Catalan-Aragonese expansion in the Mediterranean, conquering Muslim Mallorca and Valencia, and making Menorca a tributary. The Book of Deeds *is his autobiography, written in Catalan after he abdicated in 1276 in favor of his sons, Pere (Peter) the Great (1276–1285) and Jaume II of Mallorca (1276–1311). In 1264 the Muslim subjects of Andalucía and Murcia rose up against Alfonso X of Castile (1252–1284). Fearing the revolt would spread to recently conquered Valencia, Jaume intervened and captured Murcia for his kinsman, the king of Castile.*

Then we sent a frontier-guide with a Muslim, to tell the governor [of Murcia] to come out to us as we wished to speak to him for his good and that of the townspeople. And he sent word to us that we should send him a knight, and we sent him a knight by the name of Domingo López, who was a settler in Morvedre and knew Arabic, and Astruc [Bonsenyor], a Jew who was our scribe for Arabic.[1] The governor came with one of his most powerful knights of the town. Both of them had been made knights by King Alfonso [X] of Castile. And when we learnt that they were coming, we had our house draped with good cloths and fine couches prepared. And we ordered that they should have live fowl, sheep and goats prepared, so that when they arrived these might be slaughtered and that the guests should remain with us.

We were sitting on our seat, and they came and they greeted us, and they knelt before us and kissed our hand. And we ordered everybody to leave our chamber, except them and Astruc, the Jew we have mentioned above, who was our interpreter.

And we told them that we had sent for them for this reason: Because they well knew that there were many Muslims in our land (those whom our lineage had in Aragon and Catalonia in times past, and that we had in the kingdoms of Majorca and Valencia), and all practiced their religion just as if they were in the land of the Muslims. And there were the ones who had come to our mercy and had surrendered themselves to us; whereas those men who had

---

1. The Bonsenyor family—one of a number of prosperous, royally connected Jewish families—served as royal translators of Arabic and as physicians.

not wished to surrender themselves, we had taken by force, and we populated their lands with Christians. And because we did not wish their harm or death, "We wished to speak with you first of all so that you might help us to protect the Muslims of Murcia and the kingdom." For we would obtain for them three things from the king of Castile; firstly, that he maintain the charters he had with them; the other, that we would make them uphold and observe the agreements that they made with us; thirdly, that we would have them pardoned for all the things they had done to him. . . . However, we reassured them that we did not wish their death or destruction, rather we wished that they might live for always under the king of Castile, and that they could preserve their mosques and their religion, just as they had agreed with him in the initial charters.

b. Intervention in Tunis
Catalan • 1325–1328 CE • Xirivella, Valencia

Ramon Muntaner (1265–1337) was a Catalan knight who was close to the Aragonese royal family and fought in many of their campaigns. Late in life he composed a historical memoir in Catalan that focused on Aragonese expansion in the Mediterranean and the exploits of the mercenary troop known as the Catalan Company. In his Chronicle *Muntaner describes Pere the Great's reaction to the death of al-Mustansir (here, "Mostansar"), the Hafsid caliph (1249–1277) just as Pere came to power.*

The lord-king Pere had visited all of his kingdoms and all of his territories. And so it happened that he was in Barcelona and he was thinking it was time to collect tribute from the house of Tunis, and that, given that Mostansar (who was the best Muslim in the world after the Miramamoli of Morocco, and after Salah al-Din, the sultan of Babylon) had just died, it was not a good idea to delay on the said tribute.[2] And he called a great meeting of his council, and in particular, the nobleman Sir Corral Llança, and in front of everyone he told him.[3]

"Mr. Corral, as you know you went last year to demand the tribute from Tunis after al-Mustansir had died, who was a great friend of our father, and you know that they have not sent the said tribute, for which they have displeased us. Thus, it is necessary that we should do them some harm and show them our power. And so we have decided to depose the king who is there and put in his place Mirabussac, his brother, as king and lord.[4] And in doing so we will have done right and brought great honor to the House of Aragon. . . .

. . . I want you to know that al-Mustansir, just as I have told you, was a great friend of the king our father, and he sent him many jewels and his tribute every year. Now it is true that he has died, and that he did not leave any son [to rule]; there only remain two brothers of his: that is the older, Mirabussac, and the younger, Miraboaps (Abu Hafs). And the said Mirabus-

---

2. "Miramamoli" is Amir al-Mu'munin or "Commander of the Faithful," one of the titles used by the Almohad caliphs.

3. Corrado Lancia was one of a number of Italian noblemen in the service of the Crown of Aragon.

4. "Mirabussac" is "the *amir* Abu Ishaq."

sac, the older brother, had gone with great hosts of Christians and Muslims towards the Levant to wage war there, and Miraboaps remained in Tunis. And with al-Mustansir dead and having left his kingdom to Mirabussac, Boaps, who was in Tunis, and without waiting for his brother, took the throne of Tunis falsely and evilly.[5] And when Mirabussac learned of the death of his father he set out for Tunis, and when his brother Boaps learned he was coming he sent word that he not approach and that he ought to know that if he did it he would bring him to ruin. And so Mirabussac turned to Gabés with his fleet, and is there still and does not know what to do. Thus, we will do a great favor by helping justly and directly to fulfill the will of al-Mustansir. Thus, we will arm ten galleys [to send] and we want you, Mr. Corral, to be the captain and commander."

To Consider

1. In each case Christian Aragon is imposing its authority on Muslims. How does religious identity feature in these documents?

2. How did the Aragonese kings legitimize their interventions, and why?

3. Louis IX's fatal crusade of 1270 against Tunis failed. Why was the Aragonese approach successful?

Adapted from

a. James I of Aragon. *The Book of Deeds of James I of Aragon: A Translation of the Medieval Catalan Llibre Dels Fets*. Trans. Damian J. Smith. Burlington, VT: Ashgate, 2003. P. 315 [chap. 436]. Reproduced with permission of The Licensor through PLSclear.

b. Muntaner, Ramon. *Crònica de Ramon Muntaner*. Ed. Ferran Soldevila and Maria Teresa Ferrer i Mallol. Barcelona: Institut d'Estudis Catalans, 2011. Pp. 69–70 [chap. 30; Catalan]. An antiquated English translation can be found in Ramon Muntaner, *The Chronicle of Muntaner*, trans. Anna Goodenough, 2 vols. (London: Hakluyt Society, 1920–21).

6.2 VISIONS OF THE EAST

Beginning in the mid-eleventh century Latin Europe began a process of development and expansion that would more fully integrate it politically, economically, and culturally into the Mediterranean world, and particularly with Islamic North Africa and the Middle East. To a large extent this contact was framed as religious conflict with Islam, although it was largely trade that drove Latin expansion. Latin merchants strove to gain access to the sources of the lucrative "spice trade," which included rare minerals and plants, as well as manufactured goods (notably silk textiles) from Central, East, and South Asia, and spices. With the establishment of a pagan Mongol empire by Chinggis Khan (ca. 1162–1227) that stretched from Europe to China, Latin merchants and missionaries began to travel the Silk Road, and

---

5. Muntaner is confused. It was not Abu Ishaq's brother who took power in Tunis, but al-Mustansir's son, Yahya al-Wathiq, who would be deposed by Abu Ishaq (1279–1283) with Aragonese help.

encountered a world far more diverse, prosperous, and advanced than their own, prompting them to reassess their place and that of Christendom within creation.

a. Prester John Describes His Kingdom
Latin • 1160s CE • Germany

In the mid-twelfth century rumors began to circulate in Europe regarding Prester John, a Christian priest-king descended from the Three Wise Men, who ruled a great and powerful kingdom in the East (usually India, and later Ethiopia). This forged letter, ostensibly to the Byzantine emperor Manuel Komnenos (1143–1180), was written as anti-papal propaganda in the 1160s at the court of the German emperor, Frederick Barbarossa (1155–1190).

Prester John, Lord of Lords by the power and strength of God and of our Lord Jesus Christ, to Manuel the ruler of Rome, rejoice in our greeting and by the grace of our gift pass to greater things.

. . .

If you wish to know the magnificence and the excellence of our highness, and the territorial extent of our powerfulness, learn and do not hesitate to believe that I, Prester John, am the Lord of Lords; I excel every king in every land in all the riches beneath the heavens, strength and power. Seventy-two kings pay tribute to us. I am a devout Christian and we defend and sustain with our alms poor Christians everywhere who are under the rule of our clemency. It is our intention to visit the Sepulcher of the Lord with a huge army befitting the glory of our majesty in order to inflict a humiliating defeat on the enemies of the Cross of Christ while exalting His blessed name.[6]

. . .

Our magnificence rules over the Three Indies, stretching from Farther India, resting place of the Apostle St. Thomas, through the desert as far as the rising of the sun and back through the setting sun to the Babylonian desert near the tower of Babel.[7] Seventy-two provinces, only a few of which are Christian, obey us, each ruled by a king who is tributary to us.

. . .

It takes almost four months to cross our land in one direction, while nobody can calculate how long it would take in the other. If you can count the stars in the heavens and the grains of sand in the sea then you can calculate our influence and our power.

b. A Description of Suzhou
Franco-Venetian • 1299 CE • Genoa

The merchant Marco Polo departed Venice in 1271 for Mongol lands, returning in 1295. Polo claimed to have spent much of this time in the employ of the Great Khan in China, eventually

---

6. The Church of the Holy Sepulcher in Jerusalem.
7. The "Three Indies" included Ethiopia, India, and Southeast Asia ("Farther India").

returning to Venice via Southeast Asia and the Indian Ocean. His controversial account of his journey was dictated to Rustichello da Pisa, Polo's cellmate when both were prisoners of the Genoese in 1298–1299. Here, he describes the city of Suzhou (about sixty miles northwest of Shanghai).

Suzhou is a large and very noble city. They are idolators, belong to the Grand Khan, and have notes as currency. They have huge quantities of silk: they live from trade and crafts. They make a lot of silk cloth for their clothing; there are great rich merchants there. It is so large that it is about 40 miles around; there are such very great numbers of people that no one can know the number. And I tell you that if the men of Mangi were men-at-arms, they would conquer the whole rest of the world; but they are not men-at-arms.[8] But I tell you they are wise merchants and subtle men of all the arts, and they have great philosophers and natural physicians who know a lot about nature. I tell you in truth that in this city there are a good 6,000 stone bridges that 1 or 2 galleys could well pass under. I also tell you that in the mountains of this city, rhubarb and ginger grow in great abundance; for I tell you that for a Venetian groat you could get a good 30 pounds of fresh ginger, which is very good.[9] Know that it has 16 very large cities of great trade and great craft under its rule.

c. Prologue to Five Letters on the Fall of Acre (1291)
Latin • ca. 1292 CE • Baghdad

Riccoldo da Monte di Croce (ca. 1243–1321) was a Dominican friar from Florence who traveled as missionary to the court of the Mongol Ilkhans who ruled what had been the ʿAbbasid Caliphate of Baghdad, and among the Eastern and Syriac Christians of Iraq from 1288 to 1291. His account of his travels condemns Islam as false, but expresses much admiration for Muslims. This passage is from a series of letters he wrote to God, the Virgin Mary, and the patriarch of Jerusalem as he grappled to understand how God could allow the Crusades to be defeated by Islam.

And so it came to pass that I was in Baghdad "among captives on the banks of the Chebar," the Tigris.[10] A part of me delighted in the charm of the verdant place in which I found myself, for it was like paradise with its abundant trees, fertility, and various fruits. The garden was irrigated by the waters of paradise, and houses of gold had been built all around. But the other part of me was urged to sadness over the slaughter and servitude of the Christian people and their degradation after the lamentable loss of Acre, at which time I saw Muslims prosperous and flourishing and Christians squalid and dismayed as their daughters, young children and elders were taken away crying amid rumors they

---

8. "Mangi" from Manzi is a pejorative term to describe the "barbaric" people of southern China ruled over by the Song Dynasty (960–1279).

9. The groat, or *grosso*, was a coin of just over two grams of near-pure silver.

10. This is from the Old Testament (Ezekiel 1:1)—a reference to the exiled Israelites.

were to be forced into prison and slavery among barbarian nations in the remotest parts of the East.[11]

In the midst of this great sadness, I was suddenly seized by a strange wonder. I was stupefied in thinking about God's judgment concerning world governance, and most especially concerning Muslims and Christians. Why had such slaughter and degradation befallen the Christian people, and such temporal prosperity been granted to the perfidious race of the Muslims?

At this point, since I was unable to prevail over my wonder nor find a solution, I decided to write to God and the celestial court to express the source of my wonder.

To Consider

1. What tensions and anxieties would travel to the East engender among Europeans, and why?

2. How do these sources reflect the agendas and priorities of Latin Europe as it "globalized"?

3. Why would a figure like Prester John loom so large in the Latin imagination?

Adapted from

a. Barber, Malcolm, and A. K. Bate. *Letters from the East: Crusaders, Pilgrims, and Settlers in the 12th–13th Centuries.* Burlington, VT: Ashgate, 2010. Pp. 62–68 (#33). Reproduced with permission of The Licensor through PLSclear.

b. Marco Polo. *Marco Polo, The Description of the World.* Trans. Sharon Kinoshita. Indianapolis: Hackett, 2016. P. 132. Reproduced with permission of The Licensor through PLSclear.

c. George-Tvrtković, Rita. *A Christian Pilgrim in Medieval Iraq: Riccoldo da Montecroce's Encounter with Islam.* 2012. Pp. 137–38. Republished with permission of Brepols Publishers N.V. Permission conveyed through Copyright Clearance Center, Inc.

6.3 A ROUGH GUIDE TO PILGRIMAGE

By the eleventh century there was a robust tradition of geography and travelogue-writing in the Islamic world, including memoirs of *hajj* pilgrimages, such as that of the Andalusi pilgrim Muhammad ibn Jubayr (d. 1217), who left vivid impressions of the Frankish and Muslim Near East and Norman Sicily. Jewish travelogues appear in the twelfth century, including Benjamin of Tudela's (d. 1173) survey of Jewish communities from Iberia to Iraq, and the book of Petahyah of Regensburg in Germany, who reached Persia in the 1170s and 1180s. A few decades earlier, the *Book of Saint James* (known also *Codex Calixtinus*) was compiled, containing the first guidebook for Christian pilgrims on the road to Santiago de Compostela, which included much ethnographic information and practical advice for travelers. In the twelfth century European clerics began to produce descriptions of Jerusalem and the holy sites, and the thirteenth century saw missionaries writing memoirs of their travels to Persia

---

11. In 1291 the Mamluk sultan Al-Ashraf Khalil (1290–1293) conquered Acre, the last mainland territory held by Crusaders in the Holy Land.

and Central Asia. Around 1300 Marco Polo's account of his travels to China and India appeared.

a. A Syrian Pilgrim's Guide
Arabic • ca. 1200 CE • Aleppo

Ali ibn Abi Bakr al-Harawi (d. 1215) was a mystic, poet, magician, and diplomat who served the Salah al-Din (1174–93) and his Ayyubid successors. His Lonely Wayfarer's Guide to Pilgrimage *is a memoir of all of the pilgrimage sites he visited in the Near East, North Africa, and the Christian Mediterranean. At one point, his papers were confiscated by Richard the Lionhearted (1189–1199), who promised to return them if al-Harawi would come to see him. The book stands out for al-Harawi's frank observations of religious folk practices, including those of Christians and Jews.*

In Tiberias there is a spring named after Jesus the son of Mary and the Church of the Tree. A wondrous event, which is mentioned in the Gospel, took place on this spot involving Jesus son of Mary and the Tanner. It was the first of his miracles.

> . . .

Ludd is a town where the Messiah was.[12] It contains Mary's house, which the Franks venerate.

> . . .

[Acre] contains the Spring of the Ox, about which it is said the ox went out to Adam and he used it to cultivate the lands. Over this spring is a shrine ascribed to 'Ali ibn Abi Talib, the one that the Franks made into a church, and for which they appointed a custodian to oversee its construction and serve it.[13] When [the custodian] woke up [one morning], he said, "I saw a person say, 'I am 'Ali ibn Abi Talib. Tell them to make this place revert to a mosque, otherwise whoever dwells therein shall perish.'" The custodian told the Franks, but they did not heed his words and replaced him with another. When they arose [the next morning], they found him dead. Then the Franks let it revert to a mosque, [which] it is at present.

> . . .

Bethlehem is a small town that contains the birthplace of Jesus. It is said that the tombs of David and Solomon are there. The church contains ruins and a wondrous construction of marble, gold inlaid marble and pillars. Bethlehem has been inhabited for over 1200 years. The date is etched in wood and it has not changed down to our time. It is the location of the date palm mentioned in the Noble Qur'an (19:25). . . . It contains the *mihrab* of 'Umar ibn al-Khattab.[14] The Franks have not altered it down to this day.

> . . .

---

12. Al-Lidd to Arabs, Lydda to Franks, Ludd is modern Lod, Israel, about eight kilometers southeast of Tel Aviv.

13. 'Ali ibn Abi Talib was the cousin and son-in-law of Muhammad and the fourth caliph (656–661), venerated by Shi'i Muslims.

14. 'Umar ibn al-Khattab was the second caliph (634–644).

Al-Farama [near Port Said, Egypt] contains the tomb of the physician Galen.[15] On the island of Sicily is a location called Manzil al-Amir that contains a tomb of which it is said that it is also the tomb of Galen.[16]

. . .

[In ancient Cairo] resided Joseph the Righteous.[17] It contains the Cupola of Zuleika, the prison in which Joseph was imprisoned, the shrine of Jacob, and the pyramids in which Joseph the Righteous stored the grain. Among the wonders and antiquities, it contains are the Green Chamber, which belonged to Pharaoh and which is among the wonders of the world. It is a block of green granite bearing ancient inscriptions. Its roof, floor, and walls are formed from a single piece. . . . This chamber is in the middle of a white palace constructed of marble. Therein are enormous statues and a representation of Pharaoh. . . .

Next to the wall [of Constantinople] is the tomb of Abu 'Ayyub al-'Ansari, may God be pleased with him, a Companion of the Messenger of God, may peace be upon him.[18] His given name is Khalid ibn Ziyad. When he was killed, the Muslims buried him and said to the Byzantines, "This was among the most important companions of the Prophet. Should his grave be desecrated, not a church bell will ever ring in the lands of the Arabs."

It contains the congregational mosque that Maslama ibn 'Abd al-Malik[19] and the Successors, may God be pleased with them, built; the tomb of a descendant of Husayn, may God be pleased with him.[20] It contains statues of bronze and marble, wondrous talismanic objects, columns that were mentioned previously, and antiquities the likes of which do not exist in Muslim lands. It contains also the *Aya Sofia*, which is their great church. The Byzantines say that an angel dwells therein and they made a gold railing around his location which has a wondrous history and we mention in its proper place. I shall mention [in the *Book of Wonders* . . . God exalted willing] the layout of this church, its temple, elevation, doors, height, length, width and the pillars it contains, the wonders of this city and its conditions, the representations of fish that it contains, the golden gate, the marble towers, the bronze elephants, and all the wonders, antiquities and idols in the Hippodrome, and the bounty and favor that the Emperor Manuel [I; 1143–1180] bestowed upon me. The city is greater than its name! May God make it for Islam by His grace and generosity. . . .

---

15. Galen of Pergamon (129–ca. 210) was a Greco-Roman physician whose work was foundational for Muslim, Christian, and Jewish medical thought.

16. Modern Misilmeri is about eight kilometers southeast of Palermo.

17. This is the biblical prophet Joseph, the son of Isaac, venerated in Islam.

18. The Companions of the Prophet are individuals who knew Muhammad and are venerated in a manner analogous to Jesus's disciples in Christianity. Abu 'Ayyub died of old age on a raid on Constantinople in 669/70 and requested to be buried below its walls.

19. Maslama was a son of the caliph 'Abd al-Malik (685–705), who led the forces that besieged Constantinople in 717–718.

20. Husayn was a son of 'Ali ibn Abi Talib and Muhammad's daughter, Fatima. He was martyred by the Umayyads at the Battle of Karbala (680) and is venerated by Shi'i Muslims.

Divriği is a location in Byzantium that is visited from all around.[21] It was reported to me that it contains martyrs from the era of ʾUmar ibn al-Khattab, may God be pleased with him, that do not decompose and that their heads are shaven and their nails are pared. I set out for it so that I might see the truth of it. . . .

. . . They are a group of Byzantines whose agricultural lands are at the exterior of the site and whose homes are in the interior. There is a quaint church and a mosque. If the visitor is Muslim, they conduct him to the mosque. If he is Christian, they conduct him to the church. Then he enters an alcove where there is a group of deceased peoples upon whom the traces of lance and sword wounds are still visible. . . . They are wearing cotton garments. They have not changed. . . . The Byzantines allege they are from among them, and the Muslims say that they are from among the companions of ʾUmar ibn al-Khattab . . . who died there in captivity.

To Consider

1. How does al-Harawi characterize non-Muslim beliefs, and why?

2. What sorts of nonreligious information does this account include, and why was this information chosen?

3. How does al-Harawi's guide reflect the idea of a "sacred landscape"?

Adapted from

a. Al-Harawi, ʾAli ibn Abi Bakr. *A Lonely Wayfarer's Guide to Pilgrimage: ʾAlī ibn Abī Bakr Al-Harawī's "Kitāb Al-Ishārāt Ilā Maʿrifat Al-Ziyārāt."* Trans. Josef W. Meri. Princeton, NJ: Darwin Press, 2004. Pp. 38, 42, 44, 76, 84, 86, 104, 144, 146, 154, 156.

6.4 A PILGRIM AT SEA

As crucial and common as navigation was to the Mediterranean and the world beyond in the Middle Ages, we have few accounts of actual or fictional sea travel that convey the realities of this dangerous and potentially lucrative undertaking. A rare exception to this is the *rihla,* or travelogue, of Muhammad ibn Jubayr, a poet and bureaucrat who was born in al-Andalus in 1145 and served in the Almohad administration. In 1183 he determined to make the *hajj* pilgrimage to Mecca—perhaps as cover to propagandize and spy for the Almohads— and set out on board a ship for Alexandria, from there continuing on to Mecca. Returning via Iraq and Syria, he embarked for home in Crusader Acre, laying over in Norman-ruled Sicily as the result of a shipwreck. His account is written in lively, candid first-person prose, depicting life at sea vividly and at great length. Subsequently, Ibn Jubayr embarked on a second *hajj* in 1189 and a third in 1205/6, after which he settled in Alexandria, where he died in 1217.

---

21. Modern Sivas-Divriği is located in the highlands of central Anatolia.

a. Life at Sea
Arabic • ca. 1186 CE • Granada

Ibn Jubayr crossed over from al-Andalus to Ceuta (Sabta, Morocco) and found passage east.

On the morning of Wednesday, the 28th of [February 1183], we removed from Sabta [Ceuta, Morocco], where we found a *Rumi* [Latin Christian] Genoese ship about to sail to Alexandria, by the power of the Great and Glorious God, and with his help we embarked. . . .

Having concluded his planned travels, Ibn Jubayr boards ship in Crusader Acre.

On Saturday [October 6, 1184] with the favor of God towards the Muslims, we embarked on a large ship, taking water and provisions. The Muslims secured places apart from the Franks. Some Christians called *bilghriyin* ["pilgrims"] came aboard. They had been on pilgrimage to Jerusalem, and were too numerous to count, but were more than two thousand. May God in His grace and favor soon relieve us of their company. . . .

The journey begins, with the ship alternately suffering storms and being becalmed, until . . .

. . . The night of . . . the first of November, according to the non-Arabs, was a festival for the Christians, and they celebrated it with lighted candles.[22] Hardly one of them, big or little, male or female, but carried a candle in his hand. Their priests led them in prayers on the ship, then one by one rose to preach a sermon and recall the articles of their faith. The whole ship, from top to bottom was luminous with kindled lamps. . . . A north wind then rose, the ship resumed its course and our spirits were cheered, Praise be to God.

. . . From the time of our sailing from Acre, we had been twenty-two days on the sea, and therefore were wanting in felicity and felt only wretchedness and despair. . . . The provisions of the travelers were becoming scarce, but by the charity of God in this ship they were as if in a city filled with all commodities. All they might wish to buy could be found: bread, water, and all kinds of fruit and victuals, such as pomegranate, quince, watermelon, pear, chestnut, walnut, chickpea, broad-bean raw and cooked, onion, garlic, fig, cheese, fish, and many other things it would be too long to describe. . . . Throughout all these days, we had seen no land . . . and two Muslims died. . . . They were thrown into the sea. . . . Of the pilgrims two died also, and then were followed by many. One of them fell alive into the sea, and the waves carried him off more quickly than a flash of lightning. The captain of the ship inherited the effects of the departed Muslims and Christian pilgrims for such is their usage for all who die at sea. . . .

After a long and hard voyage and surviving several storms, the ship is wrecked off of Messina in Sicily on 8 December 1184.

---

22. This festival is the Christian Feast of All Saints.

... When it came to midnight on Sunday ... and we were overlooking the great city of Messina, the sudden cries of the sailors gave us the grievous knowledge that the ship had been driven by the force of the wind towards one of the shorelines and had struck it. ... Dreadful cries were raised on the ship, and the Last Judgement had come. ... The Christians gave themselves over to grief, and the Muslims submitted themselves to the decree of the Lord. ... When we were sure that our time had come, we braced ourselves to meet death. ... Cries and shrieks arose from the women and the infants of the *Rum.* ... [23]

We, meanwhile, were gazing at the nearby shore in hesitance between throwing ourselves in to swim and awaiting, it might be, relief with the dawn from God. ... The sailors lowered the longboat into the sea to remove the most important of their men, women, and effects. They took it on one journey to the shore but were unable to return, and the waves threw it in pieces on the beach. Despair then seized our spirits. ...

The sun then rose and small boats came out to us. Our cries had fallen on the city, and the King of Sicily, William [II; 1166–1189] himself, came out with some of his retinue to survey the affair.[24] We made speed to go down to the boats, but the violence of the waves would not allow them to reach the ship. We at last descended into them at the end of the terrible storm. ... Some of the chattels belonging to the men had been destroyed, but "they took comfort that although without plunder, they had returned in safety."[25] The strangest thing we were told was that the *Rumi* King, when he perceived some needy Muslims staring from the ship, having not had the means to pay for their landing because the owners of the boats were asked so high a price for their rescue, ... ordered that they be given one hundred *ruba'i* of his coinage in order that they might alight.[26] All the Muslims were thus saved and cried, "Praise be to God, Lord of the Universe."

To Consider

1. Why would a Muslim travel exclusively on Christian ships? What implications might this have for him?

2. How might Christian-Muslim-Jewish relations have been different on ship than on land?

3. Why would the king of Sicily take such an interest in Muslim travelers? What does this suggest about Mediterranean culture?

---

23. Rum, Arabic for "Roman," was a generic term for either Byzantines or Christians in general.

24. Later, Ibn Jubayr visited Palermo, and was impressed that the king spoke Arabic, followed Islamicate customs, and staffed his palace with Muslim servants and officials.

25. This is a riff on an Arabian proverb.

26. The *tari rub'* or quarter-*dinar* was a Sicilian Muslim coin imitated by the Normans.

Adapted from

a. Ibn Jubayr. *The Travels of Ibn Jubayr, Being the Chronicles of a Mediaeval Spanish Moor Concerning His Journey to the Egypt of Saladin, the Holy Cities of Arabia, Baghdad the City of the Caliphs, the Latin Kingdom of Jerusalem, and the Norman Kingdom of Sicily*. Trans. Ronald J. C. Broadhurst. London: J. Cape, 1952. Pp. 26, 325, 328, 329, 336–38.

6.5 COLLABORATION AND CREDIT

Trade, whether local, medium-distance, or long-distance, was essential to the Mediterranean region. However, trade could be an expensive, high-risk venture. Challenges included raising or borrowing capital for investment, foreseeing the changing value of commodities, transporting material and money safely over long and difficult sea and land routes, and avoiding being cheated by unscrupulous partners. Further complicating the situation was that there was no single law code that applied to or could be enforced across the entire region, people of different faiths within the same region were subject to different legal codes, one might almost never see one's partners or associates in person because of the distances involved, and a whole variety of languages were in use and cultural expectations and norms at play.

By the twelfth century Italian merchants had developed the *commenda*, a commercial contract designed to protect an investor's stake in a trade venture and ensure both the investor and the agent received a share of the profit, as well as sidestepping prohibitions on lending among Christians. The origins of the *commenda* are obscure, but it was almost certainly influenced by the Byzantine *chreokoinōnia* (debt partnership) and the Islamic *qirad*, and, possibly, the similar Jewish *'iqsa*. The *commenda* was an important step in the development of contract law and the emergence of the investment group (*societas maris;* "sea society") and company (*compangnia*) in the Latin West, which allowed enormous amounts of money to be raised and confidently committed to commercial ventures—a necessary element in the emergence of European dominance in Mediterranean trade in the later Middle Ages.

a. A Letter to 'Arus ben Yehosef
Judeo-Arabic • 1088–1116 CE • Mahdia, Tunisia

This letter was written by a Jewish merchant to 'Arus, a fellow Jew who had relocated from Mahdia to Fustat (Cairo), regarding a shipment of purple-dyed cloth to Almería (in al-Andalus). The writer insists he should not have to swear an oath on any agreement—oaths were seen as sacrilegious, and to be required to swear one as part of an agreement was a sign one's word was not trusted.

Every one of our friends knows that I am trustworthy, never giving an oath, and that I do not accept responsibility for risks on voyages.

I shall be travelling on a Spanish boat, and . . . May God let me and you partake in its blessings.

. . .

Send money for the freight and customs and write me who has the papers of the ship-ment, namely the paper for the customs house, and that for the commission for no goods can leave unless they have a sign that they are cleared; otherwise, everyone has to pay the dues again. The purple-maker 'Abd al-Rahman said . . . the wool was worth 6 *dinars* per Egyptian *qintar* and that it weighed 5 *qintars*, which makes 30 *dinars*, to which will be added the sum you will send for freight and customs.[27] 'Abd al-Rahman asked me also to write to you in his name to pay to Hasan 1 *dinar* and 2 *qirats* for the packing.[28]

When you have done what I am asking you to do in this letter, write to 'Abd al-Rahman to deliver the wool to me and send me the testimony. For he said to me, "Take the wool as a *qirad*." I answered: "I shall not accept anything before I receive an answer to what I am writ-ing to him." This is what impeded my accepting delivery from him: I have sworn that I shall not enter into any agreement with anyone in this world unless he makes a legally binding declaration that I am trustworthy, and that I am free from any responsibility.

b. A Genoese *Societas*
Latin • September 29, 1263 • Genoa

The following is a passage from a contract in which two Genoese form a partnership to trade in Tunis.

Witnesses: Simone Buccuccio, Ogerio Peloso, Ribaldo di Sauaro, and Genoardo Tasca. Sta-bile and Ansaldo Garraton have formed a *societas*, in which, as they mutually declared, Sta-bile contributed 88 Genoese *librae* and Ansaldo 44 *librae*. Ansaldo carries this *societas*, in order to put it to work, to Tunis or to wherever goes the ship in which he shall go—namely, the ship of Baldizzone Grasso and Girardo. On his return he will place the proceeds in the power of Stabile or of his messenger for the purpose of division. After deducting the capital they shall divide the profits in half. Done in the chapter house, September 29, 1163. . . .[29]

In addition, Stabile gave his permission to send that money to Genoa by whatever ship seems most convenient to Ansaldo.

c. A *Commenda*
Latin • August 9, 1252 • Barcelona

The following is a contract in which a merchant from Barcelona sets out for the Levant on behalf of investors.

---

27. 'Abd al-Rahman was a Muslim business associate of 'Arus. A *qintar* was either 99 pounds or 148 pounds, depending on the commodity.

28. A *dinar* was a gold coin (about 0.15 ounces) originally modeled on the Roman *denarius;* the *qirat* (whence "carat") was a silver coin of about 0.03 ounces.

29. Evidently, the contract was sworn out at the chapter house of either the cathedral or a monastery.

Be it known to all that I, Arnau Fabriz, am carrying in *comanda* from you, Bernat Fuentes, though you are absent, and from yours in this present voyage which I am making in the ship of Ferrer Descoll and partners to the Lands Beyond the Sea, or wherever the said ship shall make port in this present voyage for the purpose of commerce, 140 *librae*, 4 *solidi*, and 5 *denarii* of Barcelona invested in five pieces of cloth of Saint-Quentin and six Muslim [female slaves].[30] And I promise you to sell all of this well and faithfully there, and to invest in good faith the proceeds obtained from it in useful merchandise just as I see and understand best. And after this voyage is made to return into your possession and into that of your people said merchandise, this is, the capital and the profit, just as God shall have granted to preserve them, so, however, that after deducting your said capital for you I am to have one fourth of all of the profit that God shall have granted in this *comanda* of yours. But you are to have the three remaining parts of the said profit in addition to your said capital, your *comanda* itself, however going and being held and returning anywhere at your risk and fortune. This was done on the fifth day of the Ides of August, in the year of our Lord, 1252.[31]

To Consider

1. What are some of the differences between these documents, and what might these tell us?

2. How could one be sure such agreements would be honored?

3. How do these resemble, if at all, modern business agreements?

Adapted from

a. Goitein, S. D. *Letters of Medieval Jewish Traders.* Princeton: Princeton University Press, 1972. Pp. 233–34 (#48). Republished with permission of Princeton University Press. Permission conveyed through Copyright Clearance Center, Inc.

b–c. Lopez, Robert S., and Irwin W. Raymond, eds. *Medieval Trade in the Mediterranean World.* New York: Columbia University Press, 2001. Pp. 179 (#84), 181 (#87).

---

30. "Lands Beyond the Sea" refers to the Levant or Syria. The monies referenced are modeled on Roman currency: silver pounds, shillings, and pennies. One *libra* equaled twenty *solidi*, or 240 *denarii*. The cloth was from Saint-Quentin, in northeastern France, a town famous for its woolen textiles.

31. Many official documents continued to use the Roman calendar, which was gradually replaced by the day-of-the-month system we use today.

SEVEN

Mediterranean Societies

In the period between 1050 and 1350 the Mediterranean was a robust and diverse marketplace of products, ideas, cultures, and peoples, as newcomers from Africa, Asia, and Europe settled in the region in increasing numbers and native peoples circulated in search of salvation, wealth, or knowledge, or resettled as a consequence of colonialization, conquest, or slavery. On one level the region remained partitioned in three religio-cultural spheres: Byzantine, Latin, and Islamic; but these divisions were only evident in certain contexts. Muslims, Christians, and Jews of different denominations, ethnic affinities, and regional origins lived together side by side in societies that were impressively integrated despite legal and political frameworks that aimed to reinforce segregation and domination. Diversity presented opportunities, but also generated tensions, which could easily escalate into popular or official violence against any who were seen as "outsiders," and communal leaders among both majority and minority populations tended to look at fraternization among different confessional communities with suspicion.

The readings gathered here relate to various aspects of the social complexities resulting from diversity. Muslim market inspectors, for example, saw themselves as upholding public morality broadly construed. Authorities in both Christendom and Dar al-Islam looked with suspicion on the minority members who often took on crucial roles in domestic administration. Mediterranean social customs, such as public bathing, could be opportunities for intercommunal camaraderie, but also threatening episodes of acculturation. Ideal rulers were seen as rising above this messy multiconfessionalism, and were presented as distillations of orthodox faith, while heretics and schismatics were targeted with violence far more brutal than that visited on infidels. In any event, contemporaries often did not see themselves as

Muslims, Christians, or Jews but as members of ethnic communities that cut across or fractured those larger affiliations.

7.1 MORALITY IN THE MARKETPLACE

As far back as classical Athens it was recognized that marketplaces need to be supervised and rules ensuring fair trade and public safety enforced. The ancient Greek market inspector or *agronomos* was adapted first in the Eastern Roman Empire, and then as the *sahib al-suq* (market master) by Muslim Arabs, who by the ninth century transformed it into the *muhtasib*. In thirteenth-century Spain, Christian regimes would adapt the office, calling it the *mostassaf* or *zabazoco*. In medieval Italy, urban officials who supervised infrastructure and public health were called *viarii* (from *via*, "road," or "street"). The Arabic word is related to *hisba*, which refers to accounting and being held accountable. *Muhtasibs* could be found across the Islamic world, and a number of treatises written by them and describing their duties have survived, primarily from the western Mediterranean.

a. Moral Accounting
Arabic • 13th century • al-Andalus

Virtually nothing is known about 'Umar al-Jarsifi, other than that he exercised the office of muhtasib *somewhere in al-Andalus during the late thirteenth century. His name may suggest eastern Moroccan origin. Of the surviving* hisba *manuals, his is rather short. It is written in an overwrought and florid style and emphasizes the moral and religious dimensions of the office.*

The true nature of *hisba* may be summarized as an admonition to honorable actions and a prohibition of reprehensible conduct. . . . Its purpose is to straighten out whatever is crooked and to bring that which has wandered off back to the corral, measuring, weighing, and counting what should be, and keeping commerce safe from pilfering and fraud and outright cheating. . . .

. . .

The first and chief of the duties of *hisba* is to certify instruments of measurement and weight by accurate inspection; to organize those things which are disorganized, and to prevent any kind of dishonest practice and deception as regards commerce and manufacture. . . .

. . .

The *muhtasib* must also keep an eye on every aspect of the livelihoods of Muslims, so as to make them righteous and enable them to reach their full potential, monitoring prices where and when is appropriate. . . .

. . .

The *muhtasib* must pay great attention to the cleanliness of food, drink and clothing for sale, and so on. Vigilance must be taken as regards mosques and their courtyards, the streets adjoining them, the waterways appointed for customary and ritual purification, and places of public gathering. He must order the covering of people's private parts, wherever possible, in places like public baths. He must prevent women from following behind dead bodies in funeral processions or visiting graves, and from going out for pleasure, unless accompanied by a husband or close relative, especially in the case of young girls, for this involves a gratuitous display, such as is prohibited. Similarly, he must prevent the mixing of men and women, whenever and wherever is possible, such as at weddings and funerals. . . . Moreover, that which is required in the case of beautiful women applies also to attractive boys, because of the suspicions that might be raised as a consequence of the depravity of the times. . . .

    . . .

It is his duty to inspect the Muslims' streets and markets, looking out for whatever messes up the streets, or makes passage through them difficult, or darkens or blocks them, such as things sticking out or vaulted passages. . . .

    . . .

He must prevent *dhimmis* from looking down into the homes of Muslims and infringing on their privacy; likewise, from displaying wine and pork in Muslim markets, from riding horses with saddles and in outfits more suitable for Muslims, or showing arrogance.[1] He should make them wear a badge to distinguish them from Muslims. . . . He should also prevent Muslims from performing for *dhimmis* anything that would bring disgrace and humiliation upon themselves, such as cleaning up after them, transporting wine-making equipment, looking after pigs, and so on, for this implies the superiority of heathenism over Islam. . . .

    . . .

He must, furthermore, forbid whatever disturbs the dead . . . and forbid anyone to be exhumed or moved from the grave. . . . He shall also warn vendors against keeping people waiting and abusing them with snubs and impudent remarks. . . .

    . . .

He shall in general restrict all annoying persons, such as hashish-sellers, dealing in all sorts of poisonous substances. . . . And he must forbid monkey-trainers from entering homes because they terrify pregnant women and small children, and also door-to-door salesmen, who deceive people, and anyone given to frivolities, or who indulge in sinful behavior and trick folk—such as fortunetellers, soothsayers, herbalists, clowns, hermaphrodites, and people of loose morals; or anyone claiming a profession . . . but who doesn't know how to practice it, such as unqualified midwives. . . . He shall forbid gamblers, wine-merchants, and drunkards from frequenting the markets, and shall chastise anyone indulging publicly in such activities. . . .

    . . .

The *muhtasib* must not be remiss in supervising the affairs of merchants, or entrust his duties to people of bad reputation. Rather, he should carefully vet his subordinates, taking

---

1. *Dhimmis* are non-Muslims who live as secondary but legitimate subjects under Muslim rule under the "pact of protection" (*dhimma*). In al-Andalus, this included Christians and Jews.

the very greatest care in this matter, lest his authority be undermined by their swindling and bribe-taking and so on. If this happens, there will be disorder, and he will lose the respect of the *imam,* and the merchants will quickly become corrupt and commit illegal and rebellious acts. Whenever he requires a merchant to change the price of his wares because they have been diluted or are worthless, a sign shall be put up giving notice of this, to prevent any further fraud. . . .

. . .

When the *muhtasib* encounters someone who will not obey orders, and on whom warnings have no effect, instructions will be given to expel him from the market and deprive him of selling and using commercial space in public. . . . Again, let this authority be strictly enforced in the case of those concerning themselves with all kinds of food, for this is the pivot of the whole matter, first and last. . . .

A lengthy passage follows explaining by way of metaphor how the muhtasib *should mete out punishment. For repeat offenders (nonlethal) crucifixion is recommended.*

The *muhtasib* should not in such cases withhold food or drink from or the ritual ablution for prayer: the crucified man can pray by nodding his head, and when he is let go, he can perform the prayers again. The crucifixion should not last more than three days.[2] When he metes out on-the-spot punishment it is permissible to strip a man of his clothes, save for that which covers his private parts; and he shall be displayed in public, and his crime shall be publicly proclaimed, if it has been repeatedly committed and he has not mended his ways. His hair may be shaved, but not his beard; jurists disagree as to whether his face should be blackened with soot, the most allowing it and a few forbidding it.

To Consider

1. Why would commerce and hygiene be seen as related to morality?
2. How does a *hisba* treatise like this allow us to imagine life in an Islamic city at this time?
3. In what sense might we say this was a Mediterranean institution?

Adapted from

a. Wickens, G. M. "Al-Jarsifi on Hisba." *Islamic Quarterly* 3 (1956): 176–87.[3]

---

2. Crucifixion was a common punishment across the Islamic world, and was not necessarily fatal. As can be seen here, it appears akin to the Latin custom of displaying miscreants in the stocks.

3. Al-Jarsifi's text is often not very clear, and Wickens's literal and antiquated translation has issues. This loose adaptation was made with reference to John Derek Latham, "Observations on the Text and Translation of Al-Jarsifi's Treatise on 'Hisba,'" *Journal of Semitic Studies* 5 (1960): 124–43,

7.2 THE LIMITS OF LEGITIMACY

Members of religious minorities were integrated into the administrative and military structures of kingdoms across the Mediterranean, and deeply enmeshed in their broader social and economic milieux. While the legitimacy of these minorities was seldom questioned in principle (except in Byzantium), the participation of "infidels" in the institutions of power at times provoked anxieties among religious authorities and the majority populace. Tensions were exacerbated when elements within the majority accrued the skills and the ambition to work within the administration, provoking promulgations demanding the marginalization of religious minorities.

a. *Dhimmis* and the Deep State
Persian • 1091–1092 CE • Isfahan

Al-Hasan al-Tusi (1018–1092), known as Nizam al-Mulk (Organizer of the Kingdom), was the Persian wazir *of the sultans Alp Arslan (1063–1072), and Malik Shah (1072–1092). In the course of establishing the administrative foundations of the Seljuq sultanate he ruled as a virtual shadow-sultan until he fell afoul of his patron and was assassinated in 1092. The Manner of Kings (Siyar al-Muluk) was one of several treaties written at the request of Malik Shah.[4] Books of counsel or "Mirrors of Princes" were a popular genre in court literature. Here, he speaks against employing* dhimmis *in administration. In his private life, the* wazir *employed a Jewish financial administrator, as did Malik Shah.*

Furthermore, the kingdom is kept in order by its tax-collectors and army officers; and the head of all the tax-collectors and civil servants is the *wazir*. Whenever the *wazir* is corrupt, treacherous, oppressive and unjust, all taxmen are likewise, maybe worse. A taxman may be well-versed in his duties, he may be a secretary, an accountant or a business expert such that he has no peer in all the world; but if he is a member of a bad sect or a bad religion, such as a Jew, Christian or Zoroastrian, he will despise the Muslims and afflict them with hardships on the pretext of taxes and accounts. If the Muslims are oppressed by that heretic or infidel and complain about him, he must be dismissed and punished. One must not be concerned with what his intercessors may say—they may say there is no secretary or accountant or tax-collector in the world like him; they may say that if he is removed from office, the work will all come to grief, and there is nobody to take his place. This is all lies and such words must not be heeded; it is imperative to change that man for another, as The Commander of the Faithful 'Umar once did (may God be pleased with him).

---

and the Arabic edition in Évariste Levi-Provençal, *Trois traités hispaniques de hisba* (Cairo: Imprimerie de l'Institut Français d'Archéologie Orientale, 1955), 119–28.

4. The book is often referred to as the *Siyasat-nama*, or "Book of Government," but this is not the title that appears in manuscripts.

b. Banning Non-Christians from Office
Latin • 1215 CE • Rome

Innocent III (1198–1216) was the pope who perhaps most dramatically extended the papacy's power through an aggressive policy of Crusade, feudal expansion, and church reform and reorganization. The Fourth Lateran Council laid out his legislative program. Several canons (promulgations) deal with Jews and Muslims, including this one (69), prohibiting the service of Jews and pagans (including Muslims) in positions of power over Christians. This law was broadly ignored in the kingdoms of the Mediterranean, which had substantial Muslim and Jewish populations.

Since it would be absurd for a blasphemer of Christ to exercise power over Christians, We therefore renew this canon, on account of the boldness of the offenders, what the Council of Toledo providently decreed in this matter: we forbid Jews to be appointed to public offices, since under this pretext they harm Christians greatly.[5] If, however, anyone does commit such an office to them, let him, after an admonition, be curbed by the provincial council, which we order to be convened each year, by means of appropriate sanction. Any official so appointed shall be denied interaction with Christians in commerce and in other matters, until whatever he gained from Christians is given over for the use of the Christian poor according to the judgement of the bishop of the diocese, and he is dismissed from this office, which he had improperly taken up, in shame. This also we apply to pagans.[6]

c. Treacherous *Dhimmis*
Arabic • ca. 1242 CE • Cairo

'Uthman al-Nabulusi (d. 1262) was a bureaucrat in Ayyubid Egypt who was embittered after losing his job in retaliation for whistleblowing. One of his several books, The Sword of Ambition, *is a manifesto against corruption and for administrative reform, including the dismissal of dhimmis from public office. This is a passage from the second chapter, "A Description of the Copts and Their Perfidies in Fifteen Sections," entitled "Why the Copts Specialize in Secretaries and Neglect Other Professions."*

It is important that I note here how it is passed down in the annals of history that when the rule of Egypt was wrested from the Copts and they entered into the pact with Islam, they devised a strategy to ensure that their own voices would be heard by the Muslims and that their new overlords would be compelled to look after their interests. The wisest and

---

5. He refers to the Third Council of Toledo (589), in which the church in the Visigothic kingdom enacted various policies against Jews, including banning them from public offices in which they would have the power to punish Christians.

6. This is likely a reference to the pagan Cumans of the Kingdom of Hungary, but would have referred to Muslims as well.

greatest of the Copts said to their people, "You were once masters of this land. But the glory of the sword has been wrested from you. Strive, therefore, to attain the glory of the pen." "How shall we do this?" they asked. Their wise men said to them, "By teaching your children the secretarial art that they may share with the Muslims in their property, their interest, and their decisions." They all agreed upon this plan, and the result is plain to see. They gained power over the Muslims' administration and did as they please in the government. How apposite are the lines a poet composed to describe the Jews and Christians, observing that the former train their children in medicine, the latter theirs in secretarial art, as follows:

> God curse the Christians and Jews!
> They have attained what they wanted to get from us:
> They have emerged as doctors and secretaries
> that they might seize both souls and property.

To Consider

1. Why would having members of minority religious groups in official positions be a flash point?

2. What sorts of rationales underlie the call to prohibit unbelievers from formal office?

3. Why is it that these promulgations and protestations seemed to have so little effect on the situation of minority communities?

Adapted from

a. Nizam al-Mulk. *The Book of Government: Or, Rules for Kings; The Siyar al-muluk or Siyasat-Nama of Nizam Al-Mulk*. Trans. Hubert Darke. Boston: Routledge & Keegan Paul, 1978. P. 170 (#27). Reproduced with permission of The Licensor through PLSclear.

b. Tanner, Norman P., ed. *Decrees of the Ecumenical Councils*. 2 vols. Washington, DC: Georgetown University Press, 1990. Vol. 2, pp. 266, 268 [Latin on pp. 255, 258] (#69). © Tanner, Norman P., Burns & Oates, an imprint of Bloomsbury Publishing Plc.

c. Yarbrough, Luke B. *The Sword of Ambition: Bureaucratic Rivalry in Medieval Egypt*. New York: NYU Press, 2016. P. 34.

7.3 KEEPING IT CLEAN

Bathing was integral to Mediterranean culture and society. Public and private baths were features of both the Roman and Sasanian worlds, and the Arabs adopted the Roman model for their own. Washing was important for both ritual and physical cleanliness, for health and medical treatment, but also as a leisure and social activity. One could pass the day in the baths, eating, drinking, and being bathed and massaged. Bathhouses were an environment in which differences of class and religious community became ambiguous; as such baths provided a forum for both socialization and the temptations of vice. Bathing was encouraged by public authorities and promoted by rulers, enjoyed by people of all walks of life, and frequently condemned by moralists. As northern European Franks integrated into Mediterranean society, they too became aficionados of the bathhouse.

a. Bathing by the Monastery
Arabic • late 10th century • Cairo

Abu'al-Hasan al-Shabushti was a librarian to the Fatimid caliph al-'Aziz (976–996), for whom he composed a Book of Monasteries—*a sort of guidebook for visiting rural monasteries, which Muslim rulers used as retreats as if they were hotel-spas. Here he describes Mar Hanna in the province of Giza, "one of the monasteries of Egypt that are frequented for drinking and amusement," which was popular as a riverside recreational spot.*

And this monastery is situated on the shore of the pond of al-Habash near the river. By its side, there are orchards, of which the *amir* Tamim, brother of the Commander of the Faithful al-'Aziz b'illah—Peace be upon the both!—has founded some together with a council room on pillars, well-built and of good craftsmanship, accessible by means of a staircase, which the *amir* Tamim has also established.[7] Near this monastery is a well, known as the well of "Nagati" over which there is a sycamore tree, and people assemble and drink at it. This is therefore one of the places of amusement and the resorts of diversion and pleasure, agreeable at the time of the Nile flood and the filling of the pond, beautiful to look at and with pleasant surroundings. So it is also during the days of cultivation and blossom. It is rarely free from cheerful people and pleasure-seekers.

b. The Dangers of Bathing
Arabic • ca. 1097 CE • Alexandria [?]

Abu Bakr Muhammad al-Turtushi ("from Tortosa," in al-Andalus; 1059–1126) was recognized as one of the great jurists and moralists of his day. In 1084 he traveled east in search of knowledge and eventually settled in Alexandria. As a member of the Maliki school of legal interpretation he was particularly wary of anything that departed from the original message of Islam, as reflected in the cautionary title of this tract, The Book of New Things and Innovations.

The women enter the baths without coverings, together with "women of the Book"; Muslims go to the baths with the unbelievers. The bath is *bid'a* ["innovation"] and a luxury.[8]

c. Cleanliness Next to Godliness
Latin • ca. 1145 CE • France [?]

The "Route for Pilgrims to Compostela" from The Book of St. James *was a guide for pilgrims to Western Christendom's most popular destination, the purported resting place of the apostle James*

---

7. Al-'Aziz was the fifth Fatimid caliph (955–996).

8. "People of the Book" refers to members of scriptural religions who were eligible for *dhimma*: Jews and Muslims, as well as Zoroastrians and, at times, members of other religions.

"the Muslim-Killer." Attributed to Pope Calixtus II (1138–1145) but probably written by an author from northern France, it contains a wealth of practical information and ethnographic observations.

A certain river two miles from the city of Santiago, in a wooded place which is called Lava-colla ("The Arse Wash"), because in it French people, making the pilgrimage to Santiago, are in the habit, out of love of the Apostle, of washing not just their genitals, but of removing the dirt from their entire bodies, having taken off their clothes.

d. A Close Shave with an Infidel
Arabic • 1180s CE • Damascus

'Usamah ibn Munqidh was a Syrian nobleman, poet, warrior, and diplomat, whose autobiography, The Book of Contemplation, *provides an intimate picture of Muslim-Christian relations in the Crusade-era East (see chapter 5, document 3, "Franks and Muslims in Crusade-Era Palestine and Syria"). Here he recounts an anecdote reported by a bathhouse attendant from Muslim-ruled Marrat al-Nu'man (south of Aleppo).*

I once opened a bath in al-Ma'arrat [al-Nu'man, south of Aleppo] in order to earn my living. To this bath there came a Frankish knight. The Franks disapprove of girding a cover around one's waist while in the bath. So this Frank stretched out his arm and pulled off my cover from my waist and threw it away.[9] He looked and saw that I had recently shaved off my pubes. So he shouted, "Salim!" As I drew near him, he stretched his hand over my pubes and said, "Salim, good! By the truth of my religion, do the same for me." Saying this, he lay on his back and I found that in that place the hair was like his beard. So I shaved it off. Then he passed his hand over the place and, finding it smooth, he said, "Salim, by the truth of my religion, do that same to madame (*al-dama*)" (*al-dama* in their language means the lady), referring to his wife. He then said to a servant of his, "Tell madame to come here." Accordingly, the servant went and brought her and made her enter the bath. She also lay on her back. The knight repeated, "Do what thou hast done to me." So I shaved all that hair while her husband was sitting looking at me. At last he thanked me and handed me the pay for my service.

e. Dangerous Liaisons
Latin • after 1215 CE • Acre

Jacques de Vitry (d. 1240) was a French theologian who served as bishop of Acre from 1214 to 1225 and was appointed cardinal in 1229. During his time in the East, he participated in the Fifth Crusade. His popular History of the East *was part of a larger project on the history of*

---

9. In Islamic bathhouses men always wear a towel around their waist, unless within the confines of a private washing alcove.

Jerusalem, which he began in 1215. Here, he rails against the dangers of the bathhouse for Frankish women.

Nevertheless, three times per week [the Franks] allow their wives to go off to the baths with great care. These, moreover, who are among the powerful and wealthy, as they appear to be Christians and they may have some excuse (for having Mass said), make altars to be set up next to the beds of their wives, managing to have masses celebrated there by certain pitiful chaplains and ignorant little priests. Meanwhile, moreover, the wives of the *Pullani* huddle close together and busy themselves and apply so zealously to find prospects (for advancement) by a thousand wiles and infinite schemes.[10] Indeed, they are instructed in innumerable abominations and spells and, indeed, fortune-tellings by Syrian (Christian) and Muslim women, incredibly and beyond measure.

f. The Right to Bathe
Catalan • 1272–1279 CE • Tortosa

Municipal law codes of medieval Spain often contained clauses governing access to municipal baths, and typically dictating on which days men and women of different faiths could bathe.[11] The Customs of Tortosa, the Catalan-language law code in the port town of Tortosa at the mouth of the Ebro River, which had significant Muslim and Jewish communities, contained no such stipulations.

The baths of Tortosa and its boundaries belong and shall belong to the citizens and the municipality. And all of the citizens and inhabitants, including Muslims, Jews, as well as Christians ought to bathe in them. And the income or whatever else comes out of them is decreed for the citizens to contribute to the construction or repair of the walls of the city of Tortosa. And let it be known that each townsman with his servant, or each townswoman with her servant, slave or other dependent and with her child can, if she has one, bathe there for a *meala*, which will be given to whoever is running the baths for the citizens and the municipality.[12] Thus, everyone who bathes there shall pay a *meala*, even if they are there as servants.

To Consider

1. What sorts of things would lead moralists to condemn the baths?
2. How might have bathing affected intercommunal cultural and social relations?

---

10. *Pullani* referred to locally born individuals of Frankish descent and sometimes specifically to the offspring of Frankish men and indigenous women.

11. See, for example, James F. Powers, *The Code of Cuenca: Municipal Law on the Twelfth-Century Castilian Frontier* (Philadelphia: University of Pennsylvania Press, 2000), 40–41.

12. A *meala* was a silver-alloy coin worth half a *dinar* ("shilling").

3. Why would rulers and authorities have established baths and encouraged their use?

Adapted from

a. Atiya, Aziz Suryal. *Some Egyptian Monasteries According to the Unpublished Ms. of Al-Shābushtī's "Kitāb Al-Diyārāt."* Cairo: Institut Français d'Archéologie Orientale, 1939. Pp. 25–26.

b. Melville, Charles, and Ahmad Ubaydli. *Christians and Moors in Spain.* Warminster, Eng.: Aris & Phillips, 1988. Vol. 3, *Arabic Sources*, p. 121. Reproduced with permission of The Licensor through PLSclear.

c. Krochalis, Jeanne, and Alison Stones. *The Pilgrim's Guide to Santiago de Compostela: A Critical Edition.* London: Harvey Miller Publishers, 1997. P. 21. Republished with permission of Brepols Publishers N.V. Permission conveyed through Copyright Clearance Center, Inc.

d. Hillenbrand, Carole. *The Crusades: Islamic Perspectives.* New York: Routledge, 2000. Pp. 593–94.

e. Vitry, Jacques de. *Iacobi de Vitriaco . . . Libri duo, quorum prior orientalis, siue Hierosolymitanae.* Douai: Balthazaris Belleri, 1597. Pp. 188–89 (Latin). Reproduced with permission of The Licensor through PLSclear.

f. Massip i Fonollosa, Jesús, ed. *Costums de Tortosa.* Barcelona: Fundació Noguera, 1996. P. 13 (1.1.15) (Catalan).

7.4 POWER AND PIETY

Relatively few rulers in either Christendom or the Islamic world were known for their piety. After betraying his lord, Nur al-Din, Yusuf ibn Ayyub Salah al-Din (1137–1193) successfully united Egypt and Syria under his rule in 1174. Using a platform of holy war against the Franks, he galvanized his fickle subordinates and reconquered Jerusalem for Islam in 1187, very nearly extinguishing the Crusader presence in Syria and Palestine. Nevertheless, his own dynasty was overthrown in Egypt in 1250 and in Aleppo in 1260.

Louis IX (1214–1270) came to the throne of France at age twelve (1226), setting out to tame his rebellious nobility and reform the kingdom's administration. The Cathar Crusade was concluded soon after his coronation, and he presided over 1240's "Trial of the Talmud," which led to a mass book-burning in 1242. His crusade to Egypt in 1249 was a debacle, resulting in the capture of his entire army. Defying ill-health and good counsel, he launched a Crusade against Tunis in 1270, only to die of dysentery outside its walls shortly after arriving.

a. A Paragon of Virtue
Arabic • ca. 1228 CE • Damascus

Baha al-Din (1145–1234) was a religious scholar who was invited by Salah al-Din to join his retinue, becoming a close friend and inseparable companion. After the sultan's death he composed this hagiographic biography, The Deeds of a Sultan and the Virtues of Joseph, *cementing the latter's reputation as a model Islamic ruler up to today.*[13]

---

13. The title of the work embodies a double entendre, evoking the virtuous patriarch Joseph ("Yusuf") of Old Testament tradition.

[Salah al-Din's] creed was good and he was much mindful of God Almighty. He took his creed from proof by means of study with the leading men of religious learning and eminent jurisconsults. . . . His creed followed the straight path, agreed with the canon of true discernment and was approved by the greatest of the '*ulama*'.

. . .

He was extremely assiduous in the performance of prayer communally. Indeed, he mentioned one day that for years he had only prayed in company. If he fell ill, he would summon the imam on his own and force himself to stand and pray in company. . . .

. . .

When he died, he possessed nothing for which he owed any alms. As for superogatory charity, that exhausted all the property he owned.[14] He ruled all that he ruled, but died leaving in his treasury in gold and silver only forty Nasiri *dirham*s and a single gold piece of Tyrian.[15] He left no property, no house, no estate, no orchard, no village, no farm, not a single item of property of any sort. . . .

. . .

He fell a little short in respect of fasting on account of illnesses that he successively suffered in numerous Ramadans. Al-Qadi al-Fadil undertook to keep a record of those days and he began (God have mercy on him) to fulfil those missed obligations at Jerusalem the year he died.[16] He strictly kept the fast for more than a month, for he had missed some Ramadans which illness and also prosecution of the *jihad* had prevented him from keeping. Fasting did not agree with his constitution, but God inspired him to fast to make up what he had missed . . . and he continued until he had fulfilled what was due.

. . .

He always intended and planned [to go on *hajj*], especially in the year of his death. He confirmed his determination to perform it and he ordered preparations to be made. Provisions were got ready and all that remained was to set out. However, he was prevented because of lack of time and the unavailability of what was proper for such a person. He therefore put it off till the next year, but God decreed what He decreed. Everyone, high and low, knew about this.

. . .

Saladin was just, gentle and merciful, a supporter of the weak against the strong. Each Monday and Thursday he used to sit to dispense justice in public session, attended by the jurisconsults, the *qadi*s and the doctors of religion. The door would be opened to litigants so that everyone, great and small, senile women and old men, might have access to him.

---

14. This refers to charitable giving above and beyond the obligatory alms taxes.

15. A *dirham* was a silver coin of approximately three grams in this era.

16. Al-Qadi al-Fadil (1135–1200) was Salah al-Din's close adviser and the head of his chancery.

. . .

Saladin's generosity was too public to need to be recorded and too famous to need to be recounted.

b. From Jean de Joinville's *Book of Pious Words and Good Deeds of Our Saint King Louis*
Latin • 1305–1309 CE • Joinville, France

Jean de Joinville (d. 1317) was a nobleman from Champagne who joined Louis IX's ill-fated 1248 Crusade to Egypt, and became a trusted adviser and friend to the king, but refused to take part in his final and fatal Crusade against Tunis in 1270. Joinville was called on to testify as part of the king's canonization, which began in 1271 and was concluded in 1297, later writing a biography at the request of Jeanne de Navarre, countess of Champagne and queen of France (1285–1305), which emphasized Louis's piety. Louis is regarded popularly as perhaps the greatest king of medieval Europe.

Right from the time of his childhood King Louis had compassion on the poor and suffering. It was his custom, wherever he went, to entertain a hundred and twenty poor persons every day in his own house, and feed them with bread and wine, meat or fish. In Lent and Advent the number of poor was increased; and it often happened that the king served them himself, setting their food before them, carving their meat, and giving them money with his own hand as they left.

. . .

In addition to this, every day the king used to give generous alms to poor monks and nuns, to ill-endowed hospitals, to poor sick persons, and to religious communities with little money. He was equally generous in his gifts to men and women of gentle birth in need, to homes for fallen women, to poor widows and to women in labor, as also to poor craftsmen who through age or sickness could no longer ply their trade. . . .

. . .

From the moment he came into possession of his kingdom and recognized what he had in his power to do King Louis had begun to erect churches and many religious houses. . . . He built hospitals in several places. . . . He founded the abbey of Saint-Mathieu at Rouen, to house sisters of the Order of Preachers; and also the Abbey of Longchamp, for nuns of the Order of Minors.[17] To each community he assigned an ample revenue for their livelihood.

. . .

There were times when some of those who were most in his confidence found fault with the king for spending so lavishly on what seemed to them over-generous benefactions. On such occasions he would answer: "I would rather have such excessive sums as I spend

---

17. He refers here to the Dominican order and the Order of Saint Claire (the female branch of the Franciscans).

devoted to almsgiving for the love of God than used in empty ostentation and the vanities of this world."

To Consider

1. This Muslim and this Christian are presented as ideal rulers. How do their supposed qualities differ or align, and why?

2. Why might these biographers have chosen to present their subjects as extraordinarily pious?

3. How can historians use biographies that are so clearly biased?

Adapted from

a. Richards, D. S. *The Rare and Excellent History of Saladin, or, al-Nawādir al-Sulṭāniyya wa'l-Maḥāsin al-Yūsufiyya.* Trans. D. S. Richards. Burlington, VT: Ashgate, 2001. Pp. 18–25. Reproduced with permission of The Licensor through PLSclear.
b. Shaw, Margaret R. B. *Chronicles of the Crusades.* New York: Penguin, 1963. Pp. 370–71.

7.5 THE CHALLENGE OF HERESY

One of the things the Crusaders reputedly brought back from the eastern Mediterranean was a new Christian religion called Catharism (from the Greek, *kataros* or "pure"). This was a dualistic religion rooted in Manicheism, and related to Armenian Paulicianism and Balkan Bogomolism. Cathars saw the world as the theater of conflict between Good (spirit) and Evil (matter), and rejected the ritual and authority of the church. Their leaders were called *Perfecti* ("Complete Ones") or "Good Men." The same factors that drove the Gregorian Reform (clerical corruption, church worldliness, and pastoral neglect) drew people to Catharism. In Languedoc, Count Raymond IV of Toulouse (1194–1222), who was Catholic, protected his Cathar vassals and subjects, prompting Innocent III to take action, including founding the Franciscan and Dominican orders to preach against heresy, and authorizing a Crusade in 1209 with the promise of salvation to any knight who fought for forty days. Under the leadership of the northern French count, Simon de Montfort, Crusaders from across northern Europe terrorized Languedoc. De Montfort failed, but as a consequence of the Crusade Languedoc was absorbed by France by the late thirteenth century. The heresy lived on for another century or so, persecuted by the Inquisition, even after the last *perfectus* was burned at the stake in 1321.

a. From William of Tudela's *Song of the Crusade*
Occitan • 1210–1213 CE • Saint-Antonin-Noble-Val (Languedoc)

The war poem The Song of the Crusade *was composed by William of Tudela, a Navarrese cleric who lived in Languedoc and accompanied the Crusaders. This passage relates to the capture of Béziers in July 1209. Faced with an ultimatum, the Catholic townsfolk refused to hand over their Cathar neighbors, and in the ensuing storming of the town all of the townsfolk were deliberately massacred, with many, according to one source, burned to death in the Church of Mary Magdalene, where they had taken refuge.*

[Verse 20] The townsfolk saw the crusaders drawing near, saw the chief of the servants leading the attack and his lad jumping down into all the moats, breaking down the ramparts and opening the gates, they saw the great mass of the French host making ready for battle and they know in their hearts they could not hold. Hurriedly they took refuge in the high church. The priests put on vestments for a mass of the dead and had the church bells rung as for a funeral. And in the end the servant lads could not be kept out but forced their way into town.[18] They took what houses they liked, and could have taken ten each had they wanted to. They were in a frenzy quite unafraid of death, killing everyone they could find and winning enormous wealth. . . .

[Verse 21] The lords from France and Paris, laymen and clergy, princes and marquises all agreed that at every castle the army approached, a garrison that refused to surrender should be slaughtered wholesale, once the castle had been taken by storm. They would meet no resistance anywhere as men would be so terrified at what had already happened. . . . That is why they massacred them at Béziers, killing them all. . . . And they killed everyone who fled into the church; no cross or altar or crucifix could save them. And these raving beggarly lads, they killed the clergy too, and the women and the children.

b. Exemplary Punishment
Latin • 1212–1218 CE • Yvellines [?], France

Peter des Vaux de Cernay (d. ca. 1218) was a Cistercian monk from the north of France who was present on the Crusade and whose family was connected to the leadership. In this passage from his Albigensian History, *he recalls how a minor nobleman, Giraud de Pipieux, who initially supported the Crusade, betrayed the Crusaders in 1210, after his uncle was killed by a northern Frenchman.[19] For his part, Simon de Montfort deliberately perpetrated similar atrocities on nobles, knights, and commoners in order to instill terror among the local people.*

Leaving Puisserguier [west of Béziers] the Count [de Montfort] razed to the ground numerous forts belonging to Giraud and after a few days returned to Carcassonne. But the traitor Giraud, after taking the Count's knights [whom he had captured] to Minerve, made light of the promise he had made and gave no regard to his oath [to return them safely]; certainly he did not kill them, but, more cruelly, he put out their eyes; more than that, he cut off their ears and noses and upper lips and sent them off naked to find their way back to the Count.

---

18. The attack was apparently led by squires, or non-noble infantry.

19. The Catholics referred to Cathars as "Albigensians," in reference to the town of Albi, where a Cathar council was said to have been held in 1167.

He threw them out at night, exposed naked to the wind and cold (the weather was very severe), and one of them (the story cannot be heard without tears) died in a dung pit. The other, as I heard from his own mouth, was taken by a poor man to Carcassonne. A wicked crime, unheard-of cruelty! This was the beginning of the sorrows.

c. The Nature of Heresy
Latin • ca. 1321 CE • Toulouse

After the military defeat of the Cathars in 1229, the Dominican order was charged with carrying out an Inquisition. This traveling court moved through the region seeking out suspected heretics, interrogating them, torturing them if necessary, and if repentance and correction were impossible, handing them over to the authorities of execution. Bernardo Gui, who served as Inquisitor of Toulouse from 1307 to 1323 or 1324, authored a manual, The Techniques of Inquisition into Heretical Depravity, *describing the heresies of the time (including Catharism) and outlining techniques for questioning. This passage is from the chapter "The Manicheans of Today," meaning the Cathars.*

Concerning the Errors of the Manicheans of the Present Time.

The sect and heresy of the Manicheans and the supporters of its aberration declare and confess that there are two gods and two lords, to wit, a beneficent God and an evil one. They assert that the creation of everything visible and corporeal was wrought, not by God the Heavenly Father, whom they term the beneficent God, but by the devil, or Satan, the wicked God—for him they call the evil god, the god of this age, and the prince of this world. Thus, they postulate two creators, namely, God and the devil; and two creations, that is, one invisible and incorporeal, the other visible and corporeal.

Also, they pretend that there are two churches: The beneficent one, they say, is their sect, which they declare to be the Church of Jesus Christ. But the other they call the evil church; this they hold to be the Roman Church, which they shamelessly refer to as the mother of fornication, the great Babylon, the harlot and cathedral of the devil, and the synagogue of Satan. They despise and distort all its offices, its orders, its ordinations, and its statutes. They call all who hold its faith heretics and sinners, and they declare as dogma that no one can be saved in the faith of the Roman Church.

To Consider

1. Why would heterodoxy have been so threatening to the Latin Church?
2. Why would ordinary people have been attracted to heresy, and why would others go to war against them?
3. The Cathar Crusade seems far more brutal than wars waged against Muslims. Why might that be?

Adapted from

a. *The Song of the Cathar Wars: A History of the Albigensian Crusade.* Trans. Janet Shirley. 2001. Pp. 19–20 (chaps. 20–21). Republished with permission of Taylor & Francis Informa UK Ltd – Books, from *The Song of the Cathar Wars: A History of the Albigensian Crusade,* 2001; permission conveyed through Copyright Clearance Center, Inc.

b. Peter of Les Vaux-de-Cernay. *The History of the Albigensian Crusade: Peter of Les-Vaux-de-Cernay's Historia Albigensis.* Trans. W. A. Sibley and M. D. Sibley. Woodbridge, UK: Boydell, 1998. P. 70 (chap. 127). Reproduced with permission of The Licensor through PLSclear.

c. Wakefield, Walter L., and Austin P. Evans. *Heresies of the High Middle Ages: Selected Sources, Translated and Annotated.* New York: Columbia University Press, 1991. P. 379.

7.6 PRIDE AND PREJUDICE

Religious community was only one mode of identity in the medieval Mediterranean, and people also saw themselves as belonging to groups defined by profession, regional or local affiliation, gender, intellectual orientation, and ethnic origin or linguistic affinity. These modes of identity often either crossed or split religious communities. These texts betray social, cultural, and political tensions among members of the major faiths of the Mediterranean—Islam, Christianity, and Judaism—who saw themselves as members of different ethnic or sectarian communities.

a. A Muslim against Arabs
Arabic • before 1084 CE • Denia

The prestige of Arabic language and culture provoked a reaction among the Persian elite of the 'Abassid Caliphate in the ninth and tenth centuries in the form of anti-Arab literature known as shu'ubiyya. We see an echo of this in eleventh-century al-Andalus in the Treatise *of Ahmad ibn Gharsiya ("the son of García") al-Bashkuni ("the Basque") (d. 1084), a Muslim poet of Christian heritage who found patronage in the taifa kingdom of Denia, which was ruled by former slaves of Iberian or Eastern European origin. While praising Arabic literature, he criticized the Arabs as inferior to his people. His* Treatise *provoked five separate rebuttals from pro-Arab contemporaries.*

Am I to suppose that you have maligned or despised this respected non-Arab nation, without realizing that they are the blond, the fair-complexioned ones? They are not Arabs, possessors of mangy camels. They are skilled archers, descendants of Chosroes, of glorious ancestry, brave, heroic; not herders of sheep or cows.[20] Their nobles were removed by their concern for armor and supple spears from the pasturing of camels, and by seeking for greatness, from the milking of goats, a proud people who were descendants of Caesar and who wore helmets and coats of mail; they were occupied by their concern for putting armies to rout, in removing the fear of the frightened. Defenders of the flocks, raisers of the citadels,

---

20. Chosroes, or Khosrow (531–579), was a Sasanid "King of Kings" who defeated the forces of Byzantium and its Arab allies and conquered Yemen.

hawks in whom rosy whiteness pre-dominated, eager for glory but wooers of it by their spears.

> It did not harm them if they witnessed
> deeds of nobility or faced their
> peers on the day of war.
>
> That their complexion was not dark.

Of Roman origin and blond, Byzantine lineage, fostered by the possessors to inner virtue, lineal glory, and greatness among the blond ones, they did not pasture sheep or different varieties of beasts of burden; soft-skinned ones among whom neither the Egyptians nor the Nabateans have implanted; family honor well-guarded and noble lineage.

Your mother, O Arabs, was a slave to our mother. If you deny this you will be found unjust. There is no excess in remonstrating, for we never tended monkeys nor did we weave mantles, nor did we eat wild herbs; there is no cutting off your relationship with Hagar; you were our slaves, servants, enfranchised ones, and valets upon whom we showered our bounty by manumission, for we made you come forth from the bond of slavery and joined you to the freeborn.[21] Yet you were ungrateful for the favor, so we slapped you down and dragged you by the forelock so that this constrained you to dwelling in Hijaz and led you to utter stinging metaphorical allusions, whereas we are grave and forbearing.

b. Barbarous Berbers
Arabic • between 1108 and 1143 CE • al-Andalus

Muhammad al-Saraqusti ("from Zaragoza") al-Andalusi ("of al-Andalus") ibn Ashtarkuwi (d. 1143) was an important but fairly obscure poet and scholar. His Double-Rhymed Tales *is a cycle of tongue-in-cheek short stories featuring tricksters and duplicitous narrators. In this passage his narrator, a Muslim from the East on his way to al-Andalus, is cast ashore instead among the Berbers of Morocco. This was written at a time when the rigorous Maghribian Almoravids dominated al-Andalus and when many local Muslims struggled to overthrow them. It contrasts the sophistication of Arab Andalusis with the supposed barbarity of the North Africans. This passage is from Tale 41, "The Berbers."*

Time hurled me to the land of Tangier, whence I could survey the portals of the Frankish lands. There, I stayed among people like ostriches, and humans like wolves or hyenas, whose speech I could not understand, and with whose minds my own did not agree. I differed

---

21. Old Testament lore traces the Arabs' origin to Ishmael, Abraham's son by Hagar, the slave of his wife. Mother and son were cast into exile after Sarah gave birth to Isaac.

from those people in the manner of my dress and speech, nor did I escape being rejected and rebuffed by them. Hence, after speaking, I became dumb, and after neighing, I became satisfied with the clatter of bells, as though I were in the company of cattle, or herding free-grazing camels that would neither obey, keep the peace, nor match my understanding and forbearance. I had heard of the land of al-Andalus and of its culture, its festivities, and its refinement, and I had come to long for it with the longing of a passionate lover, and would have given old and valuable possession in exchange for it. The qualities I observed in its inhabitants used to delight me, and the virtues I came to expect from its best and finest citizens used to please me, even though I had met only its newly-weaned, rather than its experienced young camels, and merely viewed the foot of its summit. So, when I wished to attempt the crossing, and to traverse the straits preventing me from reaching al-Andalus, I came down to these shores.

c. Beware of Greeks . . .
Latin • 1150s CE • Saint-Denis, Paris

Odo of Deuil (1110–1162) was a monk from northern France who went on the Second Crusade in 1147. In his capacity as chaplain to Louis VII (1137–1180) he was an intimate witness to the planning and execution of the disastrous campaign against Damascus. Like many Latins he distrusted the Byzantines and blamed them for the Crusaders' failures. In his Journey of Louis VII to the East, *he echoes stereotypes regarding Byzantines that were widespread among Latin Christians. Here, he refers to negotiations between Louis and Manuel Komnenos (1143–1180); incidentally, the empress Irene was a Bavarian princess originally named Bertha of Sulzbach, who famously shunned the extravagances of the imperial court.*

The Greeks always reported good news, but they never showed any proof of it, and they were the less believed because on every occasion all used the same prefatory flattery. The king accepted, but considered of slight value, their *polychronia* (for that is the name of the gestures of honor which they exhibit, not only toward kings, but even toward certain of their nobles, lowering the head and body humbly or kneeling on the ground or even prostrating themselves). Occasionally the empress wrote to the queen. And then the Greeks degenerated entirely into women; putting aside all manly vigor, both of words and spirit, they lightly swore whatever they thought would please us, but they neither kept faith with us nor maintained respect for themselves. In general, they really have the opinion that anything which is done for the holy empire cannot be considered perjury. Let no one think that I am taking vengeance on a race of men hateful to me and that because of my hatred I am inventing a Greek whom I have not seen. Whoever has known the Greeks will, if asked, say that when they are afraid they become despicable in their excessive debasement and when they have the upper hand they are arrogant in their severe violence to those subjected to them.

d. The Wrong Type of Jews
Hebrew • early 13th century • Alexandria [?]

The poet and physician Moses al-Dar'i, a dedicated Karaite, was descended from a family from al-Andalus that relocated to Morocco and subsequently to Egypt. Little is known about his life other than what can be gleaned from his works. Below are passages from two of his poems, one against the Rabbanite Jews and the other on the Jewish community of Damascus.

1. Far be it for me to associate with wicked folk
    and walk in their path,
Or turn to their lies, deceptions and mockeries;
Neither will I incline to the prattle of their books
    filled with falsehood and vanity;
I will not study the "commands of men learned by rote"
    from their fellows
Or hold a desire for the "esoteric teaching from Sinai"
    the Rock commanded his people.
I declare them spurious and affirm my faith
    in the written Torah with which God endowed
    the people of his inheritance;
One Torah, do not add thereto; one law, do not change it.

2. I arrived in the city with my life at stake,
    hoping to find a cure among its people;
Instead, I found more danger than benefit;
    the drink I sought was filled with anguish;
My friends warned me: "They are stiff-necked
    like a forest wolf and a lion;
Their contempt for all passers-by
    rivals that of the wolf and lion."
"[Malign not the wolf and lion with your comparison],
    I liken them to dogs in their hatred of strangers."

To Consider

1. What factors might be at the root of the tensions?

2. How do the writers characterize their enemies, and why?

3. How does this invective differ from Muslim-Christian-Jewish polemic?

Adapted from

a. Monroe, James T. *The Shu'ubiyya in Al-Andalus: The Risala of Ibn Garcia and Five Refutations.* Berkeley: University of California Press, 1970. Pp. 23–24.

b. al-Tamimi al-Saraqusti ibn al-Ashtarkuwi, Abu al-Tahir Muhammad ibn Yusuf. *Al-Maqamat al-luzumiyah by Abū l-Tāhir Muhammad Ibn Yūsuf al-Tamīmī al-Saraqustī Ibn al-Aštarkūwī.* Trans. James T. Monroe. Leiden: Brill, 2002. P. 418. Reproduced with permission of The Licensor through PLSclear.

c. Odo de Deuil. *De profectione Ludovici VII in Orientem.* Ed. and trans. Virginia Gingerick Berry. New York: Columbia University Press, 1948. Pp. 57, 59.

d. Weinberger, Leon J. "Moses Darʿi, Karaite Poet and Physician." *Jewish Quarterly Review* 84 (1994): 461, 458–59.

EIGHT

Reading Each Others' Books

It is true that Jews, Christians, and Muslims were educated in separate schools, in different languages, focusing on different holy texts and on an enormous body of other religious books in their own learned language and meant to explicate the meaning of their own holy books. Nevertheless, thanks to the work of translators, they frequently read each other's books as well. Many of these contained popular stories intended to provide moral insight, but many were just entertaining tales. Yet they often read each other's holy books too, for the Hebrew Bible, Christian Bible, and Qur'an often found themselves in an another religion's language. This meant that scholars of all three religions could often argue with their religious opponents on the basis of real knowledge of their scriptures, and this helped lead to the flourishing of interreligious debates, whether in oral or written form.

The readings that follow take up these various themes, providing examples of the popular stories that crossed religious boundaries, but also illustrating what happened when holy books made it into a rival religion's scholarly language, including two examples of treatises that attempted to attack another religion based on knowledge of its holy book.

8.1 THE *DISCIPLINA CLERICALIS* OF PETRUS ALFONSI, 1062–1140 CE

What made it possible, of course, for Peoples of the Book to read each other's books was translation, and there was no end of it in the medieval Mediterranean. Best known today are the translations of Greek science and philosophy into Arabic in the eighth through tenth century, and translations of Greek and Arabic science and philosophy into Latin in the eleventh through thirteenth century. But translators put their hands to many other texts as well, often adapting and combining texts as they did so.

Petrus Alfonsi (fl. 1106–1120) is a good example of a translator of the latter sort. He had been born a Jew in al-Andalus (named Moses Sephardi), but converted to Christianity in the Kingdom of Aragon in the early twelfth century, and is well known for his learned attacks on the Judaism of his youth and on the Islam of the Arab world into which he was born. But he also was a great admirer of Arab science and culture. Indeed, he became a key conduit for the introduction of Arab stories and wisdom into Latin Europe through his widely read book the *Disciplina clericalis*—a title we might translate as *Clerical Education,* or *Scholar's Guide.* Strikingly enough, this treatise, directed at Latin-Christian educated priests, consists almost entirely of amusing and edifying stories of Arab origin mixed together with wise sayings and proverbs likewise of Arab-Islamic origin. Moreover, the work contains almost no references to specifically Christian doctrines, though a general monotheistic ethos predominates. Two passages follow.

a. The Parable of the Poet and the Hunchback
Latin • early 12th century • Christian Spain

A good portion of the Disciplina clericalis *consists of parables that are, according to Alfonsi's introduction, meant to help train "disciplined clergymen." Often these are lighthearted and amusing stories—and sometimes it's a little bit difficult to see what useful lesson they are supposed to teach the clergy.*

A poet presented some verses to a king, and the king praised his talent and ordered him to ask for some gift in exchange for what he had done. The poet asked the king to make him gatekeeper of his city for a month and to let him have one denarius[1] from every hunchback, every man with the itch, every one-eyed man, every man covered with impetigo sores, and every man with a hernia. The king granted it and confirmed it with his seal.

The poet, in his new capacity, sat down at the gate of the city to do his job. One day a hunchback wrapped in a cloak, carrying a staff, entered the gate. The poet stopped him and demanded a denarius of him. The hunchback refused. The poet seized him, and when he pulled the hunchback's hood back he discovered that the hunchback was one-eyed. He then demanded two denarii, instead of one, as before.

The hunchback refused to give him the money, and the poet held him fast. When the hunchback saw that there was no help, he tried to flee; but when his cloak was pulled father back and his head bared, it appeared that he had the itch. The poet immediately demanded three denarii of him. When the hunchback saw that he could not defend himself by fleeing or with the help of another, he began to struggle: and when he exposed his arms to defend himself, it became apparent that they were covered with impetigo sores. The poet demanded four denarii of him and pulled off his cloak. The hunchback fell to the ground and displayed

---

1. The *denarius* (pl. *denarii*) or shilling was a silver coin originating in the Roman Empire.

a hernia. The poet thereupon extracted five denarii from him. Thus it happened that the one who would not willingly give one denarius gave five unwillingly.

b. On Fear
Latin • early 12ᵗʰ century • Christian Spain

Other substantial passages of the book are wise sayings arranged in topical groups that tend to alternate with the parables, such as the one above. This passage comes near the very beginning of the text.

Enoch the philosopher, who in the Arabic language is called Edric [Idris],[2] said to his son: Let the fear of the Lord be your business, and profit will come to you without labor.

Another philosopher said: Who fears God is feared by everything, but he who does not fear God, fears everything.

Another philosopher said: Who fears God, loves God; who loves God, obeys God.

An Arab said in his poem: You are disobedient to God, yet you pretend to love Him, and [that] is unbelievable, for if you truly love him you will obey him, for he who loves, obeys.

To Consider

1. What sort of wisdom do these two passages impart for Latin-Christian priests?

2. Why do you think this text scarcely mentions any distinctive Christian doctrines?

3. What view of Arabs does the second passage offer?

Source

a–b. Petrus Alfonsi. *The Scholar's Guide: A Translation of the Twelfth-Century "Disciplina Clericalis" of Pedro Alfonso.* Trans. Joseph Ramon Jones and John Esten Keller. Toronto: Pontifical Institute of Mediaeval Studies, 1969. Pp. 52–53, 35.

8.2 THE MUSLIM AND CHRISTIAN BUDDHAS

Accounts of holy men and women were a widespread genre of literature among Jews, Christians, and Muslims. Indeed in the Latin and Greek worlds this genre, called hagiography by scholars, is the most abundant variety of written source surviving from the medieval period. Surprisingly, these Mediterranean monotheists were drawn to each other's stories of holy people. The most striking example of this phenomenon is the amazing travels, by way of

---

2. Idris was a pre-Islamic, monotheist prophet mentioned in the Qur'an whom Muslim scholars often identified with Enoch in the Hebrew Bible, who was said to have "walked with God" (Genesis 21–24).

translation, of the story of the founder of an entirely different religious tradition altogether: Buddhism.

From well before the Middle Ages Buddhists in India had recounted the story of their religion's founding: how Siddhartha Gautama (ca. 566–486 BCE), an Indian prince, who had been brought up in luxury in a secluded palace where the misery and death of the world were intentionally hidden from him, abandoned his privileged life, sought wisdom, and eventually experienced enlightenment under a sacred tree. Though originating far to the east of the Mediterranean, and in a religious tradition far different from Mediterranean's scriptural monotheism, this story became a huge best-seller around the Sea in the Middle. Eventually versions of it appeared in nearly every language and among all the major religious traditions of the region, as the following two passages indicate.

a. *The Book of Bilawhar and Yudasaf*
Arabic • 8ᵗʰ century • Southern Iraq [?]

Originally written in the holy language of India, Sanskrit, the story of the Buddha made it into Persian in late antiquity, and from Persian it was translated into Arabic by one of the founders of Arabic prose, Ibn al-Muqaffaʻ (724–759) or his circle. In this version the tale has been only lightly Islamicized. Indeed the word Islam is not used in it, but the true religion is called din, *a word that can mean "religion" in general but is often used as a synonym for Islam.*

There was in the country of India a great king, who, on account of his extreme love for the world, was turned away from contemplating eternity so ardently towards [the affairs of] his kingdom, that there was no one who dared to find fault with him. He alienated the adherents of [true] religion, and attracted the adherents of the idols. . . . In those days a boy was born to the king, and he was greatly delighted thereat, because he was anxious to possess male offspring. He then assembled astrologers and the learned men to [predict the course of his son's life], whereon they reported that [the son] would attain a higher station than any king of the kings of the earth. A scholar among them said thereon: "I do not think that the nobility this boy will arrive at will be the kind of nobility that is attained in the [affairs of the] world, and I am of the opinion that he will become a leader in asceticism, and of a high degree in religion among the degrees of eternity." Hereon the king's joy at [the birth of] the son disappeared; then by his order a town was set apart for him, and he selected for his service and education trustworthy guardians, whom he summoned to his presence and ordered never to mention among themselves death or eternity, neither religion nor asceticism, and neither removal [from this world] nor return [to the next world]; and that if they perceived one of themselves instilling into him doubts or complaints, they should make haste to expel him from among them, so as to cut off from their mouths the mention of the things he had prohibited them to notice. Accordingly when the boy had become able to understand speech, nothing of the kind was uttered by their tongues.

b. *The Balavariani (Barlaam and Josaphat)*
Old Georgian • ca. 1000 CE • Jerusalem

The first Christian version of the story was translated from an Arabic version early in the eleventh century by Christian monks from Georgia (an area north of Iran) who were living in Jerusalem. The monks translated the Arabic into their own language, Old Georgian. Where the Arabic versions contain few explicit references to Islam, the Old Georgian version is thoroughly Christianized, and is the origin of countless other versions in nearly every Christian language in the Greek and Latin worlds. As a result, Baarlam and Josaphat came to be considered saints of the church until the modern period when it became clear what the real origins of their story were.

There lived a certain king in the land of India . . . and the name of that king was Abenes. He was a man of strong pagan beliefs, possessing great dominions and armies countless in their numbers, fierce and terrible over all men, victorious over his foes. . . . He persecuted and hated the servants of Christ. . . . He was utterly immersed in the pursuit of the pleasures and delights of this world and enslaved by his own passions, and quite unable to exercise any restraint of indulgences which are so pernicious to the soul. . . . There was born to [the king] a son, more handsome than any child born in those times. The king was filled with great joy; and he called his name Iodasaph, and said: "This is what my idols have done for me, because I have exalted them." And he pressed on increasingly with wanton revelry along the road to ruin. Then he gathered together a multitude of astrologers, that they might determine the child's future career. And these all declared with a single voice: "This child shall attain a reign of glory with regal majesty such as nobody has ever achieved in the land of India." But among them there was one man, more expert than the others in all branches of wisdom. He declared: "My verdict is that the glory which this child shall attain is not the glory of this world: but I believe that he is to be a great guide upon the road of truth." When the king heard these words, he was filled with sorrow and his joyful mood left him entirely. He ordered a city to be built for his son in a place set apart, and the child lived inside it. And the king detailed trustworthy servants to stay with his son and look after him and afford him every indulgence. When the boy grew up in body and intelligence, Abenes replaced these men by other retainers, warning them not to make mention in the prince's presence of death, of disease, or of eternity; neither of righteousness nor of sin; neither of old age nor of youth; neither of poverty nor of wealth. . . . All these measures the king took so as to prevent the prince from seeing anything which might give him cause for wonderment, and thus lead him to make enquiry about the faith of the Christians.

To Consider

1. What do these passages suggest about how difficult it was to make this Muslim-Buddhist story into a Christian one?

2. What common religious interests do these excerpts suggest that Mediterranean Muslims and Christians had in the Middle Ages?

3. What kind of interactions between Muslims and Christians must have been necessary for the Muslim version of the story to be translated by Christians and adapted for their consumption?

Sources

a. Rehatsek, B., trans. "Book of the King's Son and the Ascetic." *Journal of the Royal Asiatic Society of Great Britain and Ireland*, 1890, 119–55. Pp. 121, 125–26.

b. *The Balavariani (Barlaam and Josaphat): A Tale from the Christian East Translated from the Old Georgian.* Trans. David Marshall Lang. Berkeley: University of California Press, 1966. Pp. 53, 59–60.

8.3 MIXED-BLOOD GREEK BORDER LORDS

One of the continuous features of the medieval Mediterranean was the existence of borders between major civilizations and the religions that were at their core. The two most notable borders were, perhaps, the shifting frontiers between the Christian kingdoms of the the north of Spain and the Arab-Muslim principalities in al-Andalus to the south, and between Christian Byzantium and Arab, Persian, and Turkish Islam to the east. We should never, however, think of these borders as hermetically sealed and uncrossable, but rather as highly porous. It was, in fact, all too easy to travel across them, and the people who lived along them frequently did so. Moreover, some people were particularly attracted to them, among them warriors. In some cases we know quite a lot about such men. Rodrigo Díaz de Vivar (1043–1099) was a Castilian knight who fought heroically for both the king of Castile and, after being banished by him, the Muslim sultan of Zaragoza. Intriguingly, he became, nevertheless, a Spanish national hero, known usually by his Arabic-derived honorific title, El Cid (from the north-African Arabic *al-sid*, meaning "the lord"), celebrated in a late twelfth-century epic poem called *The Poem of the Cid*.

Similarly, a genre of epic poems developed in Byzantium to celebrate the deeds of the *akritai*, the "border lords" who defended the frontiers between Greek Christianity and the Islamic world. The anonymous *Digenis Akritas* is the most famous of these poems, and circulated in various versions orally until it was written down in about the eleventh century. It celebrated the deeds of two heroic (though entirely fictional) warriors of this frontier, a converted Muslim known throughout the poem only as the Emir (= *amir* in Arabic, "commander"), who converts and marries a Greek-Christian wife, and his son, the Digenis Akritas of the work's title, his name meaning "Two-Blood Border Lord." These are not, therefore, stories that crossed religious boundaries, but examples of a genre of Mediterranean literature about the people who did so.

a. From *Digenis Akritas*
Greek • 11ᵗʰ century • Byzantium

Although both pledged allegiance to the Byzantine emperor, these two frontier warriors thrived on the ambiguous border crossings of the Byzantine-Arab frontier, much as El Cid did in Spain, as the following two passages suggest. In the first the originally Muslim Emir addresses the warrior brothers of his Greek-Christian beloved, soon to become his wife, and in the second, we are told about their heroic son's way of life.

1. "My good young men,"[3] the Emir replied, "I'm son
Of Chrysoverges[4] and of Panthia;
Amron's grandson; nephew of Karoës.
My father died while I was still an infant;
My mother gave me to my Arab kinsmen
Who brought me up a good Muslim.
Seeing me fortunate in all my wars,
They made me ruler of all Syria,
And gave three thousand chosen lancers to me.
I quelled all Syria and captured Kufah
(In telling you the truth I boast but little.)
Later I wiped out Heracleia, taking
Amorium up to Iconium,
And subdued hordes of thieves and all the beasts.
No generals could withstand me, and no armies;
A lovely woman, though, has conquered me.
Her beauty fires me and weeping quenches;
Her sighing burns; I don't know what to do!
On her account I wished to test your courage,
Because she never ceased to weep for you.
I will confess to you and tell the truth:
If you won't scorn me as your brother-in-law,
I will become, because she's so delightful,
A Christian, and come to Romania.[5]

2. Then, since the youth[6] had shown that he was worthy,
And had become renowned in his exploits,
For he'd made good in almost all the world,
He chose to live alone upon the border,
And took his girl and his own servants with him.
He had an endless longing to live alone,

---

3. The Emir speaks here to the brothers of his future Greek-Christian wife.

4. This and the following three names are Greek and indicate, therefore, that the Emir himself had a Greek-Christian father.

5. Byzantium.

6. Digenis Akritas, the Two-Blood Border Lord, son of the Emir and his Greek-Christian wife.

And walk around alone with no one with him.
In fact, where he had gone he had his own tent
In which he and the girl lived all alone.
Her two maidservants had another tent,
The Border Lord's Companions still another,
And each was a great distance from the others.
Now many of the outlaws heard about this,
And hatched a plot to carry off the girl.
He overcame them, and he slew them all
Just as he conquered all of Babylon,
Tarsus, Baghdad, the Mavorchonionites,[7]
And other parts of dread Ethiops' land.[8]

To Consider

1. Does it seem credible that two great border lords on the Byzantine-Arab frontier were both of mixed religious ancestry?

2. Why would a popular Greek epic poem celebrate these heroes' mixed background?

3. How credible do you think these portrayals are of the Byzantine soldiers who actually lived on the border with the Islamic world?

Source

a. *Digenis Akritas, The Two-Blood Border Lord: The Grottaferrata Version.* Trans. Denison B. Hull. Copyright © Athens: Ohio University Press, 1972. Pp. 11, 59. This material is used by permission of Ohio University Press, www.ohioswallow.com.

8.4 THE MUSLIM JESUS

Muslims considered Jesus not only to be a prophet in the chain of biblical and other prophets that culminated in Muhammad, the final prophet, but to have a particular reputation for holiness—in fact, it was (and is) not uncommon for Muslims to view Jesus as the holiest of all the prophets. This meant that there was much interest, particularly among Sufis and other ascetics and mystics, not only in the Qur'anic stories of Jesus, but also in biblical accounts. While the Bible circulated in many Arabic versions among Jews and Christians living in the Islamic world, and while some Muslim scholars were acquainted with these Arabic Bibles, oral transmission was a much more common channel through which biblical stories about Jesus became widely known among Muslims.

---

7. These appear to be an entirely made-up people.
8. "Ethiops' land" is Ethiopia.

a. Sayings of the Muslim Jesus
Arabic • 8th century (#1–#3), 9th century (#4), 11th century (#5) •
The Arab World

A vast body of stories about Jesus, many based directly on biblical passages, many not, circulated among Muslims in the Middle Ages, and were eventually written down in treatises offering spiritual guidance. A few examples follow.

1. Jesus said, "If it is a day of fasting for one of you, let him anoint his head and beard and wipe his lips so that people will not know that he is fasting. If he gives with the right hand, let him hide this from his left hand. If he prays, let him pull down the door curtain, for God apportions praise as he apportions livelihood." (Compare Matthew 6:3–4, 16–18.)

2. Jesus said, "Strive for the sake of God and not for the sake of your bellies. Look at the birds coming and going! They neither reap nor plough, and God provides for them. If you say, 'Our bellies are larger than the bellies of birds,' then look at these cattle, wild or tame, as they come and go, neither reaping nor plowing, and God provides for them too. Beware the excesses of the world, for the excesses of the world are an abomination in God's eyes. (Compare Matthew 6:25–34.)

3. Jesus said, "Place your treasures in heaven, for the heart of man is where his treasure is." (Compare Matthew 6:21.)

4. Jesus used to say, "Charity does not mean doing good to him who does good to you, for this is to return good for good. Charity means that you should do good to him who does you harm." (Compare Matthew 5:46.)

5. Jesus said to his disciples by way of counsel, "If you do what I did and what I told you, you will be with me tomorrow in the Kingdom of Heaven, abiding with my Father and yours, and will see His angels around His throne, extolling his praises and sanctifying Him. There you will partake of every pleasure, without eating or drinking." (Compare Luke 23:43.)

To Consider

1. Though rooted in the Christian Gospels, these stories circulated among pious Muslims. Why would they have seemed unobjectionable to them?

2. How would you explain how Muslim Sufis and ascetics came to have knowledge of this gospel material?

3. What kind of religious leader is Jesus in these passages?

Source

a. Khalidi, Tarif, ed. and trans. *The Muslim Jesus: Sayings and Stories in Islamic Literature.* Cambridge, MA: Harvard University Press, 2001. Pp. 53, 60, 71, 73, 141. Copyright © 2001 by the President and Fellows of Harvard College. Used by permission. All rights reserved.

8.5 THE LATIN-CHRISTIAN ENCOUNTER WITH THE TALMUD

Translation, as we have seen, was essential for the Peoples of the Book to be able to read each other's books. For various reasons scholars and missionaries sometimes translated their own holy books into other languages. Thus it was that Saadia ben Joseph (882–942) translated the Torah into Arabic so that the large group of Jews who primarily spoke that language could have access to it, and that Umar ibn Muhammad al-Nasafi (d. 1143) translated the Qur'an into Persian rhymed prose so as to help convert Persian speakers and to serve the already large community of Persian Muslims. In other cases, however, religious scholars learned the languages of another religion's holy book so that they could translate it and make it accessible to those who wanted to defend their own religion against its claims, as in the case of the anonymous Greek translation of the Qur'an that circulated in Byzantium from about 870 on.

Latin-Christian scholars were particularly active in the latter sort of translation in the twelfth and thirteenth centuries, having translated both the entirety of the Qur'an (two different times) and substantial portions of the Talmud, the massive accompaniment to the Torah that stood at the center of Rabbanite Judaism. In all these cases the translations were made in order to assist Christians in refuting Islam and Judaism and in defending Christianity. The French Dominican translators of the Talmud, some perhaps converts from Judaism, wanted to make this material available for Christian readers so that they would understand the "errors" of the Jews. Indeed, they were caught up in a series of events that led to the pope actually condemning the Talmud and requiring that it be burned, which it was, in countless copies, in Paris in 1241–1242.

a. Letter from Odo of Chateauroux, bishop of Tusculum, to Pope Innocent IV
Latin • mid-13th century • Paris

This letter by the chancellor of the University of Paris, who played a key role in these events, gives some sense of what Latin Christians thought made the Talmud so dangerous.

To the most holy father and lord, Innocent, supreme pontiff by the grace of God, Odo, by divine compassion bishop of Tusculum, legate of the Apostolic See.

It has recently pleased Your Holiness to issue orders to me that I have the Talmud and other books of the Jews delivered up to me and inspected and, diligently inspecting the same, I should tolerate them in those matters in which I found they ought to be tolerated in the sight of God without damage to the Christian faith and should restore them to the masters of the Jews. But lest the legal proceedings that were once held concerning the aforesaid books be unknown to Your Holiness and so that it may not happen that anyone be deceived in this matter by the cunning and lies of the Jews, Your Holiness should know that in the time of Pope Gregory of happy memory a certain convert by the name of Nicholas[9] made known to the said

---

9. Nicholas Donin, a well-educated Jew from southern France who converted to Catholicism and was the central figure in the condemnation and burning of the Talmud in Paris.

supreme pontiff that the Jews, not content with the old Law, which the Lord gave in writing through Moses, indeed utterly neglecting the same, maintain that the Lord also proclaimed another law, which is called the Talmud, i.e. teaching, and that, having been passed on orally to Moses and inserted in their minds, they say, it was preserved for a long time without being written down, until certain people came along, whom they call sages and scribes, who rendered it in writing so that it would not slip from men's minds through forgetfulness, the book of which exceeds the text of the Bible in size. In it are contained so many falsities and offensive things that they are a source of shame to those who repeat them and horror to those who hear them, and this [it is said] is the main reason that keeps the Jews stubborn in their perfidy. . . . Indeed when the aforesaid examination was made and all the masters of theology and canon law as well as many others deliberated, in accordance with the apostolic mandate all the aforesaid books that could be found at that time were then burned in a bonfire.

To Consider

1. The Babylonian Talmud was completed in late antiquity. What does this passage suggest about Christian familiarity with this work that was already more than 500 years old?

2. Aside from assertions that the Talmud contains falsity, is Odo factually correct in what he says about it and its role in Jewish belief and practice?

3. What about the Talmud might have made it seem especially dangerous to Latin Christians?

Source

a. Friedman, John, Jean Connell Hoff, and Robert Chazan. *The Trial of the Talmud, Paris, 1240.* Toronto: Pontifical Institute of Mediaeval Studies, 2012. Pp. 98–100.

8.6 *THE BOOK OF THE COVENANT* BY JOSEPH KIMHI

Having read each other's holy books, the Mediterranean monotheists often found themselves arguing with each other over their contents in informal conversations, organized debates, or written treatises, using their knowledge of their opponent's holy book to attack it and defend their own religion. In general, as a small minority throughout the Mediterranean, Jews were much less likely to engage in such conversations, whether oral or written, than Muslims and Christians. The idea was to keep one's head down and not attract unwanted attention from the dominant religion. Yet we do have a series of Jewish treatises that do this, including the work from which the following passage derives.

a. From Joseph Kimhi's *The Book of the Covenant*
Hebrew • 12th century • France

A rabbi born in al-Andalus who lived much of his life in southern France, Joseph Kimhi (1105– 1170) was something of a polymath: he was a biblical commentator, Hebrew lexicographer, trans-

lator of Arabic works into Hebrew, and poet. He also wrote a Hebrew critique of Latin Christianity called The Book of the Covenant. *In it he advances many of the standard Jewish objections to Christian doctrine. The following passage focuses on the doctrines of the Trinity and Incarnation.*

[The believer said: the Christians] profess and believe in the Trinity—Father, Son, and Spirit—and claim that the Creator is the Father of all and that He created the entire world. At the beginning of the Book of Genesis, it states, *and the Spirit of the Lord hovered over the face of the waters* (Gen. 1:2). Hence: Father and Spirit.[10] We reply: I believe that wisdom corroborates them and reason is on their side. He is the Father of the world, having engendered it and brought it into being *ex nihilo*,[11] and the [existence of] the Holy Spirit [may be seen in this verse also]. But who will constrain me to believe that he has a son [in the same way that] reason constrains me [to believe] in the Father and Spirit?

The [Christian] unbeliever said: You have judged wisely and spoken well by accepting belief in the Father and the Spirit, [both] from Scripture and from reason. I cannot prove [the existence of the Son] from reason, but in any event I can from Scripture. All the prophets spoke prophecies concerning the Son. . . . Isaiah said, *A Child is born to us, a son is given to us, and the* principatus *will be upon his shoulders; and his name will be called Wonderful Counsellor, Mighty God, Everlasting Father, Prince of Peace* (Isa. 9:5). It is not possible that these names refer to a human being. Therefore, [this] has constrained me to believe in the Son [of God].

[The believer said:] There is an error in the verse which you cited [which was introduced] by Jerome, your translator.[12] The [grammar] does not indicate a reading of *he shall be called God*, but *the Wonderful Counsellor, Mighty God, Everlasting Father shall call his name the prince of peace*. This [refers to] Hezekiah the righteous whom God called prince of peace.[13] . . . These names were mentioned according to the circumstances [of his life]: *Wonderful*, for He wrought wonders with him; *Counselor*, for he counselled him to walk in the ways of the Lord, for his father was wicked; *Mighty God*, for he caused him to grow mighty over his enemies; *Everlasting Father*, for he added fifteen years to his life, for He is the Master and Father of eternity. Further, if, as you say, he spoke this verse in reference to the Son, he should have made this quite explicit, for in the case of a non-rational doctrine, the prophets would set it forth clearly in a plain statement. Who will believe that the Holy One, blessed be He, entered the womb of a woman and took on flesh? Is it not said concerning flesh: *He remembered that*

---

10. "Hence: Father and Spirit," i.e., hence Christians argue that God has a Holy Spirit because of this mention of the Spirit of the Lord hovering over the face of the deep at the very beginning of Genesis.

11. *Ex nihilo* means "out of nothing."

12. Saint Jerome's (347–420) Latin version of the Bible, called the Vulgate and translated from the original Hebrew, Aramaic, and Greek, became the standard Bible of Latin Europe.

13. Hezekiah was king of the Jewish kingdom of Judah from 716 to 697 BCE.

they were but flesh, a wind that passes and does not come again (Ps. 78:39). Who will believe that the Lord of the world was *born of woman, of few clays and full of trouble* (Job 14:1)?

To Consider

1. The great majority of the Christian Bible is Jewish—the Old Testament, the Hebrew Bible, that is, comprises about 75 percent of it. What, according to this passage, does Joseph Kimhi think about how Christians interpret the Hebrew Bible?

2. To what extent is his critique of Christianity a critique of Christian biblical interpretation?

3. Does Kimhi advance nonscriptural arguments against Christianity here?

Source

a. Kimhi, Joseph. *The Book of the Covenant of Joseph Kimhi.* Trans. Frank Talmage. Toronto: Pontifical Institute of Mediaeval Studies, 1972. Pp. 27–30.

8.7 IBN TAYMIYYA CRITIQUES CHRISTIANITY—AND OTHERS

Though countless treatises attacking Islam or Christianity or Judaism were written in the Middle Ages, and while these treatises on the surface seem focused entirely on attacking one religion, very often these texts functioned in rather complex ways. For one thing, if, say, a Greek Christian wrote a treatise attacking Islam in the Greek language, it is probably the case that he meant the treatise to be read primarily not by Muslims—who only very rarely had reading knowledge of Greek—but by his own coreligionists, whose faith he was attempting to firm up. Furthermore, there were countless cases in which in attacking another religion, the author was also, or even primarily, attacking his coreligionists with whom he disagreed. This seems to have been the case, for example, among the Syrian Miaphysite Christians in the early Middle Ages, whose extensive attacks on Judaism often were very clearly directed at their Christian enemies, the Dyophysites.[14]

a. From Ibn Taymiyya's *Correct Answer*
Arabic • ca. 1316 CE • Damascus

One of the most influential thinkers in Islamic history, Taqi al-Din Ahmad ibn Taymiyya (1263–1328) also wrote the longest Muslim polemical attack on Christianity in the Middle Ages: The Correct Answer against Those Who Changed the Religion of Christ. *This huge work is aimed*

---

14. Miaphysitism and Dyophysitism were mutually hostile positions on the exact nature of Jesus Christ as Son of God, an issue that rent the church in late antiquity. The former held that Christ had only one nature, and survives today in what are called the Oriental Orthodox Churches, while the latter insisted that he had two separate natures, divine and human, and survives today in the Church of the East.

at Christians, who of course existed in very large numbers in Syria and Egypt, where Ibn Taymi-
yya spent his adult life, and certainly many if not most Christian scholars in these regions could
read Arabic, so Ibn Taymiyya may very well have had a Christian audience in mind, hoping to
persuade them of the truth of Islam. It is, nevertheless, clear that Ibn Taymiyya had other enemies
in mind as well—various kinds of Muslims with whom he disagreed, and there were many of
these—as this passage on the Christian doctrine of the Trinity makes clear.

[The Christians] claim that they only arrived at belief in the Trinity . . . from the viewpoint of religion—from [the texts of] the prophets and the revealed books and not on the authority of reason. . . . They report that the sacred books, according to their thinking, have delivered these views, not that rational argumentation has indicated them. This is in spite of the fact that there is nothing in the divine Books which indicates such things; rather they contain what proves their contrary, as we will show, God willing. They do not distinguish between what the mind imagines and proves false and knows to be impossible and that which the mind is unable to conceive since it knows nothing about it, and has no information on it either by affirmation or denial. The prophets have informed mankind about the second of these. It is not possible for the first type of information to have been reported. The Christians do not differentiate between the absurdities of reason and its pearls. . . .

The innovators and the wayward among those who associate themselves with Islam resemble the Christians in this matter and can be likened to them. These are people who hold a view like that of the Christians which exaggerates concerning the prophets, people of the family of the Prophet, shaykhs, and others. Whoever claims pantheism and divine ind- welling, or a specified particular divine union like that held by the Christians, is in this category—thus the view of Shi'i extremists on 'Ali and that of the sect concerning the family of the Prophet like the Nusayris[15] and those like them who claim divinity for 'Ali, like the claim of some Isma'ilis of divinity for al-Hakim.[16] . . . The views of all these people are of the same kind as those of the Christians, and some of them are worse than those of the Christians. Most of these people when presented with an argument showing the falseness of their opinion say something like the statement of the Christians, that this is a matter beyond reason.

To Consider

1. What is the substance of Ibn Taymiyya's argument?

---

15. The Nusayris, known today as the Alawis, were (and are) a syncretistic sect in Syria closely associated with Shi'i beliefs, whose doctrines included a belief in the semidivinity of Muhammad and his closest companions, including 'Ali.

16. The Isma'ilis were (and are) a branch of Shi'i Islam, and some groups of medieval Isma'ilis claimed divinity for al-Hakim bi-Amr Allah (985–1021), one of the Fatimid (Isma'ili) caliphs of Egypt.

2. What are "the prophets and the revealed books" and "the sacred books" that he refers to?

3. Who is Ibn Taymiyya more worried about, Christians or the other groups that he mentions? How would you tell?

Source

a. Ibn Taymiyya. *A Muslim Theologian's Response to Christianity: Ibn Taymiyya's al-Jawab al-Sahih.* Ed. and trans. Thomas F. Michel, SJ. Delmar, NY: Caravan Books, 1984. Pp. 256–57.

NINE

A Sea of Technology, Science, and Philosophy

Since the Renaissance, it has been fashionable to think of the Middle Ages as backward, barbaric, and irrational—it was, of course, Renaissance thinkers who invented that idea! And this characterization of the period has long been discredited by scholars, though it lives on quite persistently in popular culture. It is true, of course, that like every period in history, the medieval period contained its share of irrationalism, but a substantial strand of thorough-going rationalism, inherited from the Greeks, ran right through it and expressed itself in the invention and spread of remarkably contrived technologies, careful scientific observation and theorizing, and rigorous rationalist philosophy. There were, of course, disputes about how far reason could take the human mind, but even some of the greatest religious teachers of the period believed that reason alone could verify many things that religion taught.

The readings in this chapter are meant to exemplify this strand of medieval rationalism by featuring perhaps the most sophisticated medieval technology, the astrolabe; exploring the biography of a scholar who dedicated his life to translating rationalist scientific and philosophical works from Arabic; examining how one learned medicine and prepared medicines; looking at a critic of the excessive use of reason; and pointing out that alongside the period's fascination with well-designed tools and rationalist thought, there was indeed a lot of nonrational thought in the air as well.

9.1 HACKING THE ASTROLABE ACROSS THE MEDITERRANEAN

The astrolabe was a scientific technology used all around the Mediterranean, and we have surviving examples inscribed (they needed to have a lot of information recorded on them) in the major scholarly languages of the Middle Ages—Arabic, Hebrew, Greek, Latin. While its main function was to calculate local time, it was actually a multi-functional tool that could be used for surveying, calculating the height of buildings or mountains, or estimating the distance a hostile army must cross to reach the point of battle. As the astrolabe circulated around the Mediterranean so too did many guidebooks for its use, written not only in classical languages, but in vernaculars as well, as the two passages that follow indicate.

a. From Geoffrey Chaucer's *A Treatise on the Astrolabe*
Middle English • 1391 CE • England

This first passage is from the preface to a Middle English manual for the astrolabe written by the poet Geoffrey Chaucer (1343–1400) for his son, Lewis. As it happens, Chaucer's treatise is based closely on a Latin translation, called On the Operation and Use of the Astrolabe, *that was itself translated from an Arabic manual written in al-Andalus in the early eleventh century.*

This treatise is divided into five parts and is written clearly and in plain English, because your Latin is still not good enough, my little son. But the facts are the same in English as Greek was to the Greeks, Arabic to the Arabs, Hebrew to the Jews and Latin to the Romans, who learned them first from other diverse languages and rewrote them in Latin. And, as God wills, all of these facts have been completely learned and taught in all these languages, but by different methods, much as all roads lead to Rome. Now I ask every person who reads or hears this little treatise to excuse my crude editing and my excessive use of words for two reasons. First, it is hard for a child to learn from complex sentences. Second, it seems better to me to write a good sentence twice for a child so he will not forget the first.

And Lewis, I get my satisfaction if my English treatise presents as many and the same facts as any Latin treatise on the astrolabe. And praise God and save the king, who is lord of this language, and all who obey him, each in his own way, more or less. But consider well that I have not claimed to create this work from my own work or energy. I am but a lewd compiler of the labor of old astronomers (astrologers) and have translated it into English only for your use. With this statement I slay envy.

b. From an Anonymous Greek Treatise on the Astrolabe
Greek • 14ᵗʰ century • Byzantium

The second passage is from a Byzantine-Greek treatise on the astrolabe that was translated from the same Latin treatise that Chaucer was working with in the same period, a treatise that itself had been translated from an earlier Arabic work written in al-Andalus. In this part of the treatise, the author explains some of the other astrolabic operations besides telling time.

In order to find the degree of the sun, by means of day and month—just as you will know the day by means of the degree (of the sun)—by which you want to know the degree of the sun.

Place the alidade[1] on the point of the month, according to the day, for two degrees. At the utmost part of the point of contact you will find the degree of the sun on the sign where it stands. On the other side of the spider[2] is the degree, identical to its height, on the point diametrically opposed, that of the seventh sign. You will find the day of the month thanks to the degree of the sun and the day sought will be known.

In order to find the height of the sun.
When you want to know the height of the sun hang (the astrolabe) by its ring, with your right hand on your left side, since the sun rises from the east at your left side. Move the alidade until the sun's ray passes through each of the holes of the [sighting plates] located on [each end of] it. Afterwards, measure the number of degrees by which the alidade rises on the eastern line; this will be the height of the sun. At night, proceed the same way with a star, without having the height of the sun or its elevation.

In order to find the sign of the horoscope[3] at night by means of a star.
If you desire to know the horoscope at night, take the height of one of the fixed stars positioned on the spider which crosses the eastern or western part. Afterwards, place the point (which indicates) the height of the star on the parallel of its own height and the degree of the sun will tell you the hours of the night. On its opposite (side) will be the hours of the day. Do the same for the other (stars) as mentioned above.[4]

To Consider

1. On the basis of these two sources, what sorts of people would have been interested in using astrolabes?

2. What kinds and level of knowledge does the second passage assume that the user of the astrolabe has?

3. What are some of the practical uses to which the astrolabe could be put according to these examples?

---

1. The movable sight on the back of an astrolabe by which users can measure the angle above the horizon of celestial objects.

2. That is, the *rete,* as it was known in the Latin world: the rotating map of the locations of the brightest stars and the path of the sun that overlays the astrolabe's *tympanum* and gives the coordinate lines of the dome of heaven.

3. "Horoscope" in this case means the sign of the zodiac that is ascending on the eastern horizon at a particular moment. This ascending sign (often called simply the "ascendant") played a big role in how astrologers, for example, used the exact configuration of the stars and planets to predict the personal characteristics of someone based on when exactly they were born.

4. In this case, the author of the treatise left out the final step (perhaps because he reckoned that the user would already know to do this): determining from the front of the astrolabe, having done the steps described above, what sign was crossing the path of the sun at that time—that is, the ascendant sign, or what is called here the "horoscope."

Sources

a. Chaucer, Geoffrey. *A Treatise on the Astrolabe.* In "Chaucer's Astrolabe Treatise," ed. and trans. James E. Morrison, http://www.chirurgeon.org/files/Chaucer.pdf.

b. Tihon, Anne, Régine Leurquin, and Claudy Scheuren, ed. and trans. *Une version Byzantine du traité sur l'astrolabe du Pseudo-Messahalla.* Louvain-la-Neuve Belgium: Bruylant-Academia, 2001. Many thanks to Romain Thurin for his English translation of these passages. Reproduced with permission of The Licensor through PLSclear.

9.2 THE LIFE OF A SCIENTIFIC TRANSLATOR: GERARD OF CREMONA (CA. 1114–1187 CE)

From the late eleventh century into the early thirteenth century a number of Latin scholars traveled from north of the Pyrenees to northern, Christian Spain in search of the sophisticated scientific and philosophical learning of the Arabs, which they had somehow heard about (we don't know how) and wanted to acquire. For many this meant sojourning in Spain for many years or the rest of their lives, learning Arabic and translating Arabic works on mathematics, astronomy and astrology, medicine, and, increasingly as time went on, philosophy. In general we know very little about these scholars other than their names and in some cases where they came from. Indeed it is striking how widely dispersed their origins were: Robert of Ketton from England, Plato of Tivoli from Italy, Herman of Carinthia from what is now southern Austria.

a. From the *Life* of Gerard of Cremona
Latin • late 12th century • Toledo

Though we know little about most of the scholar-translators of the period, the Italian-born Gerard of Cremona, the most prolific and famous of these wandering scholars, is an exception because his students and colleagues composed a brief account of his life that they attached to his translation of one of the Greek scientist Ptolemy's second-century medical treatises, the Tegni *or* Ars Parva *(which Gerard had translated from an Arabic version).*

As a light shining in darkness must not be set under a bushel but rather upon a candlestick, so too the splendid deeds of the great must not be held back, buried in timid silence, but must be made known to listeners today, since they open virtue's door to those who follow, and in worthy memorial offer to modern eyes the example of the ancients as a model for life. Thus, lest master Gerard of Cremona be lost in the shadows of silence, lest he lose the credit that he deserved, lest in brazen theft another name affixed to the books translated by him (especially since he set his name to none of them), all the works he translated—of dialectic as of geometry, of astronomy as of philosophy, of medicine as of the other sciences—have been diligently enumerated by his associates at the end of this *Tegni* just translated by him, in imitation of Galen's enumeration of his own writings at the end of the same book; so that if an admirer of their works should desire one of them, he might find it quicker by this list, and be surer of it. Although he scorned fame, although he fled from praise and the vain pomp of this world; although he refused to spread his name in a quest for empty, insubstantial things, the fruit of his works diffused through the world makes plain his worth. For while he enjoyed good fortune, possessions or their lack neither delighted nor depressed him; manfully sustaining whatever chance brought him, he always remained in the same state of constancy. Hostile to fleshly desires, he clove to spiritual ones alone. He worked for the advantage of all, present and future, mindful of Ptolemy's words: when approaching your end, do good increasingly. He was trained from childhood at centers of philosophical study and had come to a knowledge of all of this that was known to the Latins; but for love of the *Almagest*[5] which he could not find at all among the Latins he went to Toledo; there, seeing the abundance of books in Arabic on every subject, and regretting the poverty of Latins in these things, he learned the Arabic language, in order to be able to translate. In this way, combining both language and science; (for as Hamet says in his letter *On Proportion and Proportionality*,[6] a translator should have knowledge of the subject he is dealing with as well as an excellent command of the languages from which and into which he is translating), he passed on the Arabic literature in the manner of the wise man who, wandering through a green field, links up a crown of flowers, made from not just any, but from the prettiest; to the end of his life, he continued to transmit to the Latin world (as if to his own heir) whatever books he thought finest, in many subjects, as accurately and as plainly as he could. He went the way of all flesh in the seventy-third year of his life, in the year of our Lord Christ 1187.

To Consider

1. As a young man Gerard traveled a long way—more than 1,000 miles—from northern Italy to Toledo, where he spent the rest of his life. What motivated him?

2. What subjects was Gerard interested in?

3. What subjects commonly studied in medieval schools and monasteries are not mentioned here?

Source

a. McVaugh, Michael, trans. In *A Sourcebook of Medieval Science*, ed. Edward Grant. Cambridge, MA: Harvard University Press, 1974. P. 35. Copyright © 1974 by the President and Fellows of Harvard College. Used by permission. All rights reserved.

---

5. The *Almagest* is the most famous work of Claudius Ptolemy (100–ca. 170), a mathematical-astronomical treatise on the apparent motions of the planets and stars.

6. Ahmed ibn Yusuf (835–912), born in Baghdad, was a Arab mathematician and astronomer called Hamet in Latin Europe, where many of his works were known in Latin translation, such as the one mentioned here, translated by Gerard of Cremona himself.

9.3 LEARNING MEDICINE, FINDING MEDICINES

Medicine was understood and practiced basically the same way all around the Mediterranean. Based on the ancient Greek theory that illness was caused by an imbalance among four major liquids in the body (blood, phlegm, black bile, and yellow bile), the work of a physician was to find ways to restore that balance. One could bleed a patient who showed signs of excess blood, but many ailments required prescribing medicines that would help rebalance the humors. In the Middle Ages, the most influential textbook that one studied to master this form of medicine was the *Canon of Medicine*, written in Arabic by the great Muslim philosopher-physician Ibn Sina (980–1037), but translated into Latin in the thirteenth century (and used as the standard medical textbook in Europe till about 1800). To become a competent physician one needed to master both humoral theory and how to find and compound medicines appropriate to the patient's symptoms. The following passages provide a window into both processes.

a. From Ibn Sina's *Poem on Medicine*
Arabic • early 11th century • Bukhara

Ibn Sina also composed a much shorter overview of medicine called al-Urjuzah fi-al-Tibb *or* Poem on Medicine. *Like his* Canon of Medicine, *this poem was read widely in the Middle Ages in many Mediterranean languages. The following excerpted lines from the* Poem *outline some of the basic principles of humoral medicine.*

80. The body is made up of humors of different colors and of distinct temperaments.

81. They are phlegm, yellow bile, blood and black bile.

243. Among the causes of sickness it is believed that the temperament of an organ can be changed when the humors seep away.

244. In this regard one must bear in mind the pressure of the humor and the weakness of the nourisher, and the quantity of this malignant humor.

245. And also the width of the vessels and the weakness of the nourishment, and all this is the whole matter.

997. Here I mention the remedies that expel humors from feces.

998. Those that dominate the temperament, those that make a humor depart.

999. Those that open obstructions or soften, those that burn, those that corrupt.

1000. Those that mature, those that fortify, those that block, those that attract.

1001. Those that liquify, those that stimulate, those that inflame the flesh, those that heal.

1003. Scammony[7] expels yellow bile powerfully.

1004. The proper dose is a third of a *qirat*;[8] it has a powerful influence over humors.

---

7. A plant related to the morning glory whose bitter roots are an excellent purgative.

8. A measure equivalent to four grams.

1006. Aloe is administered in a dose of one *dinar*,[9] and if it doesn't work, double the dose.

1007. As in the case of bedellium[10] or tragacanth.[11]

b. From *The Alphabet of Galen*
Latin • 4th–6th century • Western Europe

Having mastered the humoral principles, a physician would then need to turn to much more comprehensive treatises on the properties of a whole range of substances—minerals, plants, parts of animals—that could be used as medicines to help balance the humors. This and the following two passages provide examples from across the Mediterranean, and across the medieval centuries.

Dittany of Crete is a soft plant that shoots branches that are round, pale, and oblong, with lots of nodules upon them, around which sprout little leaves that are similar to mint, but are paler and more narrow, and on the small branches near the top there appears a small, pink flower, inside this flower is a black seed that has full fragrance a little similar to that of wormwood but more pleasant, with a bitter taste that slowly begins to warm the mouth. Dittany has heating and gently astringent properties, and is particularly useful for stimulating urination or menstruation. It also expels a dead foetus, and its odour kills off vipers and snakes.

c. From the *Judeo-Syriac Medical Fragment*
Syriac written in Hebrew letters • ca. 1000–1200 CE • Syria

While it is highly uncommon to find Syriac written in Hebrew characters, as in this text, this passage is otherwise quite typical of the medieval pharmacopeia—texts that explain how to find and compound medicines.

Scales of copper: And its power is dry like iron and silver, but iron to a great extent restrains the menstruation of women and heals the stomach, and sometimes without dismissing that which she conceives utterly. And it happens that copper is useful for eyes that are weak and shed tears, and that silver dries sores and itching. . . . *Mandrakes:* They possess cold power in the third order, and their fruit possess a little moisture, and when they ripen the insides turn yellowish and poisonous, and the peel of their root causes vomiting and restrains blood.

d. From a Byzantine Commentator on Dioscorides
Greek • before 1400 CE • Byzantium

Dioscorides (ca. 40–90) was a Greek physician and pharmacologist, who wrote a five-volume pharmacopeia usually referred to by its Latin title De materia medica. *Perhaps the most influential*

---

9. A *dinar* is an Arab-Islamic coin whose weight is used here to calibrate the dose.

10. An aromatic gum.

11. Gum made from the dried sap of the Middle Eastern astragalus plant.

such work, it was still being read closely thirteen centuries later by an anonymous Greek scholar who wrote a commentary on it.

Growing in rocky soil, asparagus or "spiky-mushroom," which some term a sage, has a stalk which, boiled and eaten, softens the bowels and is also a diuretic. When drunk, the decoction of its roots is helpful for those having difficulty urinating, and for those afflicted by jaundice or sciatica; when decocted with wine, the roots are helpful for those bitten by a poisonous spider, and those suffering from toothache are benefitted when the decoction is applied to the painful tooth.

To Consider

1. Why would Ibn Sina compose an overview of medicine in poetry?

2. What kinds of knowledge of the world and the human body did Ibn Sina and the authors of these guides to medicines expect physicians to master?

3. To what extent do these works suggest that illnesses are the result of natural causes?

Sources

a. Ibn Sina. *Poema de la medicina = 'Urǧuza fī 'ṭ-ṭibb*. Ed. and trans. Najaty S. Jabary and Pilar Salamanca. Salamanca: Junta de Castilla y León, 1999. Pp. 44–45, 66–69, 164–65. English translation by Thomas E. Burman in reliance on the Spanish version and notes.
b. *The Alphabet of Galen: Pharmacy from Antiquity to the Middle Ages*. Ed. and trans. Nicholas Everett. Toronto: University of Toronto Press, 2012. P. 213. Reprinted with permission of the publisher.
c. Bhayro, Siam. "The Judaeo-Syriac Medical Fragment from the Cairo Genizah: A New Edition and Analysis." In *Collecting Recipes: Byzantine and Jewish Pharmacology in Dialogue,* ed. Lennart Lehmhaus and Matteo Martelli. Boston: Walter de Gruyter, 2017. Pp. 273–300 at 280, 282–83.
d. Adapted slightly from John M. Riddle's translation in his *Byzantine Commentaries on Dioscorides,* Dumbarton Oaks Papers 38 [Symposium on Byzantine Medicine, ed. John Scarborough] (Washington, DC: Dumbarton Oaks Research Library and Collection, 1985). P. 95.

9.4 THOMAS AQUINAS'S THIRD WAY

When Will Durant published his best-selling 1,196-page history of the Middle Ages in 1950, he entitled it *The Age of Faith*. This title at once alluded to a romantic vision of the medieval period as an epoch of noble virtuousness and simple piety, and tendentiously marked off the Middle Ages from the supposedly more rational periods to follow: eleven years later Durant published *The Age of Reason Begins,* his similarly lengthy history of the sixteenth century. While no scholar these days would argue that the sixteenth century was any more or less rational than the thirteenth, the cultures of the Middle Ages continue to be depicted, especially in popular culture, as particularly religious and, in consequence, uninterested in or hostile to rational methods of exploring ultimate questions. It is true, of course, that in some ways the Middle Ages was more religious than the modern world. Religious institutions were, indeed, often remarkably powerful—they everywhere, as we have seen, dominated advanced education in the Mediterranean. But if, in that sense, the Middle Ages was an "Age of Faith," many of the leading religious thinkers of the eleventh, twelfth, and thirteenth centuries were nevertheless devout believers in the power of reason. Indeed, they argued strenuously that at least some religious beliefs could also be shown to be true by rational argument alone.

This included the core belief of Mediterranean religion: that God exists and is one. It is true that this was a doctrine that the average Jew, Christian, and Muslim was required to accept on faith, but for the small class of learned scientist-philosophers it was also a matter of rational knowledge. They believed, in fact, that it could be demonstrated like a scientific proof. The passage that follows is a reworking of an argument originally propounded by the great Muslim philosopher-physician Ibn Sina (980–1037) by the greatest medieval Latin theologian, Thomas Aquinas (1225–1274), who was deeply influenced by the Muslim and Jewish philosophy of the Arab world.

a. Thomas Aquinas's Third Way of Demonstrating God's Existence
Latin • 1265–1274 CE • Italy, France

In his most famous work, called the Summa theologiae,[12] *Thomas Aquinas, a Dominican friar and theologian, offered five proofs for the existence of God. Not surprisingly these proofs appear very near the beginning of this vast, though unfinished work (Aquinas died while working on it).*

The third way is taken from possibility and necessity, and runs thus. We find in nature things that are possible to be and not to be, since they are found to be generated, and to corrupt, and consequently, they are possible to be and not to be. But it is impossible for these always to exist, for that which is possible not to be at some time is not. Therefore, if everything is possible not to be, then at one time there could have been nothing in existence. Now if this were true, even now there would be nothing in existence, because that which does not exist only begins to exist by something already existing. Therefore, if at one time nothing was in existence, it would have been impossible for anything to have begun to exist; and thus even now nothing would be in existence—which is absurd. Therefore, not all beings are merely possible, but there must exist something the existence of which is necessary. But every necessary thing either has its necessity caused by another, or not. Now it is impossible to go on to infinity in necessary things which have their necessity caused by another, as has been already proved in regard to efficient causes. Therefore we cannot but postulate the existence of some being having of itself its own necessity, and not receiving it from another, but rather causing in others their necessity. This all men speak of as God (*Summa theologiae* I.q.2.a.3).

---

12. Meaning something like the "Complete Summation of All Theology."

To Consider

1. Whether you are persuaded by it or not, what makes this argument for God's existence rational?

2. One modern historian referred to scholastic thinkers such as Aquinas as "physicist-theologians." Explain how cosmological proofs for God's existence exemplify that identification.

Source

a. Aquinas, Thomas. *Summa theologiae*. Trans. Fathers of the English Dominican Province. https://www.newadvent.org/summa/1002.htm. NewAdvent.org.

9.5 GREGORY PALAMAS ON THE DANGERS OF PHILOSOPHY

As the previous source suggested, some Jewish, Christian, and Muslim intellectuals in the High Middle Ages believed strongly that reason alone—especially in the form of Aristotelian philosophy—could not only explain the nature of the created world, but could even demonstrate the rational truth of religious doctrines, such as the existence of God. But there were other views about the usefulness and Godliness of reason. Other thinkers, and there are examples from all the Mediterranean religious traditions, were in many ways devoted to the use of reason where appropriate, but didn't think that it extended quite as far as Aquinas. Some, like the Latin-Christian philosopher William of Ockham (1287–1347), expressed serious doubts that such arguments as Aquinas's (and Ibn Sina's) demonstrations of God's existence were actually rationally persuasive. They loved the tool of reason, but had a more limited view of its scope. But there were other reasons to be worried about this rationalist tendency. To think that reason could tell humans much about the transcendant God of Jews, Christians, and Muslims seemed like dangerous vanity to other intellectuals, as the following passage demonstrates.

a. From Gregory Palamas's *Triads*
Greek • mid-14th century • Byzantium

Perhaps the most influential Byzantine thinker of the fourteenth century, Gregory Palamas (1296–1359) had been a monk on Mt. Athos, where he studied Aristotle and received an excellent education otherwise. He later became the bishop of the Thessaloniki (Salonica). In one of the key theological disputes of his century, he was the powerful (and quite successful) defender of Hesychasm, the Byzantine tradition of mysticism. Here is what he had to say about the dangers of reason in matters of faith.

In the case of secular wisdom, you must first kill the serpent, in other words, overcome the pride that arises from this philosophy. How difficult that is! "The arrogance of philosophy has nothing in common with humility," as the saying goes. Having overcome it, then, you must separate and cast away the head and tail, for these things are evil in the highest degree. By the head, I mean manifestly wrong opinions concerning things intelligible and divine and primordial; and by the tail, the fabulous stories concerning created things. As to what lies in between the head and tail, that is, discourses on nature, you must separate out useless ideas by means of the faculties of examination and inspection possessed by the soul, just as pharmacists purify the flesh of serpents with fire and water. Even if you do all this, and make good use of what has been properly set aside, how much trouble and circumspection will be required for the task! Nonetheless, if you put to good use that part of the profane wisdom which has been well excised, no harm can result, for it will naturally have become an instrument for good. But even so, it cannot in the strict sense be called a gift of God and a spiritual thing, for it pertains to the order of nature and is not sent from on high. This is why Paul,[13] who is so wise in divine matters, calls it "carnal" for, says he, "Consider that among us who have been chosen, there are not many wise according to the flesh."[14] For who could make better use of this wisdom than those whom Paul calls "wise from outside"? But having this wisdom in mind, he calls them "wise according to the flesh," and rightly too.

To Consider

1. To what extent is Palamas an antirationalist?

2. What are his gravest concerns about the usefulness of reason?

3. To what extent is Palamas employing logic and reason to make this argument on the dangers of philosophy?

Source

a. Saint Gregory Palamas. *The Triads*. Trans. John Meyendorff. New York: Paulist Press, 1981. P. 29. Used with permission of Paulist Press. www.paulistpress.com.

9.6 NONRATIONALISM THRIVES!

While there was a strong rationalist, especially Aristotelian, bent in Mediterranean culture in the High Middle Ages, it would be a grave mistake to ignore other forms of thought that flourished in this period, even though they eschewed Aristotelian logic and physics and merrily embraced nonrational, often mystical approaches to knowing (something we will explore further in chapter 13). Sometimes rationalism and nonrationalism flourished side by side. A university-educated physician in the Latin world might attend a woman in labor, who valued having his elite medical learning brought to bear on her birth experience, but he might at the same time have her wear a birth girdle across her abdomen with phrases of

---

13. The apostle Paul, author of many of the books of the Christian New Testament.
14. 1 Corinthians 1:26.

the Bible on it in hopes that divine intervention might protect her and her child. Similarly, well-educated Muslims might turn to a fine physician to help with their bodily maladies, but might also drink water from a bowl decorated with Qur'anic verses and magical symbols to speed their recovery.

Indeed, there were scholars all around the Mediterranean who devoted their whole lives to exploring and elucidating fundamentally nonrational modes of knowing, especially in regard to the divine realm. In civilizations deeply in the thrall of written scriptures whose very languages and alphabets became important markers of religious boundaries, it is not surprising that deep currents of what might be called letter mysticism developed. This was especially true of notable Jewish and Muslim groups, of whom the author of the following passages, the Sufi Ahmad al-Buni (d. 1225), is quite representative. He became well known in Egypt for works that explained how contemplation of the individual letters of the Arabic alphabet, the very language of heaven, as Muslims believed, could lead to deep spiritual insight.

a. From al-Buni's *Subtle Instructions Concerning the Celestial Letters*
Arabic • 1225 CE • Cairo

What follow are three passages from one of al-Buni's influential treatises, Subtle Instructions Concerning the Celestial Letters. *In the first passage, he tells how God wrote different forms of Arabic letters—metaphorical "luciform" letters, spiritual letters, corporeal letters—right into the fabric of the cosmos. The construction of the cosmos from Arabic letters, in consequence, is what makes letter mysticism possible. In the second two passages he explains the value of contemplating two letters in particular, alif (A) and ra 'R).*

1. The spiritual force of every star is determined by the lights of every one of the luciform letters. And as the celestial spheres, in their track through the zodiacal signs, are classified according to degree and minute and so on, so the effect manifests sequentially, and this is the cause of [the effect's] duration. Likewise, these twelve spiritual lettristic faculties take from the lights of the luciform letters, stage after stage, in accordance with the mystery of the gradated sequence and the astrological mystery. As the spheres are encircled over the dense inferior world, making manifest in it the divinely originated workmanship and the definitiveness of the divine power of predetermination, so the corporeal letters are like the earth in relation to the spiritual letters, except that all their provisioning from the spiritual letters is gathered together in the "earth" of the corporeal letters, owing to the manifestation of the superior forces in the earthly sphere.

2. The *alif.* It is the first of the letters to be created, and with it are 3,180 angels. [God] brought about in it all the levels of the cosmos in combination. Here I represent it to you [as it is] in the superior worlds and how it is established there, and in the inferior worlds as well. This is the figure of the *alif* and of how God arranged in it all the parts of the cosmos, natural and religious, superior and inferior, of the Dominion and of the Kingdom. Whoever real-

izes what is in its hidden and apparent essence will ascend to the rank of the heirs [of the prophets]. And whoever realizes what is in its apparent and hidden worlds, God will make all beings to serve him and His speech will enjoin him. And that relationship [with God] is the bliss of the garden which he bestows upon the saints, the ones near to God.

3. He who meditates upon the secret of *ra* and how God disposed its inscription in the tablet-world will witness the marvels of the handiworks of God (Most High) and discover the secret of the spirit, of how it was established in accordance with the divine command by the secret of regulation and took the form of a sphere encompassing all the superior and inferior parts of the cosmos. He who writes it on a parchment after eight days of fasting, [maintaining] cleanliness, [reciting God's names], and [maintaining the state of] sincerity, writing with it "Our Lord [*rabbuna*], give us good in this world and good in the hereafter" and every verse in the Qur'an in which [the phrase] "Our Lord" [*rabbuna* occurs], as well as this figure and image,[15] with the verses [written] above the image in a circle around it—one who carries this inscription, God will not inflict the dread of poverty within him, and God will ease the sensory constraints for him and make clemency and mercy manifest in his interior.

To Consider

1. What similarities and differences are there between al-Buni's approach and preoccupations here and those of other texts in this chapter?

2. To what extent does al-Buni seem to understand and rely on the kinds of non-mystical thought that flourished in this period?

3. Many scholars in the medieval Mediterranean might be both rationalists in some aspects of their thought and esotericists, like al-Buni, in others. How is that possible?

Adapted from

a. Gardiner, Noah. "Esotericism in a Manuscript Culture: Al-Buni and His Readers through the Mamluk Period." PhD diss., University of Michigan, 2014. Pp. 216, 221, 223.

---

15. Al-Buni recommended the use of cryptograms and other images as a part of his letter mysticism.

PART THREE

THE CONTEST FOR THE MEDITERRANEAN (1350–1650 CE)

TEN

Imperial Rivalry and Sectarian Strife

The political history of the 1350–1650 era was marked by the rise of two great empires, the Ottoman and Spanish empires, centered, respectively, in western Anatolia and Castile. Though they conquered, at least ostensibly, for reasons of faith, the victims of their imperial expansion were as often coreligionists as infidels. Other great powers, such as the Venetian and Mamluk empires, as well as weaker polities in Italy, the Balkans, and the Maghrib, conducted themselves similarly, resulting in a dizzying array of alliances that frequently cut across religious boundaries. By 1520, after Spain had become the dominant power in Italy and the Ottomans had conquered Mamluk domains, the two empires were engaged in a struggle for Mediterranean hegemony. Yet also by then the German monk Martin Luther had initiated the Protestant Reformation, irreparably fracturing Latin Christendom, and the Shi'i Safavid dynasty had established a new empire in Iran. These sectarian divisions made the web of alliances that much more complex, as the Ottomans, for instance, allied with Protestant realms and even with Catholic France against Catholic Spain.

The readings in this chapter explore the role of religious concerns in the conduct of politics. We see Ottoman sultans and their Western rivals, the Moroccan Sa'dids, representing themselves as Sunni "holy warriors" to enhance their legitimacy; Christian reactions to the Ottoman conquest of Byzantine Constantinople; Christian and Muslim responses to Fernando and Isabel's conquest of Muslim Granada; Machiavelli's thoughts on political pragmatism and the place of religious ideology; and the use of religious propaganda by the Ottomans and Spanish in their wars against sectarian enemies.

10.1 ISLAMIC DISCOURSES OF LEGITIMACY

Since the early Middle Ages *jihad* propaganda composed by chroniclers and court scribes provided Muslim rulers with a powerful means of propping up their legitimacy. Ottoman chroniclers of the fifteenth and sixteenth centuries continued this tradition and portrayed the earliest princes of the House of Osman as pious Muslim *ghazis*. The term *ghazi* had a shifting significance, sometimes simply signifying a "frontier warrior," other times connoting a warrior who was religiously motivated, roughly synonymous with *mujahid*. The first reading consists of passages from the *Joy of Histories*, written by the chronicler Şukrullah (1388–1488) during the reign of Mehmed II (1444–1446, 1451–1481), the conqueror of Constantinople. The passages look back on the deeds of Bayezid I (1360–1403) and Murad II (1421–1444). Because Bayezid suffered a disastrous defeat and death in captivity at the hands of Timur-Lenk (Tamurlane), Şukrullah needed to show that his misfortunes were not the result of moral corruption. Murad, who had done much to restore Ottoman power, was easier to praise. The second reading consists of two poems from the historical chronicle of Aşikpaşazade (1400–1484), *History of the House of Osman*, composed at the behest of Bayezid II (1481–1512), a ruler known more for his institutional and military reforms than for his conquests. The first poem focuses on deeds of the sultan Murad I (1362–1389), who, after capturing important cities in the Balkans, died in the Battle of Kosovo in 1389, even though his army defeated the Serbian enemy. The second poem celebrates the whole Ottoman dynasty. In the Maghrib, the Sa'did sultan Ahmad al-Mansur (1578–1603) upheld his authority by combining his role as *mujahid* with claims to the status of caliph, based partly on his dynasty's supposed descent from the Prophet Muhammad. The erudite courtier Ibn al-Qadi (1553–1616), who had studied in the Islamic East, composed the third reading, a panegyric illuminating the achievements of his patron.

a. Şukrullah
Persian • ca. 1460 CE • Constantinople

The ghazi sultan [Bayezid I] began to exercise pious asceticism and devotion. Moreover, he abandoned anything done by former emirs and sultans that was contrary to holy law such as musical parties and debauchery . . ., all these things being the devil's temptations.

He [Murad II] performed five ghazas. First, he conquered Thessaloniki,[1] second, was his ghaza at the pass of Izladi,[2] third, the ghaza of Varna,[3] fourth, the ghaza of Germe,[4] and fifth, the ghaza of Kosovo.[5] . . . In no other age has there been as many good and pious deeds

---

1. The city fell in 1430.

2. The battle at Zlatitsa or Izladi Pass in Bulgaria, in 1443, in which Murad and his Janissaries halted the advance of a Hungarian army led by John Hunyadi.

3. Murad's defeat of a crusading army led by King Vladislav I of Hungary and John Hunyadi at Varna, in Bulgaria, in 1444.

4. The reference is unclear; perhaps it is to Murad's successful campaign against his rebellious vassal, Constantine, the Byzantine Despot of Mistra, in the Peloponnese in 1447.

5. The defeat of John Hunyadi at Kosovo in October 1448, after Hunyadi had again invaded Ottoman domains.

as during the blessed reign of this religion-nurturing monarch—deeds such as ghazas, conquests of the lands of infidelity, seizure of castles and fortresses from apostates, the building of schools, mosques, hospices, pulpits, etc.

b. Aşikpaşazade
Turkish • early 1480s CE • Constantinople

In the name of God they marched to battle [at Kosovo, in 1389]
The ghazis came together and realised their promise
The ghazis prayed on horseback
The sultan [Murad I] prayed fervently to God
To God: "the faith of Islam is yours
Submission to you without fault is my aim."

The sons of Osman are constantly waging ghaza
The infidels of the lands have been converted to Islam
They only showed mercy to those who begged for it
Not to those who tried to escape
This family became world-class ghazis
Even [the Prophet] Süleyman[6] envied this dynasty.

c. Ibn al-Qadi
Arabic • 1587–1590 CE • Marrakesh

I know that our lord fights true holy war for God in his military expeditions. . . . For he—may God assist him—is the most vigorous of kings in the path of God, and the most extensive in determination for good deeds. Through jihad, he safeguards the people of his land, and expands his new acquisitions as well as his inherited possessions. For [he places] overwhelming importance [on jihad], and diligently strives for success. His heroic javelins are stars of guidance, and racing missiles on that day. The lion cubs [are protected in their den] by them, and the Right is made victorious by them.

. . . The subjects of our lord—may God assist him—have agreeable and pleasant lives—may God preserve his days for the Muslims and guide his standards and banners—As for the governance of the shari'a, there is never any variation or change in it, [unlike what] is customary in the lands of the Mashriq [Islamic East]. . . . For our lord . . . excels in his dealings with his subjects, and he has brought lasting justice to them, and a way of righteousness. When there appears any violation of the shari'a against anyone, he punishes and reproves the perpetrator, and he never neglects this. . . . He does not take anyone's [position] into consideration, and cannot be criticized in this, for he delineates the truth, and even if it

---

6. The Israelite king Solomon, who in Islamic tradition had prophetic status and was a great ruler.

were himself or his sons or his relatives—may God assist him—he administers the shari'a and adheres to the requirements of truth. . . .

There is no secret about the perfection of his discernment and his righteous nature. . . . He has been mentioned among councils in Egypt, Alexandria, Upper Egypt, Jedda, Mecca, and Medina . . . for the hearts of the [Eastern Muslims] are troubled because they are broken by affection and the desire to become among his flock and among those who enter into his oath [of obedience]. Many of the influential people of the Mashriq have sworn to me, with binding oaths that cannot be reversed, that if even a slave girl entered [their lands] with a call to submission and obedience to [al-Mansur], they and their people would be the first to submit to it in an instant . . . and this would not be the case were it not for their longing for his sublime appearance.

To Consider

1. To what extent do the chroniclers' portraits of the early Ottoman sultans accord with what modern historians know of their actual deeds and policies? How would you explain the chroniclers' embellishments?

2. For both Ottoman and Sa'did writers, what kinds of deeds and characteristics marked a Muslim ruler as an ideal ruler?

3. How does Ibn al-Qadi advance al-Mansur's claims to be the caliph of all Muslims, East and West?

Sources

a. Anooshahr, Ali. *The Ghazi Sultans and the Frontiers of Islam: A Comparative Study of the Late Medieval and Early Modern Periods*. London: Routledge, 2009. Pp. 138, 163.
b. Özdemir, Lale. *Ottoman History through the Eyes of Aşıkpaşazade*. Istanbul: The Isis Press, 2013. Pp. 133, 154. Reproduced with permission of The Licensor through PLSclear.
c. Cory, Stephen. *Reviving the Islamic Caliphate in Early Modern Morocco*. Surrey: Ashgate, 2013. Pp. 74–75, 82–83. Reproduced with permission of The Licensor through PLSclear.

10.2 CHRISTIAN VIEWS OF THE FALL OF CONSTANTINOPLE

The fall of Constantinople on May 29, 1453, to the forces of the Ottoman sultan Mehmed II sent shock waves throughout the Christian world. Many Eastern and Western Christians wrote accounts of what seemed to them a great catastrophe. The first reading is excerpted from *A Brief Treatise on the Capture of Constantinople,* which the humanist bishop of Siena, Aeneas Silvius Piccolomini, penned in Latin shortly before he became Pope Pius II (1458–1464). The treatise is a reworking of several eyewitness accounts. Once pope, Aeneas would try unsuccessfully to organize a European crusade against the Ottomans. Kritovoulos (ca. 1410–1470), a Greek Christian, authored the second reading, the *History of Mehmed the Conqueror,* in Greek. Although Kritovoulos was not present when Constantinople was captured, he visited the city shortly afterward and entered the service of

Sultan Mehmed, who eventually appointed him as governor of his native island of Imbros in the Aegean.

a. Aeneas Silvius
Latin • ca. 1457 CE • Rome

This Mehmed . . . now thinks of nothing other, I hear, than immediate war. That has been Mehmed's state of mind and has guided him in his recent conquest of Constantinople. . . .

[Before the conquest] the Greeks . . ., because they had no faith in their own strength, they turned to the Latins and sought help with wails and tears. It is shameful to admit but the ears of our princes turned deaf, their eyes turned blind, as they failed to recognize that the fall of Greece heralded the imminent destruction of what remained of the Christian religion, and I believe that their private feuds and short-term convenience forced them to neglect the commonwealth.

[Aeneas recounts the final moments of the siege.] And since part of the wall had already been demolished by the bronze cannons . . . they [the Turks] climbed over the very ruins, overran the outer defenses, and forced the Greeks to flee. . . . The emperor [Constantine XI] perished, not by fighting (which would have been appropriate for a king) but when he fell in the narrow passage to the gate, where he was trodden on and trampled to death. . . .

Suddenly the city had fallen; all those who dared to offer resistance were slain; and the troops turned to plunder. . . . Their [the Turks'] cruelty could not be checked by anyone's dignity, age, or sex. Orgies mixed with slaughter, slaughter mixed with orgies. . . . The church of [Hagia] Sophia . . . was stripped of its holy apparatus and admitted pollution. All the precious bones of the martyrs which were housed in that city were offered to dogs and swine. . . . The enemy [Mehmed] snatched the very image of the crucified one whom we worship and declare to be the true God and . . . he spat upon it; he polluted it; and to make sport of our faith, he crucified it again. . . .

Such behavior hurts and confuses our souls, as we, through cowardice and sloth, allow the worship of the true God to perish and in this age we have forfeited our good name and in the world to come our hope of salvation.

b. Kritovoulos
Greek • 1460s CE • Imbros

My object is . . . to present the deeds of the now reigning great Sultan Mehmed, excellent as they are and in every respect surpassing those of his predecessors.

I would not place any censure on my nation or proceed to slander or speak evil of my people. . . . For I am not so past feeling or so bitter in my judgment as to wish to condemn the unfortunate rather than to share their pain. . . .

Who does not know that since men have existed the kingly or ruling power has not always remained in the same people, nor has it been limited to one race or nation? Like the planets, rule has gone from nation to nation and from place to place in succession. . . . There is therefore nothing astonishing if . . . the Romans [Byzantines] lose their rule and prosperity, which pass on and are transferred to others. . . .

[Kritovoulos imagines Mehmed's speech to his troops before Constantinople.] "My friends and men of my empire! You all know very well that our forefathers secured this kingdom that we now hold at the cost of many struggles and very great dangers. . . . And they exhibited in it all such heroism of spirit and firmness of purpose, and greatness of mind that, from the very beginning, from their very small kingdom and power, they set their minds on the destruction of the rule of the Romans [Byzantines], and hoped to secure complete power over Asia and Europe. . . . But now we are defeated by one city. . . . And you see how it is located in the midst of our realm, finely situated by land and sea, how many great difficulties it has given us from the beginning, and still gives us now—always fighting against us. . . . A great and populous city, the capital of the ancient Romans . . ., I give it now to you for spoil and plunder. . . .

[After the capture and pillage of Constantinople] . . . the sultan entered the city. . . . When he saw what a large number had been killed, and the ruin of the buildings, and the wholesale ruin and destruction of the city, he was filled with compassion and repented not a little. . . . Tears fell from his eyes. . . .

Then, with the notable men, and his courtiers, he went through the city. First he planned how to repopulate it, not merely as it formerly was but more completely, if possible, so that it should be a worthy capital for him, situated, as it was, most favorably by land and sea. Then he donated to all the grandees, and to those of his household, the magnificent homes of the rich. . . . And to some of them he even gave beautiful churches as their private residences.

To Consider

1. In which respects are the accounts of Aeneas Silvius and Kritovoulos in agreement? How do they differ?

2. How does the account of Aeneas Silvius criticize both Latins and Greeks, and how does it serve as a call to arms against the Ottomans?

3. How does Kritovoulos try to reconcile himself to the conquest of Constantinople and to Sultan Mehmed's rule over it?

Sources

a. Philippides, Marios, ed. and trans. *Mehmed II the Conqueror and the Fall of the Franco-Byzantine Levant to the Ottoman Turks: Some Western Views and Testimonies.* Tempe: Arizona Center for Medieval and Renaissance Studies, 2007. Pp. 95–99, 109–15.
b. Kritovoulos, Michael. *History of Mehmed the Conqueror by Kritovoulos.* Trans. Charles T. Riggs. Princeton: Princeton University Press, 1954. Pp. 10–12, 23–24, 27, 61, 76–77, 83.

10.3 FERNANDO II OF ARAGON AND SPANISH IMPERIAL EXPANSION

Fernando II of Aragon (1479–1516) was one of the great political strategists of his time. His contemporaries as well as modern scholars have debated whether religious or political concerns were more significant in shaping his foreign policy. All would agree, however, that the capture of Granada in 1492 was a crucial achievement for Fernando and his spouse, Isabel I of Castile (1474–1504), enabling them to pursue further conquests in Muslim North Africa and Italy. The first reading comes from Fernando's response, in September 1489, to the threat of the Mamluk sultan Qaytbay (1468–1496) to harm Christian holy places in his domains after Granadan Muslims complained to him about the war Fernando and Isabel were waging against them. Fernando sent his reply, in Spanish, to King Ferrante I of Naples (1458–1494) so that Ferrante could convey the substance of it to Mamluk ambassadors in Italy. The second reading is a passage from a bull issued by Pope Alexander VI (1492–1503) in 1495 encouraging Fernando and Isabel to expand into North Africa. The third reading is the account of the Aragonese Jesuit chronicler Pedro Abarca (1619–1693) of a statement that Fernando reportedly made to a meeting of the Cortes (parliament) of the Crown of Aragon in Monzon in 1510 for the purpose of acquiring funds from it to invest in his imperial projects. The fourth reading is a law concerning his Muslim subjects, the Mudejars, that the king promulgated at the same meeting. The coerced conversion of the Muslims of Granada and Castile between 1499 and 1502 had been worrying Aragonese Mudejars. The last reading is an assessment of Fernando by the Florentine political thinker Niccolo Machiavelli (1469–1527) from his treatise *The Prince*, published in 1513. By this time, Fernando had not only conquered Granada and various North African ports; he had also defeated the French monarchy in the contest for the kingdom of Naples.

a. Fernando to Qaytbay (through Ferrante of Naples)
Spanish • 1489 CE • Jaén (Spain)

And as for the reasons we have for making war against the Muslims *[moros]* of Granada . . . the great Sultan should know how a little more than seven hundred years ago, when our progenitors and ancestors the kings of Spain were lords of and in peaceful possession of these kingdoms of Spain . . . without being at war with or inflicting harm on the Muslims who were living in Africa, a great mass of them [Muslims], without just cause for doing so, entered with armed hand in this our Spain and occupied a great part of it; from most of which they [Muslims] have been ejected by the kings of glorious memory, our ancestors; and many of the said Muslims returned to Africa and others have withdrawn to this kingdom of Granada. . . . They [Granadan Muslims] have made and continually murder or make captives of our Christians and commit many other evils . . . which are so serious that they cannot be tolerated. But wishing to treat them with full clemency, we have many times sent to demand and we continually demand that they leave our land, and that if they wish to live in it under our lordship . . . we will leave them with all their property living in their law [religion] and dwelling securely in their houses and lands, and having their houses of prayer and mosques, and we will protect them in peace and justice and not permit them to be molested by anyone, as we do with the other Muslims who have for a long time lived in our kingdoms.

b. Bull of Alexander VI
Latin • 1495 CE • Rome

As is very well known throughout the world, you have . . . with divine aid subjugated the Muslims [Saracens] of the Kingdom of Granada. . . . [Now] with apostolic authority . . . we grant you the investiture of Africa itself and all its kingdoms, lands, and dominions . . . so that you, your heirs and successors should possess them in perpetuity if, as we hope, you conquer them . . . and there the name of our Savior will be honored and the Catholic faith exalted and augmented.

c. Pedro Abarca
• Spanish • ca. 1682 CE • Salamanca

He [Fernando] made the proposal, referring to the auspicious glory of the conquest of the Kingdoms of Tunis and Bijaya, which was already so far advanced, and promised the success of yet another conquest even greater than that of Africa, penetrating Asia as far as Jerusalem . . . which belonged to him by right, as King of Aragon, due to the links between Naples and Jerusalem.[7]

d. Fernando's Decree in the Cortes
Catalan • 1510 CE • Monzon

We [Fernando] are making a new law: that the Muslims residing and living in royal cities and towns, and in other cities, towns, and villages of clergy, nobles, knights, [and] citizens . . . may not be expelled . . . nor may they be constrained or forced to become Christians.

e. Machiavelli on Fernando
Italian • 1513 CE • Sant' Andrea in Percussina, Italy

Nothing gives a prince more prestige than undertaking great enterprises and setting a splendid example for his people. In our day we have Fernando of Aragon, the present king of Spain. He may be considered a new prince, since from being a weak king he has risen to become, for fame and glory, the first prince of Christendom. . . . At the beginning of his rule he attacked Granada, and that enterprise was the cornerstone of his reign. . . . He kept all the barons of Castile preoccupied with it, and while they were thinking of the war, they never considered the changes he was making in the state. Thus he acquired reputation and authority over them without their being aware of it. . . . Apart from this, he made use of the pretext of religion to prepare the way for still greater projects, and adopted a policy of pious cruelty in expelling the Muslims from his kingdom and despoiling them [in 1502]; his conduct here could not have been more despicable nor more unusual. On the same pretext, he attacked

---

7. Since 1291, when the Mamluks put an end to the Crusader kingdom of Jerusalem, the papacy had continued to invest the kings of Naples with the title to the defunct kingdom, hoping that they would one day recapture Jerusalem. Fernando had, in 1504, made good on the Crown of Aragon's claims to the kingdom of Naples, which also made him the titular king of Jerusalem.

Africa; he carried out his campaign in Italy; and finally he assaulted France. . . . And his various projects have risen one out of the other, so that they have never allowed men leisure to take concerted action against him.

To Consider

1. Why would an Italian observer like Machiavelli have been inclined to see Fernando as using religion as a pretext for territorial expansion, and is there evidence in the other readings that supports Machiavelli's view?

2. Do the readings provide evidence that Fernando's imperial ambitions were mainly guided by religious concerns?

3. How should Fernando's assurances to Qaytbay that he would preserve the religious freedom of the conquered Muslims of Granada and his 1510 decree protecting the Mudejars of the Crown of Aragon figure into an analysis of his religious and political motives?

Sources

a–b. Doussinagüe, José M. *La política internacional de Fernando el Católico*. Madrid: Espasa-Calpe, 1944. Pp. 515–17, 521–24.
c. Devereux, Andrew W. "Empire in the Old World: Ferdinand the Catholic and His Aspiration to Universal Empire, 1479–1516." In *In and Out of the Mediterranean: Medieval and Early Modern Iberian Studies*, ed. Michelle M. Hamilton and Nuria Silleras-Fernández. Nashville: Vanderbilt University Press, 2015. P. 138, n. 21.
d. *Cortes del reinado de Fernando el Católico*. Ed. Ernest Belenguer Cebrià. Valencia: Universidad de Valencia, 1972. Pp. 133–34.
e. Machiavelli, Niccolo. *The Prince*. Trans. Robert M. Adams. 2nd ed. New York: Norton, 1977. Pp. 60–61.

10.4 MACHIAVELLI'S VIEWS ON POLITICS

Often regarded as one of the founders of modern political thought, Niccolo Machiavelli (1469–1527) served the republic of Florence as secretary and diplomat between 1498 and 1512. His diplomatic missions took him to several European courts and to papal Rome. He observed the French and Spanish monarchies carving up northern and southern Italy, and Cesare Borgia, the son of Pope Alexander VI (1492–1503), employing brutal tactics to bring more territory in central Italy under papal control. Machiavelli was of course very much aware of the threat that the Ottoman empire presented to the Italian Peninsula. In 1512, when the Medicis returned to power in Florence, they stripped him of office and briefly imprisoned him. Afterward, in 1513, while confined to his small estate near the city, he wrote his most famous work, *The Prince*. It was a handbook for rulers, addressed to members of the Medici family whose favor he hoped to earn. On the basis of his observation of contemporary Italian politics and his reading of classical history, Machiavelli called for a politics that was pragmatic rather than idealistic. To acquire and retain political power, he concluded, rulers needed to be deceitful and ruthless, if necessary. The first passage from *The Prince* contains Machiavelli's thoughts on whether it was better for a prince to be loved or feared. The second passage includes Machiavelli's reflections on the strength of Ottoman government. The third reading comes from Machiavelli's *Discourses on Livy*, which were written as a commentary on the Roman historian Titus Livy (64/59 BCE–12/17 CE) in 1515–1517. In this passage he considers the role of the papacy in Italian politics.

a. *The Prince*, On Love and Fear
Italian • 1513 CE • Sant' Andrea in Percussina, Italy

Here the question arises: is it better to be loved than feared, or vice versa? I don't doubt that every prince would like to be both; but since it is hard to accommodate these qualities, if you have to make a choice, to be feared is much safer than to be loved. For it is a general rule about men, that they are ungrateful, fickle, liars and deceivers, fearful of danger and greedy for gain. . . . People are less concerned with offending a man who makes himself loved than one who makes himself feared: the reason is that love is a link of obligation which men, because they are rotten, will break any time they think doing so serves their advantage; but fear involves dread of punishment, from which they can never escape.

b. *The Prince*, On Ottoman Government

The whole monarchy of Turkey is governed by a single master; everyone else is his servant; he divides his kingdom into districts, sending different administrators to each, and changing them around as he thinks best. . . . The problem in gaining control of Turkey is that you cannot hope to be invited in by the district rulers, or to make use of a palace revolt in gaining a foothold. . . . Since they are all the slaves of their master and obliged to him, there is no easy way of corrupting them. . . . Hence, anyone who attacks the Turks may expect to find them completely united, and had better count on their own strength rather than any internal disorders. But once they are thoroughly beaten and crushed so their army cannot reform, there is nothing more to fear except the family of the prince; once his line is extinct, there is no other danger, since nobody else has any standing with the people.

c. *Discourses*, On the Papacy
Italian • 1515–1517 CE • Sant' Andrea in Percussina, Italy

It is therefore the duty of princes and heads of republics to uphold the foundations of the religion of their countries, for then it is easy to keep their people religious, and consequently well conducted and united. . . . And, certainly, if the Christian religion had from the beginning been maintained according to the principles of its founder, the Christian states and republics would be much more united and happy than in fact they are. Nor can there be greater proof of its decadence than to witness the fact that the nearer people are to the Church of Rome, which is the head of our religion, the less religious they are. . . . We Italians then owe to the Church of Rome and to her priests our having become irreligious and bad; but we owe her a still greater debt, and one that may cause our ruin, namely, that the Church has kept and still keeps our country divided. And certainly a country can never be united and happy, except when it obeys wholly one government, whether a republic or a monarchy, as is the case in France and in Spain; and the sole cause why Italy is not in the same condition, and is not governed by either one republic or one sovereign, is the Church; for having acquired and holding a temporal dominion, yet she has never had sufficient power or courage to enable her to seize the rest of the country and make herself sole sovereign of all Italy. And on the other hand she has not been so feeble that the fear of losing her temporal power prevented her from calling in the aid of a foreign power to defend her against such others as had become too powerful in Italy . . . and when in our times she crushed the power of the Venetians by the aid of France, and afterwards with the assistance of the Swiss drove out in turn the French.[8]

To Consider

1. How does Machiavelli explain the strength and unity of the Ottoman empire? What role does fear play, and why does Machiavelli say nothing about Islam?

2. In his analysis of Italy's political misfortunes, why is Machiavelli so critical of the papacy? For him, what is the political function of religion?

3. Within a generation of Machiavelli's death, both Catholics and Protestants throughout Europe were condemning his views. Why?

Source

a–c. Machiavelli, Niccolo. *The Prince.* Trans. Robert M. Adams. 2nd ed. New York: Norton, 1977. Pp. 46, 12–13, 98–100.

10.5 FIGHTING SECTARIAN ENEMIES

For the monarchs of the warring Sunni Ottoman and Catholic Habsburg empires, some of the most serious challenges to their power came not from each other but from states whose rulers professed and promoted sectarian forms of their own Islamic and Christian faiths: Shi'i Safavid Iran and Protestant Tudor England. Originally the leaders of a Sunni Sufi movement that had resisted the rule of the successors of Timur-Lenk (Tamurlane), the Safavids under Shah Isma'il (1501–1524) shifted their allegiance to Shi'ism, established control over Iran, and began to violently suppress Sunnism, then the persuasion of the majority of the population. Claiming that he was the descendant of Muhammad's son-in-law 'Ali and therefore the only legitimate successor to the Prophet, Isma'il challenged the Ottomans' authority within their empire and in the wider Muslim world. England adopted

---

8. A reference to the political machinations of Pope Julius II (1503–1513), who in 1508–1509 engineered a coalition against Venice that included France and Spain, and then later formed a new coalition against the French that led to their withdrawal from the duchy of Milan and to the fall of the Florentine republic, a French vassal, and the Medici restoration in 1512.

Protestantism at least formally in 1534, when Henry VIII (1509–1547) broke with the papacy and became the "supreme head" of the English Church. His daughter Elizabeth I (1558–1603) followed his lead after her half sister, Mary I (1553–1558), who had married the future Felipe II of Spain (1556–1598), tried to restore Catholicism in England. Tensions between Elizabeth and Felipe II peaked in 1585, when the queen's support for Dutch Protestants rebelling against Spanish rule in the Netherlands became overt. The first reading is from a letter that Sultan Selim I (1512–1520) issued in response to letters from Shah Isma'il shortly before the Ottoman defeat of the Safavids in the Battle of Chaldiran in 1514. These letters were a form of propaganda, Selim's an argument for his political legitimacy. The second reading comes from sermons that the Jesuit Pedro de Ribadeneyra (1527–1611) gave to inspire the soldiers of the Spanish Armada, the massive naval force sent by Felipe II to invade England in 1588.

a. Selim I to Shah Isma'il
Persian • ca. 1514 CE • Istanbul

[T]he Caliph of God Most High in this world, . . . the warrior in the Path, the defender of the Faith, . . . to the ruler of the kingdom of the Persians, the possessor of the land of tyranny and perversion, . . . the peer of Cain, Prince Isma'il. . . .

It has been repeatedly heard that you have subjected the upright community of Muhammad . . . to your devious will, that you have undermined the firm foundation of the Faith, that you have unfurled the banner of oppression in the cause of aggression, that you no longer uphold the commandments and prohibitions of the Divine Law, that you have incited your abominable Shi'i faction . . . to the shedding of innocent blood,[9] . . . that you have rent the noble stuff of Islam with the hand of tyranny. . . .

Indeed, as both the *fatwas* [legal opinions] of distinguished *'ulama'* who base their opinions on reason and tradition alike and the consensus of the Sunni community agree that the ancient obligation of extirpation, extermination, and expulsion of evil innovation must be the aim of our exalted aspiration . . . action has become necessary and exigent. . . . If God almighty wills, the lightning of our conquering sword shall uproot the untamed bramble grown to great heights in the path of the refulgent Divine Law. . . . The thunder of our avenging mace shall dash out the muddled brains of the enemies of the Faith as rations for the lion-hearted *ghazis* [holy warriors].

But . . . should you take up a course of repentance, become like one blameless and return to the sublime straight path of the Sunna of Muhammad . . . and finally should you consider your lands and their people part of the well-protected Ottoman state, then shall you be granted our royal favor and imperial patronage.

---

9. Perhaps a reference to Shi'i massacres of Sunni Muslims in Tabriz, Shah Isma'il's new capital, and other places.

b. Sermons to the Soldiers of the Spanish Armada
Spanish • 1588 CE • La Coruña

This journey, gentlemen, has in its favor all of the reasons of a just and holy war that there can possibly be in the world. And though it may at first seem an offensive rather than a defensive war, in that we are attacking another kingdom rather than defending our own, if we look more closely we will see that it is indeed a defensive war in that we are defending our sacred religion and most holy Roman Catholic faith; we are also defending the extremely important reputation of our king and lord, and that of our nation; we are also defending all of the property and wealth of all the kingdoms of Spain. . . .

So this Elizabeth . . . has made herself head of the Church of England, and being a woman, and thus naturally subject to the male, as Saint Paul says, and not being able, following God's commands, to speak in church, she wishes to be recognized as the spiritual head of the clergy. . . .

She is the one who each day promulgates new and extremely rigorous laws against the Catholic faith, executes them with extreme force, and continually spills the innocent blood of those who profess it. . . .

She is the one who, inspired by the heretics whom we have said she has in her kingdom, . . . has sought with all her skill and shrewdness to make this destructive and consuming fire spread throughout the entire world. . . .

She is the one who is supporting the long, costly, and bloody war of the states of Flanders [modern Belgium, then part of Spain's empire] against our lord the king. . . . She is the one who has taken over Holland, occupying its cities, forts, and ports, infested our seas, . . . and with her money, soldiers, arms, supplies, advice, and her tricks, has stirred those states up against . . . our king, our holy religion, and God.

This very same Elizabeth is the one who, . . . hoping to uproot our holy and Catholic religion from all of our kingdoms, has made alliances with heretical princes, . . . has sent . . . her fleets even to Constantinople to solicit the help of the Turk and to summon him against us, and to bring him to our lands to terrorize us and afflict us in our own houses.

To Consider

1. How do Sultan Selim and Ribadeneyra argue for waging holy war against the sectarian enemies of the Ottoman and Spanish empires, and why are they so careful to make these arguments?

2. Where in these readings do you see the political concerns and aims of Ottoman and Spanish rulers? Can or should we disentangle their political goals from their religious ones?

3. Why do these Sunni and Catholic authors think that the Shi'i and Protestants, respectively, are so dangerous?

Sources

a. McNeill, William H., and Marilyn Robinson Waldman, eds. *The Islamic World.* Chicago: University of Chicago Press, 1973. Pp. 338–42.

b. Cowans, Jon, ed. *Early Modern Spain: A Documentary History.* Philadelphia: University of Pennsylvania Press, 2003. Pp. 126–29.

ELEVEN

Minorities and Diasporas

During the era 1350–1650 religious minorities had markedly different histories in Catholic and Muslim realms. In Spain, many Jews were forcibly converted in 1391, and, while the Spanish Inquisition prosecuted converts who clung to Judaism, the remaining Jews were expelled in 1492. In subsequent decades, all Spanish Muslims were forced to convert, and, as Moriscos, also suffered inquisitorial prosecution for practicing Islam, and, finally, expulsion in 1609–1614. Though permitted to remain in Italian cities, from the sixteenth century Jews were confined in segregated ghettos. Yet in the Muslim world the policies of protecting religious minorities persisted, even though the Ottoman conquest of Constantinople created a diaspora of Greeks unwilling to live under Muslim rule. Muslim rulers, moreover, admitted many Jewish refugees from Spain and Portugal. This Sephardi diaspora had a major impact on Jewish culture throughout the Mediterranean and beyond. Expelled Moriscos, too, found a refuge in Muslim domains and gradually assimilated into local populations.

The readings in the chapter examine the expulsions of Spanish Jews and Moriscos and the activities of the Inquisition; the life of Italian Jews in urban ghettos; the varied experiences of Coptic Christians in Mamluk Egypt and of Christians in the Ottoman Balkans; and, finally, contemporary reflections on the phenomenon of Greeks, Jews, and Moriscos living in permanent exile from their homelands.

11.1 THE SPANISH INQUISITION AND THE EXPULSION OF THE JEWS

On March 31, 1492, three months after their conquest of Granada, the royal couple Fernando II of Aragon and Isabel I of Castile decreed that all Jews living in the lands of Castile and the Crown of Aragon must, by July 31 of the same year, either go into exile or convert to Christianity. Most Jews, perhaps 100,000 altogether, departed. Historians have debated about the monarchs' possible motives in expelling the Jews, though most would agree that there was a connection between the Spanish Inquisition's activities and the monarchs' final decision. The monarchs had begun establishing inquisitorial tribunals throughout their realms in 1480 for the purpose of eradicating the Jewish beliefs and practices, or the Judaizing, of Conversos. Baptized as Catholics, Conversos were the descendants of the thousands of Jews who had been forced to convert in the anti-Jewish violence of 1391. Inquisitors examined many witnesses in order to identify Judaizers, uncover their social and religious networks, and prosecute and punish them for their "heresies." The first reading comes from the testimony of the Converso Galceran Ferrandis in the trial of the Conversa Violant Guimera, whom inquisitors in the city of Valencia (Crown of Aragon) sentenced to death on April 24, 1490. Galceran and Violant were among a group of Valencian Conversos who had dined in the home of a Jewish couple, Jacob and Perla, in nearby Morvedre (modern Sagunto) and visited its synagogue. The second reading comes from the record of an inquisitorial trial conducted in Ciudad Real (Castile). Here the witness, the Old Christian noble Juan de Torres, recounts his conversation with the Converso Juan Falcon. The last reading includes passages from the decree of expulsion itself.

a. Testimony of Galceran Ferrandis
Catalan • 1489 CE • Valencia

In the said house of the Jew [Jacob] they [Galceran, Violant, her husband Bernat, and five other Conversos] all sat at the table . . . and the said Jew and his wife [were] at the head of the table. The said Jew took a silver cup of wine and said certain words in Hebrew, which the witness could not understand, and then the said Jew took a sip of wine, and after this the said Bernat Guimera and all the others each took a sip of wine. . . .

The Jew who had the synagogue key was a little, old man . . . and he showed all the aforesaid [Conversos] the synagogue. . . . They opened a cabinet where the Torah was kept, and the said old Jew took the Torah in his hands, and it seemed to the witness that he raised it [the Torah] above the heads of all the aforesaid [Conversos], of whom some were kneeling and others were still on their feet. Afterward, the witness saw how the said [Manuel] Çabata [a Converso] . . . gave [a] gold piece to the said Jew who had shown them the Torah, telling him that he was giving him the said gold piece for oil for the lamp of the synagogue.

b. Testimony of Juan de Torres
Spanish • 1484 CE • Ciudad Real

Juan Falcon asked this witness what were the things in this world he most desired; and this witness responded: "Salvation for my soul." The said Juan Falcon asked: "This salvation, how does one get it?" This witness replied: "I would want to perform such works that I might go to paradise, and not to purgatory or hell." . . . And the said Falcon said: " . . . to possess much wealth, enough to give and not to lack anything, is paradise; times of plenty and times of want is purgatory; known poverty, this is hell, and they should not make you believe that there is another paradise or purgatory or hell." And this witness then said: "Oh, what an evil belief!"

c. Decree of Expulsion
Spanish • 1492 CE • Granada

You know well, or ought to know, that whereas we have been informed that in these our kingdoms there were some wicked Christians who Judaized and apostatized from our holy Catholic faith . . . we procured and gave orders that inquisition should be made in our afore-mentioned kingdoms and lordships, which as you know has for twelve years been made and is being made, . . . and accordingly we are informed by the inquisitors and by other devout persons . . . that great injury has resulted and still results, since the Christians have engaged in and continue to engage in social interaction and communication they have had and continue to have with Jews, who, it seems, seek always and by whatever means and ways they can to subvert and steal faithful Christians from our holy Catholic faith and to separate them from it, and to draw them to themselves and subvert them to their own wicked belief and conviction, instructing them in the ceremonies and observances of their law . . . and persuading them as much as they can to hold and observe the law of Moses [Judaism], convincing them that there is no other law or truth except for that one. . . .

Therefore, we, with the counsel and advice of prelates, great noblemen of our kingdoms, and other persons of learning and wisdom of our council, having taken deliberation about this matter, resolve to order the said Jews and Jewesses of our kingdoms to depart and never return or come back to them. . . .

And so that the said Jews and Jewesses during the stated period of time until the end of the said month of July may be better able to dispose of themselves and their possessions . . . for the present we take and receive them under our security, protection, and royal safeguard. . . . And we likewise give license and faculty to those Jews and Jewesses that they be able to export their goods and possessions out of these our said kingdoms . . . as long as they do not export gold or silver or coined money or other things prohibited by the laws of our kingdoms.

To Consider

1. Judging from the testimony of Galceran Ferrandis, why was the presence of Jews in Spain such a threat to the Catholic faith of Conversos? And if perhaps not even half of the Converso population was still clinging to Jewish beliefs and practices in 1492, why did Fernando and Isabel and their advisers view such Judaizing Conversos to be a significant danger to Spanish Catholic society?

2. Why did Juan Falcon's views shock and disturb Juan de Torres, and how might Falcon's experience of living as a Converso between two worlds, the Christian and the Jewish, have led him to formulate such skeptical views about the existence of an afterlife?

3. Do the passages excerpted from the decree of expulsion suggest that Fernando and Isabel had economic and political motives for expelling the Jews?

Sources

a. Meyerson, Mark D. *A Jewish Renaissance in Fifteenth-Century Spain*. Princeton: Princeton University Press, 2004. P. 209. Republished with permission of Princeton University Press, from *A Jewish Renaissance in Fifteenth-Century Spain,* Meyerson, Mark D., Archivo Historico Nacional: Inquisition: legajo 545, no. 7: folio 15r-v, 2004; permission conveyed through Copyright Clearance Center, Inc.

b. Beinart, Haim, ed. *Records of the Trials of the Spanish Inquisition in Ciudad Real.* Vol. 1. Jerusalem: Israel National Academy of Sciences and Humanities, 1974. P. 556. Translated here by permission of The Israel Academy of Sciences and Humanities from the original Spanish version.

c. Constable, Olivia Remie, ed. *Medieval Iberia: Readings from Christian, Muslim, and Jewish Sources.* 2nd ed. Philadelphia: University of Pennsylvania Press, 2012. Pp. 508–13.

11.2 OPPRESSION AND EXPULSION OF THE MORISCOS

Since the time of the coerced mass conversions of Spanish Muslims between 1499 and 1526, most Moriscos—the converts and their descendants—had continued practicing their Islamic faith in some manner, most noticeably in recently conquered Granada. On January 1, 1567, the government of Felipe II therefore passed new laws prohibiting Granadan Moriscos from wearing traditional clothing, celebrating with traditional music and dance, using the Arabic language, and so forth. The aim of the laws was to bring about the assimilation of the Moriscos by suppressing all elements of their culture that the government regarded as Islamic. The first reading comes from one Morisco response to the laws: the protest, or *Memorandum,* that Francisco Núñez Muley (ca. 1490–1570), an elderly Granadan noble, wrote to royal officials in 1567. Most Granadan Moriscos, however, reacted by rising in armed revolt in 1568. Royal troops needed more than two years to defeat the rebels. The second reading is the sentence the Spanish Inquisition passed against a Morisco rebel in an *auto de fe* celebrated in Granada in March 1571. The third reading is a passage from one of the decrees calling for the expulsion of the Moriscos that Felipe III addressed to lay and ecclesiastical officials in 1609, in this case those in the kingdom of Valencia. At this juncture, Valencia had the largest Morisco population, one whose beliefs and practices were still notoriously Islamic.

a. Francisco Núñez Muley
Spanish • 1567 CE • Granada

In their reports, the prelates contend that the preservation of the traditional style of dress and footwear of the natives of this kingdom [Granada] is tantamount to a continuation of the ceremonies and customs of the Muslims. I can only say . . . these reports are wholly without merit, because the style of dress, clothing, and footwear of the natives . . . can more rightly be said to be clothing that corresponds to a particular kingdom or province. . . . All the other kingdoms and provinces have their own style of dress that is different from the others, and yet they are all Christians. In like manner, the style of dress and clothing of this kingdom is very different from the clothing of the Moroccan and Barbary [North African] Muslims. . . .

Let us return once again to the issue of whether the women of this kingdom who cover their faces do so as part of their supposed adherence to the Muslim faith. We might then ask, why do the majority of Old Christian women cover their faces? They do so in order that people not recognize them at times when they do not wish to be recognized, and New Christian women do so for the same reason, and so that men might not fall into the mortal sin of seeing the beautiful face of a woman they admire and pursuing her, by licit or illicit means, in order to marry her. That a woman covers her face is nothing but a matter of modesty meant to prevent these events from occurring. . . .

And I say . . . no ill effect can be caused by the continued use of the Arabic language. . . . The Arabic language has no direct relation whatsoever to the Muslim faith. This is so because . . . the Catholic Christians who live in the holy city of Jerusalem and throughout the Christian kingdom of that region speak Arabic and write their evangelical books and laws and all that has to do with Christianity and documents and contracts in this language. . . . If using Arabic were truly something that went against the Holy Catholic faith, then these priests and philosophers in . . . Jerusalem would not use it, as they are Christians.

b. Sentence of a Granadan Morisco
Spanish • 1571 CE • Granada

Alonso Rufian, Morisco, resident of Penillos. While in this city of Granada, he planned with others of his caste and lineage to travel to Barbary [North Africa] in order to be Muslims *[moros]* there. He actually went to Barbary with these people and had himself circumcised. He . . . went to the mosques and fasted for Ramadan. He performed the prayers of the Muslims. Learning that the Moriscos of this kingdom had risen up against the Christian religion and His Majesty the King, he returned to this kingdom with other Muslims, bringing gunpowder and weapons with them. And he joined the rebellious Muslims and performed the ceremonies of the law [religion] of Muslims. . . . It was voted [by the Inquisitors] to relax him to the secular arm [that is, execute him].[1]

c. Decree of Expulsion
Spanish • 1609 CE • Valencia

You are all aware of what I have through such long efforts tried to do toward the conversion of the Moriscos of this kingdom [Valencia] . . . and the attempts that have been made to instruct them in our holy faith, and the little that has been accomplished, for we have not seen any of them convert, and they have instead merely increased their stubbornness. . . . I ordered the junta [of clerical and lay advisers] . . . to meet to see if there was some way to avoid removing them from these kingdoms. But realizing that those of this kingdom [Valencia]

---

1. As church officials, the inquisitors could not execute sentences involving the shedding of blood. They therefore handed convicted heretics over to the secular authorities to carry out capital punishments.

and of that of Castile were continuing in their harmful intentions, and given that I have heard on sound and true advice that they were persisting in their apostasy and perdition and were seeking to harm and subvert people of our kingdoms through their envoys [to Muslim rulers] and other ways, and wishing to fulfill my obligations to assure the preservation and security particularly of that kingdom of Valencia . . . given that its dangers are more evident, and wishing for the heresy and apostasy to cease, . . . I have resolved that all of the Moriscos of that kingdom be expelled and sent to the land of the Berbers [North Africa].

To Consider

1. Would the arguments of Núñez Muley have seemed at all persuasive to royal officials? Do you think that Núñez Muley's arguments were sincere or that he was engaging in special pleading?

2. Spanish kings and their advisers feared that the Moriscos' adherence to Islam made them politically traitorous. How might government policies have contributed to making such fears a reality, at least in some cases?

3. Compare how the Spanish Christian authorities dealt with religious difference in 1609 with how they treated non-Christian subjects two centuries earlier. How would you account for the change in outlook?

Sources

a. Núñez Muley, Francisco, and Vincent Barletta. *A Memorandum for the President of the Royal Audiencia and Chancery Court of the City and Kingdom of Granada.* Ed. and trans. Vincent Barletta. Chicago: University of Chicago Press, 2006. Pp. 69–70, 87, 92. Republished with permission of University of Chicago Press. Permission conveyed through Copyright Clearance Center, Inc.

b. Homza, Lu Ann. *The Spanish Inquisition, 1478–1614: An Anthology of Sources.* Indianapolis: Hackett Publishing Company, 2006. P. 244.

c. Cowans, Jon, ed. *Early Modern Spain: A Documentary History.* Philadelphia: University of Pennsylvania Press, 2003. Pp. 145–46.

11.3 JEWS AND GHETTOS IN RENAISSANCE ITALY

When formulating policies for their Jewish populations, both native and immigrant, the ruling authorities in Italian city-states were guided by often conflicting economic and religious concerns. Although the segregation of Jews in urban ghettos in the sixteenth and seventeenth centuries generally worsened their social and material conditions, the extent of Jewish degradation ultimately depended on the intentions of the rulers who founded the ghettos. The governors of Venice established the first Jewish ghetto in 1516 as a segregated living space for Jewish and even Converso immigrants whose commerce they wished to foster. However, when Pope Paul IV instituted the Roman ghetto in 1555, with the bull *Cum nimis absurdum* ("Since it is absurd . . ."), he had in mind religious goals that were more explicitly anti-Jewish. His policy influenced how other Italian urban governments subsequently treated their Jewish populations. The first reading is the preface of Paul IV's bull, in which he explains his reasons for segregating the Jews. The second reading comes from the *Life of Judah,* the autobiography of Leon (Judah Aryeh) Modena (1571–1648), a leading Jewish intellectual in the Venetian ghetto. The descendant of an immigrant Ashkenazi family that had settled in northern Italy, Modena received a traditional Jewish education while also studying Latin, Italian, poetry, and music. Unfortunately, his impoverished father died when he was young and left him very little. He moved to Venice in 1592 after marrying his cousin, Rachel Simhah.

a. Pope Paul IV
Latin • 1555 CE • Rome

Since it is absurd and improper that Jews, whose own guilt has consigned them to perpetual servitude . . . [and] whose presence Christian piety tolerates, should be ungrateful to Christians, so that they attempt to exchange the servitude they owe to Christians for dominion over them, we—to whose notice it has lately come that these Jews, in our dear city [Rome] and in some other . . . places of the Holy Roman Church, have erupted into insolence, not only dwelling side by side with Christians and near their churches but even erecting homes in the more noble sections and streets of the cities . . . and having nurses, housemaids, and other hired Christian servants, and perpetrating many other things in ignominy and contempt of the Christian name—[and we] considering that the Roman Church tolerates the Jews in testimony of the true Christian faith and to the end that they, led by the piety and kindness of the Apostolic See, should at length recognize their errors, and make all haste to arrive at the true light of the Catholic faith, and thereby [the Jews] to agree that as long as they persist in their errors, they should recognize through experience that they have been made slaves while Christians have been made free through Jesus Christ, God and our Lord . . . and [we], desiring to make sound provisions as best we can . . . in the above matter, we ordain, by this our perpetually valid constitution, that . . . all Jews are to live in only one [quarter] to which there is only one entrance and from which there is but one exit . . . and be thoroughly separate from the residences of Christians.

b. Leon Modena
Hebrew • 1617–1648 CE • Venice

I came to Venice [in March 1607] and set up an apartment and a school on the top floor of the house belonging to the family dal Osto, the Levites. . . . I took on students and also resumed preaching in the "garden" [a study center in the Old Ghetto] and in the house of study of the Torah Study Society. . . .

In [October–November] . . . I went to live in the house of a very unpleasant person, my wife's relative, Moses Copio [who later converted to Christianity], may his name be blotted out, in order to teach his son Abraham Copio, a chip off the old block, and four other students, and to board at his table. And because no one could live cooped up with such a wild person . . . I left his house and, with students, set up a school in my apartment, which was located in the Old Ghetto on an upper floor of the house belonging to the Treves family. . . .

My son Mordecai [in November–December 1614] . . . began to engage in the craft of alchemy with the priest Joseph Grillo, a very learned man. He worked at it assiduously and became so adept that all the venerable practitioners marveled at what such a lad knew. . . . He repeated an experiment that he had learned to do in the house of the priest, which was to make ten ounces of silver from nine ounces of lead and one of silver. . . .

When the Torah portions Tazria and Metzora[2] were read in 5389 [on April 28, 1629] I preached in the synagogue of the Sephardim. . . . In attendance were the brother of the king of France, who was accompanied by some French noblemen and by five of the most important Christian preachers who gave sermons that Pentecost. God put such learned words into my mouth that all were pleased, including many other Christians who were present. All the [Jewish] congregations gave great praise and thanks. . . .

[In 1637] . . . there came an enormous anxiety, fear, and heartache the likes of which I had never before experienced. . . . About two years earlier I had given a certain Frenchman who knew the Holy Tongue [Hebrew], M. Giacomo [Jacques] Gaffarel [a Catholic orientalist and Hebraist], a certain book to read. I had written it more than twenty years earlier at the request of an English nobleman, who intended to give it to the [Protestant] king of England [James I (1603–1635)]. In it I relate all the laws, doctrines, and customs of the Jews at the present time in their dispersion. When I wrote it I was not careful about not writing things contrary to the Inquisition, because it was only in manuscript and was meant to be read by people who were not of the pope's sect.

After reading it, that Frenchman asked me to leave it with him and he would print it in France. I agreed, but did not think of editing out the things that the Inquisition in Italy might find unacceptable in a printed book. . . .

But . . . in the end the items turned out to be not so forbidden. . . . God . . . put into my mind the idea to seek the advice of the inquisitor, may he be blessed and praised, for he had always acted like one of the righteous gentiles in his dealings with me. So I made the voluntary declaration to the Inquisition, which protected me on every count.

To Consider

1. What concerns moved Pope Paul to establish a ghetto for the Jews of Rome, and what did he hope to achieve by isolating the Jews?

2. How did the crowded and confined conditions in Venice's Jewish ghetto help Leon Modena to make a living?

3. Ghettos seem to symbolize the isolation and oppression of the Jews of Italy. Does Leon Modena's autobiography suggest a different interpretation?

Sources

a. Stow, Kenneth R. *Catholic Thought and Papal Jewry Policy.* New York: Jewish Theological Seminary of America, 1977. Pp. 5–6.

---

2. Leviticus 12–13 and 14–15.

b. Modena, Leon. *The Autobiography of a Seventeenth-Century Venetian Rabbi: Leon Modena's Life of Judah.* Trans. Mark R. Cohen. Princeton: Princeton University Press, 1987. Pp. 104–5, 108, 131, 146–47. Republished with permission of Princeton University Press. Permission conveyed through Copyright Clearance Center, Inc.

11.4 CHRISTIANS UNDER MAMLUK AND OTTOMAN RULE

In the post-1350 era, Christian (and Jewish) subjects usually enjoyed the protection of their Muslim rulers in accordance with the *dhimma*. Occasionally, however, they became the targets of popular Muslim violence or of especially oppressive royal policies. The first reading is the Muslim historian al-Maqrizi's (1364–1442) account of the reaction of Coptic Christians to popular and state persecution in Mamluk Egypt in 1354, one of a series of intermittent outbreaks of anti-Christian violence perpetrated or fomented by Muslim masses resentful of Coptic government officials, Coptic affluence, and the renovation of Coptic churches. In the Ottoman Balkans, even if Christians were rarely forced to contend with popular Muslim violence of this sort, they nonetheless had to make difficult adjustments to their subordinate status. The second reading comes from the English diplomat Paul Rycaut's observations on the situation of Greek Christians in the later seventeenth century. Rycaut had little prior knowledge of Islam or of the centuries of complex Muslim-Christian interaction in the Balkans. In some parts of the Balkans, however, Ottoman government did not have a great impact on Christians' daily lives. The third reading is the Ottoman traveler Evliya Çelibi's (1611–1682) description of the congregational mosque in Ohrid (modern North Macedonia), formerly the Bulgarian church of St. Sophia.

a. Al-Maqrizi
Arabic • early 15th century • Cairo

Many reports came from both Upper and Lower Egypt of Copts being converted to Islam, frequenting mosques, and memorizing the Qur'an. . . . In all the provinces of Egypt, both north and south, no church remained that had not been razed; on many of those sites mosques were constructed. For when the Christians' affliction grew great and their incomes small, they decided to embrace Islam. Thus Islam spread amongst the Christians of Egypt. . . . Many people attributed this to Christian cunning, so repugnant did most of the *amma* [common people] find them. But this was a momentous event in Egyptian history. From that time on, lineages became mixed in Egypt, for those persons who professed Islam in the rural areas married women and had children by them. Later their offspring came to Cairo, where some of them became *qadis* [judges], legal witnesses, and *'ulama'*. Whoever knew their way of life in its reality and the control they gained over Muslim affairs understood intuitively what they could not express openly.

b. Paul Rycaut
English • 1679 CE • London

It has been usual for the Turks . . . to take Greek women to wife, marrying them according to the Mahometan [Islamic] law; which custom was become so frequent, that the Christian women . . . freely enter into *Kabin* [concubinage] with the Turks, and without scruples designed the fruit of their bodies to the service of the Antichrist, and by the infidelity of their children, seemed half-content to become themselves apostates. To prevent and remedy which inconvenience, the patriarchs and metropolitans [bishops] often consulted together, but contribute little to their redress, while the Turks, who were masters of both their lives and fortunes, made the bodies of the [Christian] men subservient to their labor, and of the women to their lusts.

c. Evliya Çelibi
Turkish • 1662–1682 CE • Istanbul

Imperial mosques. First is the Aya Sofya congregational mosque. . . . In those Christian days this was their Jerusalem—saving the comparison!—but now, God be praised, it is a prayer-hall of the Muslims. Occasionally, however, Christians manage to enter the mosque by slipping a few *akçes* [coins] to the doorkeepers; they hold a quick prayer-service in honor of Jesus, then depart. . . . But it is an isolated mosque, slowly going to ruin. Several finely-wrought brass doors and wooden shutters with inlay mother-of-pearl are in a terrible condition. The reason is that the mosque is stranded in the midst of the Christians and has no Muslim congregation. . . . Only once a week, on Friday, the doors are opened, the servants sweep it out, and five or ten guards perform the Friday noon prayer. Then they shut the doors again and leave. At the time of the conquest this was the *Fethiyye* or "Conquest" mosque—may God restore it to prosperity!

To Consider

1. What were the economic, social, and religious factors that might have contributed to the anger of Muslim commoners against Coptic Christians in 1354? Why did Copts respond to Muslim violence by converting to Islam, and why did Muslims distrust the converts?

2. Explain the willingness of some Greek-Christian women to become the wives or concubines of Ottoman Muslims, knowing that their children with Muslim men would be raised as Muslims. Why was it so difficult for the Christian clergy to prevent such interfaith relationships?

3. If the conversion of Ohrid's church of St. Sophia into a congregational mosque was originally supposed to symbolize the triumph of the Ottoman conquerors and their faith, then what does Çelibi's description suggest about the strength of Ottoman rule in Ohrid in the seventeenth century? How did the Ottomans nonetheless maintain control over such largely Christian cities?

Sources
a. Little, Donald P. "Coptic Conversion to Islam under the Baḥrī Mamlūks, 692–755/1293–1354." *Bulletin of the School of Oriental and African Studies* 39 (1976): 568. Reproduced with permission.

b. Rycaut, Paul. *The Present State of the Greek and Armenian Churches, anno Christi 1678*. London: Printed for John Starkey, 1679. Pp. 314–17.

c. Çelebi, Evliya. *Evliya Çelebi in Albania and Adjacent Regions: Kossovo, Montenegro, Ohrid; The Relevant Sections of the Seyahatname*. Ed. and trans. Robert Dankoff and Robert Elsie. Leiden: Brill, 1998. P. 207. Republished with permission of Brill. Permission conveyed through Copyright Clearance Center, Inc.

11.5 RESPONSES TO EXPULSION AND EXILE

The traumatic experiences of expulsion and exile compelled many individuals to try to make sense of why, in the framework of their own people's history, they had been uprooted from their homeland, and to ponder how they and their people might make new lives for themselves in exile. It was not only the actual victims of expulsion who grappled with such questions, but also the descendants of the original exiles and even the former neighbors of the exiles who remained behind in the country from which the latter had been expelled. The first reading is from a letter of the Greek exile Basilios Bessarion (ca. 1403–1472). Appointed archbishop of Nicaea by the Byzantine emperor John VIII in 1437, his support for the union of the Greek and Latin Churches at the Council of Ferrara-Florence in 1439 earned him not only the resentment of many Greeks but also the rank of cardinal in the Roman Church. He then chose to remain in Italy. But after the Ottoman conquest of Constantinople, Bessarion devoted himself to recovering the Greek cultural heritage and patronized learned Greek refugees. In the letter, written to the exiled scholar Michael Apostolis in 1455, he explains why he was collecting Greek manuscripts. The second reading is taken from *Consolation for the Tribulations of Israel*, written by the former Portuguese Converso Samuel Usque in 1553 in Ferrara, Italy, where he had returned to Judaism. In it, Usque attempts to give Sephardi Converso and Jewish readers reasons to have hope for the future. The last reading comes from *Don Quixote*, the fictional masterpiece of the Spanish author Miguel de Cervantes (1547–1616). Cervantes had been wounded in the naval defeat of the Ottomans at Lepanto in 1571; later, from 1575 to 1580, he was the captive of corsairs in Algiers. Yet in this passage he considers the experience of expelled Moriscos through his depiction of a fictional Morisco, Ricote. Here, Ricote, who had secretly returned to Spain from exile, addresses his friend the Old Christian Sancho Panza.

a. Bessarion's Letter
Greek • 1455 CE • Bologna

As long as the common and single hearth of the Greeks [Constantinople] remained standing, I did not concern myself [with collecting Greek manuscripts] because I knew they were to be found there. But when, alas!, it fell, I conceived a great desire to acquire all these works, not so much for myself, who possess enough for my own use, but for the sake of the Greeks who are left now as well as those who may have a better fortune in the future. . . . Thus the Greeks may be able to find intact and preserved in a safe place all the records of their language which remain up to now, and, finding these, may be able to multiply them, without being left completely mute. Otherwise, they would lose even these few vestiges of these excellent and divine men . . . and they [future Greeks] would differ in no way from barbarians and slaves.

b. Usque's *Consolation*
Portuguese • 1553 CE • Ferrara

Thirdly, by scattering you [Jews and Conversos] among all peoples, He [God] made it impossible for the world to destroy you, for if one kingdom rises against you in Europe to inflict death upon you, another in Asia allows you to live. And if the Spaniards burn you in Spain and banish you, the Lord wills for you to find someone in Italy who welcomes you and lets you live in freedom. . . .

The fifth road to consolation is the great benefit which has come of your misfortunes in Spain and Portugal. . . . Since you had forgotten your ancient Law, and feigned Christianity with all your might solely to save your life and property, without realizing that you were jeopardizing your soul . . . His [God's] mercy was great in being cruel to you, for the noxious wound penetrated your body so rapidly that in a few years it would have killed the memory of Judaism in your children. . . .

The eighth is the most signal way by which you will rise to a higher degree of consolation in the great nation of Turkey. . . . Here the gates of liberty are always wide open for you that you may fully practice your Judaism. . . . Here you may restore your true character, transform your nature . . . and abandon the practices opposed to God's will, which you have adopted under the pressures of the nations in which you have wandered.

c. Cervantes's *Don Quixote*
Spanish • 1605–1615 CE • Madrid

You know very well, O Sancho Panza, my neighbor and friend, how the proclamation and edict that His Majesty issued against those of my race [Moriscos] brought terror and fear to all of us. . . . It seems to me [Ricote] it was divine inspiration that moved His Majesty to put into effect so noble a resolution, not because all of us were guilty, for some were firm and true Christians, though these were so few they could not oppose those who were not, but because it is not a good idea to nurture a snake in your bosom or shelter enemies in your house.

In short, it was just and reasonable for us to be chastised with the punishment of exile: lenient and mild, according to some, but for us it was the most terrible one we could have received. No matter where we are we weep for Spain, for, after all, we were born here and it is our native country. . . . We did not know our good fortune until we lost it, and the greatest desire in almost all of us is to return to Spain; most of those, and there are many of them, who know the language as well as I do, come back to Spain, abandon their wives and children and return, so great is the love they have for Spain. . . .

Now, Sancho, my intention is to take out the treasure I buried here . . . outside the village . . . and then I'll write to my daughter and wife, or leave from Valencia and go to Algiers, where I know they are. . . . I know for a fact that my daughter, Ricota, and my wife, Francisca

Ricota, are true Catholic Christians, and though I'm less of one, I'm still more Christian than Moor.

To Consider

1. Why does Bessarion think that recovering the Greek intellectual heritage is crucial for the Greeks' future, and how would his position as a Catholic cardinal have shaped his vision of that future?

2. For Usque, how does the long history of the Jewish diaspora become a source of strength for Sephardi exiles after 1492, and how are the Iberian expulsions and even inquisitorial prosecutions ultimately beneficial for Jews, Conversos, and Judaism?

3. Is Cervantes, through the words of Ricote, criticizing or supporting the Spanish monarchy's decision to expel the Moriscos? How do Ricote's words compel the reader to reflect on the Moriscos' complicated loyalties?

Sources

a. Geanakoplos, Deno John. *Greek Scholars in Venice: Studies in the Dissemination of Greek Learning from Byzantium to Western Europe.* Cambridge, MA: Harvard University Press, 1962. Pp. 81–82.
b. Usque, Samuel. *Consolation for the Tribulations of Israel.* Trans. Martin Cohen. Philadelphia: Jewish Publication Society of America, 1965. Pp. 227, 229, 231.
c. Cervantes Saavedra, Miguel de. *Don Quixote.* Trans. Edith Grossman. New York: Ecco, 2003. Pp. 813–14. Reproduced with permission of The Licensor through PLSclear.

TWELVE

Slavery and Captivity

Throughout the era 650–1650 slavery and captivity were features of Mediterranean life, perpetuated by the religious and economic motives of the pirates, raiders, and rulers who captured "enemies of the faith" and then either sold them to the merchants who traded in human merchandise or held the captives for lucrative ransoms. Since slavery was more widespread in the Muslim world, most noticeably in monarchs' use of enslaved soldiers, eunuchs, and concubines, the networks of slave traders, many of them Christian, were oriented more toward markets there. Yet, because Mediterranean slavery was largely domestic and urban, growing southern European cities housed larger enslaved populations after 1100. Enslaved Blacks from sub-Saharan Africa, long a presence in Muslim societies, increasingly appeared in Europe, too, after 1450. Institutions for ransoming captives developed over the centuries in tandem with the more complex political and commercial relations between Muslim and Christian realms. By the sixteenth century, ransoming "infidels" was a booming business on both Mediterranean shores.

The readings in this chapter examine the views of learned Muslims on the recruitment and importance of enslaved soldiers; and the efforts of Carolingian rulers to prohibit Christian slave merchants from selling Christians to Muslim buyers, along with the pagan Slavs they legitimately sold them. We also explore archival documents that shed light on the lives of the enslaved in Mediterranean Europe; chronicles treating captive exchanges between Crusaders and Muslim princes, and the treatment of Christian captives in sixteenth-century Algiers, a ransoming center; and Christian observations on the import of enslaved Blacks into Portugal as well as Muslim discussions regarding the legitimacy of enslaving Blacks.

12.1 SLAVE SOLDIERS IN THE MUSLIM WORLD

Military slavery was a key institution in medieval and early modern Muslim states. The first two readings are from the *Book of Lessons* (*Kitab al-'Ibar*), the universal history of Ibn Khaldun (1332–1406). The great Tunisian historian served Marinid, Nasrid, and Hafsid rulers before spending his last years in Mamluk Egypt as chief judge of the Maliki school of Islamic law. In the first reading, he explains the origins of the institution of military slavery, and in the second, the crucial role in Islamic history played by the Mamluk regime in Egypt. The third reading, from the *Seyahatname* (*Book of Travels*) of the famous Ottoman traveler Evliya Çelebi (1611–1682), presents Çelebi's observations on the institution of the *devşirme*, or "collection," of slaves from among Christian children in the Ottoman Balkans. Like the pagan Turkic youths imported into Egypt, these Christian youths were converted to Islam.

a. Ibn Khaldun on the Origins of the Use of Slave Soldiers
Arabic • 1375–1404 CE • Qal'at Banu Salama (Algeria), Tunis, Cairo

Their [the Arabs'] policy [before the 'Abbasids] was not to use their slaves in anything connected with their raids and conquests and their fighting against [other] peoples. . . . For the group feeling ['*asabiyya*] of the Arabs was then at a high peak and their vigor was firm and sharp and they and their ruler were united in ruling and their goal towards might and glory was the same. . . . [This lasted] until the ruler became excessively strong and was on the way to acquiring absolute power. . . . He needed, in order to stay in power, to have the upper hand over those who contested his authority from among his own people by means of an '*asabiyya* which must defend him alone. . . .

At that time [of the 'Abbasid caliph al-Mu'tasim (833–842)] the wars of the Muslims in the remote areas, and especially against the Turk, continued without break. . . . Waves of prisoners . . . arrived unceasingly. . . . [Al-Mu'tasim and his successors] would foster [a certain part] of them for the purpose of [developing their] loyalty. They would choose from among them [commanders] to lead the armies in war . . . as well as to heal the breaches which occur [inside the realm].

b. Ibn Khaldun on the Mamluk Regime in Egypt

[When] the Tatar infidels [Mongols] . . . abolished the caliphate and wiped out the splendor of the land[1] . . . God . . . came to the rescue of the true faith by reviving its last breath and restoring in Egypt the unity of the Muslims. . . . This He did by sending to them [the Muslims], out of this Turkish people and out of its mighty and numerous tribes, guardian *amir*s [commanders] and devoted defenders who are imported as slaves from the lands of heathendom to the lands of Islam. This status of slavery is indeed a blessing . . . from Divine

---

1. The Mongols under Hulagu Khan brought an end to the 'Abbasid caliphate in Baghdad in 1258. The Mamluks reestablished it in Cairo in 1261 to enhance their own political legitimacy, but the caliphs exercised minimal authority.

Providence. They [the slaves] embrace Islam with the determination of true believers while retaining their nomadic virtues . . . unmarred by the habits of civilization, with their youthful strength unshattered by the excess of luxury. The slave merchants bring them to Egypt in batch after batch. . . . The rulers have them paraded and bid against one another to pay the highest prices for them. The purpose of their purchase is not to enslave them but to intensify their group solidarity and strengthen their prowess. . . .

Then the rulers lodge them in the royal chambers, and foster their loyalty and give them a careful upbringing, including the study of the Qur'an. . . . Then they train them in the use of the bow and the sword, in riding, . . . in fighting with the lance, until they become tough and seasoned soldiers. . . . When the rulers are convinced that they are prepared to defend them and to die for them, they multiply their pay and augment their fiefs.[2] . . . Then they appoint them to high offices of state, and even sultans are chosen from them who direct the affairs of the Muslims, as had been ordained by the Providence of Almighty God and out of His benevolence to His creatures. Thus one group [of Mamluks] follows another and generation succeeds generation and Islam rejoices.

c. Evliya Çelebi on the *Devşirme*
Turkish • 1662–1682 CE • Istanbul

It is here [in Starova, modern Albania], in accordance with the statute of Sultan Suleyman [the Magnificent], that a colonel from the janissaries arrives in the name of the sultan and collects hundreds of select young Bulgarian and Greek boys. . . . They are dressed in red conical caps and red woolen robes and are sent to the court. . . . After being well educated and trained, they serve as recruits, then enter the service of the janissaries, then graduate to the service of the *sipahi*s [cavalry]. If God determines it, some of them can go on to become grand viziers, *mufti*s and *mullah*s [judges and legal scholars]. So this town of Starova is the mine of *devşirme* boys and a blessed and beautiful place.

To Consider

1. Why, according to Ibn Khaldun, did the 'Abbasid caliphs start using slave soldiers, and why did he view them as the saviors of Islam? Would Evliya Çelebi have shared the view of Ibn Khaldun?

2. Ottoman sultans "recruited" their slave soldiers from inside their empire, while most other Muslim rulers obtained theirs from outside the lands of Islam. How might differences in the mode of obtaining military slaves have affected the relative strength of Muslim states and the relationship between Muslim rulers and their subjects?

---

2. Grants of land the revenues from which supported individual Mamluks.

3.   Historians of slavery often describe slaves as "powerless." Is such a description accurate for Muslim slave soldiers? If not, what were the limitations of their power?

Sources

a–b. Ayalon, David. "Mamlukiyyat." *Jerusalem Studies in Arabic and Islam* 2 (1980): 340–49.

c. Çelebi, Evliya. *Evliya Çelebi in Albania and Adjacent Regions: Kossovo, Montenegro, Ohrid; The Relevant Sections of the Seyahatname.* Ed. and trans. Robert Dankoff and Robert Elsie. Leiden: Brill, 1998. P. 225. Republished with permission of Brill. Permission conveyed through Copyright Clearance Center, Inc.

12.2 EARLY MEDIEVAL EUROPE AND THE SLAVE TRADE

The profitability of the slave trade in the early medieval Mediterranean attracted merchants of many backgrounds who were prepared to obtain and sell whatever human merchandise buyers demanded. The religious faith, power, and wealth of rulers, however, often determined the routes and direction of the slave trade and the identity of the slaves marketed. The three readings here concern efforts of Carolingian rulers to place restrictions on the slave trade in Europe. The first reading is from a letter Pope Hadrian I wrote to Charlemagne (768–814) in 776 regarding the alleged involvement of Romans in selling slaves to the Muslims. After defeating the Lombards in 773, Charlemagne had become the dominant power in north-central Italy. In 800, Pope Leo III would crown him Emperor of the Romans. The second reading comes from Charlemagne's legislation of 802, which protected from enslavement all peoples who had submitted to his imperial authority. The third reading includes clauses from a treaty established between Emperor Lothar I (840–855) and the government of Venice in 840 regulating the slave trade; it is based on earlier agreements.

a. Pope Hadrian's Letter
Latin • 776 CE • Rome

We find in your [Charlemagne's] sweet letter a mention of the sale of slaves, to the effect that they were sold by our Roman people to the unspeakable race of the Saracens [Muslims]. We have never sunk to such a disgraceful act . . . nor was it done with our approval. The unspeakable Greeks [Byzantines] have always sailed along the coasts of Lombardy, and it was they who bought some families from the region and struck up friendships with the Lombards themselves and through their agency received the slaves in question. When this happened we sent straightaway to Duke Allo, instructing him to prepare a large fleet, arrest these Greeks and destroy their ships by fire; but he would not obey our command, because we have neither the ships nor the sailors to make the arrest. Nevertheless . . . we strove mightily in our desire to prevent this scandal; the ships belonging to the Greeks we had burned in the harbor of our city of Citavecchia, and we kept the Greeks in prison for some considerable time. But, as we have said, many families were sold by the Lombards at a time when famine was pressing them hard; indeed, some of the Lombards went on board the Greek ships of their own accord, having no other hope of staying alive.

b. Charlemagne's Legislation
Latin • 802 CE • Aachen

Concerning those whom the lord emperor wishes, with Christ's blessing, to have peace and protection in his kingdom, that is, those who have thrown themselves upon his mercy, those who, whether Christians or pagans, have desired to offer any information, or who from poverty or hunger have sought his intervention: let no one dare to bind them in servitude or take possession of them or dispose of them or sell them, but rather let them stay where they themselves choose, and live there under the lord emperor's protection and in his mercy. If anyone should presume to transgress this instruction, let him know that a man so presumptuous as to despise the lord emperor's orders must pay for it with the loss of his life.

c. Lothar's Treaty with Venice
Latin • 840 CE • Rome

We [the Venetians] promise you [Emperor Lothar] in return that we knowingly will neither buy nor sell nor, through whatever stratagem, transport Christian people from your empire or realm under your dominion with the result that they endure captivity or their lord loses them; but nor will we under any pretext transport any Christian from anywhere to here [Venice] with the result that she or he falls into the possession of the pagans [Muslims]. And if we discover that anyone is bringing them [Christian captives] into our duchy [of Venice], we will by all means deliver to you [for punishment] the one who has brought the Christian slaves to be sold; and the one who apprehends them [the slave dealers] will receive everything that he [the slave dealer] was bringing with him.

Indeed, concerning captives, if they are found in our duchy: we will deliver to you [for punishment] those persons who transported those captives with all their goods and families; and if this is not done, then the judge of that place, where those slaves were sought, will take an oath . . . that those slaves will neither be received there nor transported from there.

To Consider

1. What were the concerns that motivated Charlemagne and Lothar I to write letters to the pope, pass laws, and make treaties with Venice about restricting the slave trade?

2. Judging from Pope Hadrian's letter, what were some of the religious, political, and economic factors that promoted the business of slave traders and facilitated their activities?

3. If Charlemagne's law of 802 was intended to make the Carolingian empire a no-slaving zone, how effective does the law appear to have been, and why would it have been so difficult to enforce?

Sources

a. Loyn, Henry R., and John Percival, ed. and trans. *The Reign of Charlemagne: Documents on Carolingian Government and Administration.* New York: St. Martin's Press, 1976. P. 129.
b. Geary, Patrick, ed. *Readings in Medieval History.* 5th ed. Toronto: University of Toronto Press, 2015. P. 264.
c. *Pactum Hlotharii I.* In *Monumenta Germanica Historica: Legum Sectio II. Capitularia Regum Francorum,* vol. 2, ed. Alfred Boretius. Hanover: Bibliopilii Hahniani, 1883. Pp. 130–31.

12.3 SLAVE LIFE IN LATE MEDIEVAL MEDITERRANEAN EUROPE

Late medieval documents from the archives of Mediterranean Christian states bear witness to the diverse origins of enslaved men and women, to their varied labors, and to their relationships with their owners and with local populations. Since these chattel slaves were the property of their owners, the latter could sell them or lease out their services in notarized contracts, and free them, or otherwise dispose of them, in their notarized wills. Yet the laws that protected the owners' rights to their "property" also acknowledged that enslaved persons were human beings entitled to fundamental legal protections. Hence municipal governments or even monarchs might intervene on behalf of the enslaved. The passages from the documents below, which are arranged in chronological order, are but a tiny sampling of the many thousands of pieces of evidence that historians draw upon when reconstructing the experience of enslaved people in the premodern Mediterranean.

a. Letter of Alfonso IV, King of Aragon
Latin • 1335 CE • Valencia

Considering that Guillem Straery, silk-weaver and citizen of Valencia, had once promised—in a notarial document . . . dated 18 May 1325—to Mahomet Abendenu, then his slave and captive, that if the said Mahomet taught him, or whomever he wished, how to make and work silk . . . and to dye it of such a color . . . so that it would not change or lose its color, he [Mahomet] would, after the passing of twelve years from then, remain free . . . from all servitude . . . without [paying] any ransom, but with the condition that said Mahomet could not make or dye silk of the said color . . . nor teach anyone else how to do it. . . . Therefore, considering that it had been established in the [notarized] agreement between Guillem Straery and Mahomet that Guillem could not sell him within the said twelve-year period . . . [but] that Mahomet, within the twelve-year period, was [later] sold and offered for sale by Jaume Straery, guardian of the children of the said [deceased] Guillem, in violation of the aforesaid agreement and promise, . . . We [King Alfonso] grant you [Mahomet] license . . . to work silk and to make and dye it in the aforesaid color throughout our lands and dominion without any impediment.

b. Lease of an Enslaved Man's Labor
Latin • 1340 CE • Palermo, Sicily

Jacoba, widow of Guillem Buccetti, butcher, citizen of Palermo, willingly leased the labor and services of the person of Demetrius, her Greek slave . . . to Benedict de Perri . . ., butcher,

her co-citizen, acting on behalf of himself and his associates, . . . for the entire month of next August. . . . Jacoba promised . . . that the said Demetrius will stay with the same associates for the whole time of the leasing and perform all the tasks pertinent to the occupation of butchering in Palermo or wherever else in Sicily the same associates may take him. [The amount that Benedict will pay Jacoba for "renting" Demetrius' services is then stipulated.]

c. Letter of the Merchant Francesco Datini, to His Agent in Genoa
Italian • 1393 CE • Prato, Italy

Pray, buy for me a little slave-girl, young and sturdy and of good stock, strong and able to work hard . . . so that I can bring her up in my own way, and she will learn better and quicker and I shall get better service out of her. I want her only to wash the dishes and carry the wood and bread to the oven, and work of that sort . . . for I have another one here who is a good slave and can cook and serve well.

d. Letter of an Italian Slave-Owner, Aglio degli Agli, to a Friend
Italian • ca. 1393 CE • Prato, Italy

I had a very good [slave], but, for her misfortune, she became pregnant and had a boy child— and since the father could not be found I took it and sent it out to a nurse. But my Monna Lucia [his wife] was seized with jealousy, and said it was mine; and though I told her it was only mine as a calf belongs to the man who also owns the cow, she still will not believe me. . . . And she has won the quarrel, and the slave has been turned out, and we now have an old woman who is more like a monkey than a female; and this is the life I lead.

e. Municipal Legislation, Barcelona
Catalan • 1414 CE • Barcelona

The councillors and leading men of the city ordain: in order to avoid and put a stop to the great dishonesties and grave sin of carnality which have been occurring for some time . . . for reason of the slave women whose masters [men or women] demand of them such great and immoderate prices for their manumission that they give over their bodies to the said sin of carnality in order to earn [money] from it so that they can pay the said manumission prices. And, moreover, for reason of some other slave women who . . . are permitted by their masters [men or women] to engage in the said sin, such that from the earnings that they make from engaging in the said sin, their said masters [men or women] get part of it. [Masters are threatened with a fine of 100 sous, while enslaved women are to be fined 30 sous on the first offense and whipped through the city should they offend again.]

f. Clause from the Will of the Tanner Garcia d'Agramunt
Catalan • 1476 CE • Valencia

I grant freedom to my [converted Muslim or Black African] slaves Francesc, Pere and Jordi on condition that they serve and be obligated to serve my said wife for two years, to be counted from the day before my death, so that they clean and be required to clean the hides for my said wife. And if within the said two years they run away and/or do not want to work, in such a case the one or ones who act against [my will] should remain enslaved . . . and may be sold by my said wife.

g. Judicial Testimony of Maymo ben Çabit, Mudejar (Minority Muslim) Tailor
Catalan • 1492 CE • Valencia

Among Muslims *[moros]* of the present kingdom [Valencia] such is the practice and custom that, encountering [foreign Muslim] captives, they give [alms] to them for the love of God, and better yet to those who are in irons. And it can be shown manifestly and is shown that in recent years in the present kingdom diverse captives have been ransomed by the Muslims of the present kingdom, according to the said obligation of giving [alms] to them for the love of God.

To Consider

1. How did the legal systems of the states in which enslaved people found themselves contribute to their hardship, and how did they provide the enslaved with some forms of protection?

2. Consider the varied origins of enslaved people in Mediterranean Christian states and how and where they might have been procured. How did the slaves' origins, ethnicity, religion and/or "race" likely affect their ability to function and to fit into local societies before and after their manumission?

3. How did the gender of enslaved persons determine the kinds of labor they were required to perform and the forms of exploitation to which they were subjected? Did the gendered roles of slaves differ greatly from those of free women and men?

Sources

a–b. Verlinden, Charles. *L'esclavage dans l'Europe médiévale.* 2 vols. Ghent: University of Ghent, 1955, 1977. Vol. 1, pp. 877–78; vol. 2, pp. 174–75. Reproduced with permission of Ghent University Library. Library, BIB.G.023801.

c–d. Origo, Iris. "The Domestic Enemy: The Eastern Slaves in Tuscany in the Fourteenth and Fifteenth Centuries." *Speculum* 30:3 (1955): 329–30, 344.

e. Mutgé i Vives, Josefina. "Les ordinacions del municipi de Barcelona sobre els esclaus." In *De l'escalvitud a la lllibertat: Esclaus i lliberts a l'Edat Mitjana,* ed. Maria Teresa Ferrer i Mallol and Josefina Mutgé i Vives. Barcelona: CSIC, 2000. P. 260.

f. Blumenthal, Debra. *Enemies and Familiars: Slavery and Mastery in Fifteenth-Century Valencia.* Ithaca: Cornell University Press, 2009. P. 199. Original source Arxiu del Regne de Valénica. Reproduced with permission of The Licensor through PLSclear.

g. Meyerson, Mark D. "Slavery and Solidarity: Mudejars and Foreign Muslim Captives in the Kingdom of Valencia." *Medieval Encounters* 2:3 (1996): 313. Republished with permission of Brill. Permission conveyed through Copyright Clearance Center, Inc.

12.4 CRUSADERS, CORSAIRS, AND CAPTIVES

Captivity was a persistent, harrowing aspect of Mediterranean life, the result of Muslim and Christian military campaigning, raiding, and piracy. For the captors, holding captives for ransom became an increasingly profitable enterprise, one closely linked to the slave trade. In the first reading, Usamah ibn Munqidh (1095–1188), a Syrian Muslim nobleman, poet, and diplomat, recounts his own efforts to ransom Muslims held captive by the Franks in the early 1140s. The second reading, from the time of the Third Crusade (1189–1192), is the Muslim chronicler Ibn Shaddad's (1145–1234) eyewitness account of Salah al-Din's treatment, in 1190, of French knights from the army of King Philip Augustus (1180–1223), whom the sultan's soldiers had just captured in an ambush. Ibn Shaddad was an officer and confidant of Salah al-Din. The third reading is from the *Topography of Algiers*, written by the Portuguese cleric Antonio de Sosa while he was a prisoner in the corsair capital between 1577 and 1581. Sosa had been traveling from Barcelona on a galley of the Knights of Malta to take up an ecclesiastical post in Sicily when a corsair squadron overwhelmed the galley, seizing him and the other passengers. In Algiers Sosa befriended the Spanish author Miguel de Cervantes, who gained freedom a year before he did.

a. Usamah ibn Munqidh
Arabic • ca. 1183 CE • Damascus

I used to travel frequently to visit the king of the Franks[3] during the truce that existed [in 1140] between him and Jamal al-Din Muhammad.[4] . . . The Franks used to bring their captives before me so that I might buy their freedom, and so I bought those whose deliverance God facilitated.

Once a real devil of a Frank called William Jiba went out in a boat of his on a raid and he captured a ship carrying Muslim pilgrims from the Maghrib, around four hundred souls, men and women. Groups of these captives would be brought to me by their owners and I would buy those of them I could afford to buy. . . .

So I bought both of them [a youth and an old man]. I also bought a few more for me and a few more for the amir Mu'in al-Din[5] . . ., all for 120 dinars. I paid out all the money I had with me and offered a guarantee for the remainder.

I then went to Damascus and told the *amir* Mu'in al-Din . . ., "I bought back some captives for you, putting them specifically under your charge, but I didn't have the full amount with which to pay for them. . . . If you want them, you can pay the remainder of the price; if not, I will."

"No, I'll pay for them," he said. "By God, there's no one who desires the spiritual rewards of such a good deed more than I."

---

3. Fulk V, king of Jerusalem (1131–1143).
4. Turkic Burid ruler of Damascus (1139–1140).
5. Successor of Jamal al-Din Muhammad in Damascus (1140–1149).

b. Ibn Shaddad
Arabic • 1188–1198 CE • completed in Aleppo

The sultan [Salah al-Din] . . . summoned the captives and ordered the herald to announce that anyone who had taken a prisoner should bring him. Our men brought in their prisoners. I was present at the gathering. The sultan honoured the nobles amongst them. He bestowed a fur robe especially on the commander of the French king's troops and ordered for each of the rest a fur top-coat, for the cold was intense and they had suffered from it. He also had food brought for them which they ate and he ordered a tent to be pitched for them close to his own. At all times he treated them generously. Sometimes he invited the commander to his table. He then ordered that they should be bound and conveyed to Damascus. They were taken there in an honoured state. He allowed them to write to their comrades and to have the clothes and other things they needed brought to them from their camp. When that was done, they traveled to Damascus.

c. Antonio de Sosa
Spanish • 1577–1581 CE • Algiers (published posthumously in 1612)

"Turks by profession" are all those renegades of Christian blood and parentage who have turned Turk of their own free will, impiously renouncing and spurning their God and Creator. These renegades and their children outnumber all their neighbors in Algiers . . . because there is no Christian nation on earth that has not produced renegades in this city. . . .

What moves some of these men to forsake the true path of God, at such great peril to their souls, is nothing more than the fainthearted refusal to take on the work of slavery. Others are attracted by pleasure, by the good life of fleshy vice in which the Turks live. . . . And the Turks wilfully turn them into renegades, persuading themselves that, as good Turks, they do this to serve both God and Muhammad. Those who have already adopted that way of life or profession naturally want others to follow and approve of their deceits, from which, in general, they all profit. . . .

Corsairs are those men who live by privateering or full-time robbery at sea. Some of these are Turks by birth and others are Moors [Muslims of North African or Iberian origin], but the vast majority consists of renegades from all nations, men very adept on the shores, riverbanks, and coasts of the whole Christian world. . . .

Few are the corsairs who do not have at home the slaves needed for . . . all the jobs necessary to put together a corsair ship—carpenters, caulkers, ironmongers, coopers, oar builders, and others—because these are the men that corsairs try to get for themselves, and to buy at a high price, whenever they capture a Christian ship. So that if Christian workers were lacking to the Turks, there would not be perhaps one ship among them. . . .

The captain who does not own a quantity of Christians, enough to arm the vessel— because almost all of them need three men per oar, and some four . . .—can rent Christians from merchants who have them especially for hire. . . .

. . . The ration given each day to the galley slaves, and to all the *lewends* [irregular militia] and workmen on the galliot[6] is nothing more than some biscuits, a bit of watered-down vinegar, and a few tablespoons of olive oil. The Christian galley slaves are given only biscuits. . . .

The beatings with sticks or fists, the slappings, kickings, whippings, hunger, thirst, and the infinity of continuous and ruthless cruelties that the corsairs use with the poor Christians who row, without letting them rest for half an hour, are inhuman. They cruelly whip open their backs, draw blood, tear out eyes, break arms, crush bones, slash ears, cut off noses, and even brutally slit throats.

To Consider

1. What were the political, institutional, and religious developments that would explain the ability of Usamah ibn Munqidh to ransom Muslim captives and Salah al-Din's "chivalrous" treatment of captured French knights?

2. For individual Muslim and Christian captives, captivity often enough turned into a life of slavery. Which factors increased the likelihood of a captive instead being ransomed?

3. Why in Sosa's day did so many Christian captives in Algiers convert to Islam, even though the possibility of being ransomed was much greater than ever before?

Sources

a. Ibn Munqidh, Usamah. *The Book of Contemplation: Islam and the Crusades.* Trans. Paul M.
Cobb. London: Penguin Books, 2008. Pp. 93–94. Reproduced with permission of The
Licensor through PLSclear.

b. Ibn Shaddad, Baha al-Din. *The Rare and Excellent History of Saladin.* Trans. D. S. Richards.
Aldershot: Ashgate, 2002. Pp. 139–40. Reproduced with permission of The Licensore
through PLSclear.

c. De Sosa, Antonio. *An Early Modern Dialogue with Islam: Antonio de Sosa's "Topography of Algiers"*
(1612). Trans. Diana de Armas Wilson. Notre Dame: University of Notre Dame Press,
2011. Pp. 125–26, 151–57.

12.5 PERCEPTIONS OF BLACK AFRICANS IN THE EARLY MODERN MEDITERRANEAN

During the fifteenth century enslaved Black people began to arrive in Mediterranean Europe in significant numbers as a result of growing Portuguese commerce in sub-Saharan West Africa. The first reading comes from the chronicle of Gomes Eannes de Azurara (ca. 1410–1474), the royal librarian of King Afonso V of Portugal (1438–1481) whom the king commissioned to record the deeds of his uncle, Prince Henry the Navigator (1394–1460), the driving force behind Portuguese expansion into West Africa. Here, Eannes de Azurara describes the arrival of enslaved Blacks in the Portuguese port of Lagos. By this time, Black people had long been a presence in Muslim lands. Their enslavement, however, could still be controver-

---

6. A small and very fast galley with fourteen to twenty-five benches for oarsmen.

sial. In the second reading, Ahmad Baba (1556–1627), an important legal scholar from Timbuktu, issues a ruling on the legitimacy of enslaving people of the Sudan, "the land of the
Blacks." The last reading is from a letter sent by the Sa'did sultan and self-proclaimed caliph
of Morocco Ahmad al-Mansur (1578–1603) to legal scholars in Egypt justifying why he was
pressing free Black Moroccans into his army to make a slave regiment. In the letter, al-
Mansur speciously refers to the Blacks he planned to conscript as "slaves."

a. Gomes Eannes de Azurara
Portuguese • 1553–1568 CE • Lisbon

Although the sorrow of those captives was for the present very great, especially after the partition and each one took his own share aside . . . ; and although it chanced that among the
prisoners the father often remained in Lagos, while the mother was taken to Lisbon, and the
children to another part (in which partition their sorrow doubled the first grief)—yet this
sorrow was felt less among those who happened to remain in company. For as saith the text,
the wretched find consolation in having comrades in misfortune. But from this time forth
they began to acquire some knowledge of our country, in which they found great abundance,
and our men began to treat them with great favour. For as our people did not find them hard-
ened in the belief of the other Muslims *[moros]*, and saw how they came in unto the law of
Christ with a good will, they made no difference between them and their free servants, born
in our own country. But those whom they took while still young, they caused to be instructed
in the mechanical arts, and those whom they saw fitted for managing property they set free
and married to women who were natives of the land. . . . Yea, and some widows of good family who bought some of these female slaves either adopted them or left them a portion of
their estate by will, so that in the future they married right well, treating them as entirely
free. Suffice it that I never saw one of these slaves put in irons like other captives, and
scarcely any one who did not turn Christian and was not very gently treated.

And I have been asked by their lords to the baptisms and marriages of such; at which
they, whose slaves they were before, made no less solemnity than if they had been their children or relations.

And so their lot was now quite the contrary of what it had been, since before they had
lived in perdition of soul and body: of their souls in that they were yet pagans, without the
clearness and light of the holy faith; and of their bodies, in that they lived like beasts, without any custom of reasonable beings—for they had no knowledge of bread or wine, and they
were without the covering of clothes, or the lodgment of houses; and worse than all, through
the great ignorance that was in them, in that they had no understanding of good, but only
knew how to live in a bestial sloth.

b. Ahmad Baba
Arabic • 1614–1615 CE • Timbuktu

You should be aware that the cause of enslavement is unbelief, and the unbelievers of the
Sudan are like any other unbelievers in this regard—Jews, Christians, Persians, Berbers, or

others whose persistence in unbelief rather than Islam has been established—as will be demonstrated from the words of the *Mudawwana*[7] at the end of this section. This is proof that there is no difference between any unbelievers in this regard. Whoever is enslaved in a state of unbelief may rightly be owned, whoever he is, as opposed to those of all groups who converted to Islam first, such as the people of Bornu, Kano, Songhay, Katsina, Gobir, and Mali and some of [the people] of Zakzak [Zaria in northern Nigeria]. They are free Muslims who may not be enslaved under any circumstance.

c. Ahmad al-Mansur
Arabic • 1591–1603 CE • Marrakesh

We found that many of these slaves were runaways who had deserted their owners and escaped from their control. Every one of them bore the runaway mark and was known by it, either through his father or his paternal or maternal grandparents. . . . These runaways would attach themselves to other masters or to tribes, or become part of the entourage of shaykhs or big men with a following. . . . Thus they became dispersed throughout the lands and regions, especially during times of dearth and turmoil. . . . This despite the fact that they are originally unbelieving blacks, imported from over there through purchase from those who neighbor them and raid and campaign against them.

We selected those slaves to be made into soldiers . . . for Islam, because of qualities which they possess to the exclusion of others: they are a race who give little trouble, they are content with simple living conditions. . . . In addition, this race of slaves has strengthened this blessed affair of guarding the jihadist fortresses and encompassing the Islamic lands to which they were assigned and directed. They are tougher and more long-suffering. . . . They were suited to that and best fitted to undertake it most perfectly. . . .

Also, [we had] a desire to obtain a great reward from God Most High through civilizing them well and ordering them and training them and refining them. To this may be added the polishing they acquire in terms of good manners, fine qualities, and morals through . . . serving the household of the caliphate.

To Consider

1. In what ways are the Christian and Muslim explanations for the enslavement of Black Africans similar?

2. What do you think of the comments of Eannes de Azurara and al-Mansur that enslaved Blacks were willing Christians and Muslims?

3. On the basis of these sources, to what extent did religious conversion, to Christianity or Islam, overcome discrimination against Blacks on the basis of color?

---

7. *Al-Mudawwana*, a major legal work composed by Sahnun ibn Sa'id ibn Habib al-Tanukhi (776–854), a leading Maliki jurist from Qayrawan.

Sources

a. Muldoon, James. *The Expansion of Europe: The First Phase.* Philadelphia: University of Pennsylvania Press, 1977. Pp. 60–61. Reproduced with permission of The Licensor through PLSclear.

b–c. Hunwick, John. "Islamic Law and Polemics over Race and Slavery in North and West Africa (16th–19th Century)." In *Slavery in the Islamic Middle East,* ed. Shaun Marmon. Princeton: Markus Wiener Publishers, 1999. Pp. 49–50, 52–54. Reproduced with permission of The Licensor through PLSclear.

THIRTEEN

Mystical Messiahs and Converts, Humanists and Armorers

The period 1350–1650 saw a bewildering range of cultural and religious tendencies in the Mediterranean region. While mysticism flourished in various ways among the Mediterranean monotheisms all across the Middle Ages, this period witnessed both particularly striking mystical movements and especially memorable individual mystics. Mysticism, moreover, often contributed directly to a second notable tendency, a fascination with prophecies of messiahs and Last World Emperors who were soon to arrive and set things to right here on earth. Though conversion between Judaism, Christianity, and Islam had been going on for centuries—especially the conversion of the Christians of the Middle East to Islam, this period, with the expansion of the Ottoman empire, and forced (and sometimes unforced) conversion of Jews and Muslims to Christianity on the opposite side of the Mediterranean in Spain, was an age of particularly notable conversions often of quite prominent people about whom we know a great deal. Yet much of the other cultural and intellectual work that we have seen in the earlier periods continued quite energetically as well—sophisticated philosophy and science continued to flourish, though in both cases Aristotle's views were gradually diminishing in importance, and Mediterranean engineers continued to design, refine, and create amazing technologies, some quite benevolent, others, such as effective gunpowder artillery pieces, quite destructive.

The readings in this chapter give some sense of the intellectual, religious, and technological currents that shaped the Mediterranean in the late medieval/early modern period through examples of Muslim and Jewish mystics and Christian and crypto-Muslim prophets; descriptions of the public nature of conversion in the period; illustrations of the high esteem Latin Christians still had for Arabic science; and accounts of the building and firing of the most dangerous weapons of the period, the great Turkish bombards.

13.1 DESCRIBING MUSLIM AND JEWISH MYSTICS

In the sixteenth and seventeenth centuries, mystics played an outsize role in the culture and religious life of the Ottoman lands. Often Muslim Sufis (usually referred to in this period by the Persian word of the same meaning, *dervish*) were members of formal orders, of which there were many in this period. Likewise, many Jews who practiced the widely embraced form of Jewish mysticism called the Kabbalah were organized communally into orders, which were also numerous, especially in Safed, the Jewish Palestinian town that was a thriving center of intellectual and religious life for Ottoman Jews.

Moreover, the dervishes and Kabbalists of the Ottoman world often embraced unusual behaviors as they sought mystical communion with God, and some of them were deeply charismatic, larger-than-life figures who must have been unforgettable to those who met them. Two descriptions of dervishes and one of the great Kabbalist Isaac Luria follow.

a. Abu Hafs 'Umar al-Suhrawardi's Description of the Qalandars
Arabic • mid-13ᵗʰ century • Baghdad

The dervishes who were probably most notorious for their peculiar practices were members of the Qalandar order. Here they are described by the leader of a rival order of dervishes called the Suhrawardiyya.

The term [Qalandars] denotes people who are governed by the intoxication [engendered by] the tranquility of their hearts to the point of destroying customs and throwing off the bonds of social intercourse, traveling [as they are] in the fields of tranquility of their hearts. They observe the ritual prayer and fasting[1] only insofar as these are obligatory and do not hesitate to indulge in those pleasures of the world that are permitted by the Law; nay, they content themselves with keeping within the bounds of what is permissible and do not go in search of the truths of legal obligation.[2] All the same, they persist in rejecting hoarding and accumulation [of wealth] and the desire to have more. They do not observe the rites of the ascetic, the abstemious, and the devout and confine themselves to, and are content with, the tranquility of their hearts with God. Nor do they have an eye for any desire to increase what they already possess of this tranquility of the heart. The difference between the Malamati[3] and the Qalandar is that the former strives to conceal his acts of devotion while the latter strives to destroy custom. . . . The Qalandar is not bound by external appearance and is not concerned with what others may or may not know of his state. He is attached to nothing but the tranquility of his heart, which is his sole property.

---

1. I.e., the normal Sunni requirements about daily prayer and fasting in the month of Ramadan.

2. I.e., they focus not on what is required by Muslim ritual and legal practice, but on things that it allows but does not require.

3. An early medieval Muslim ascetic and mystical movement of ninth- and tenth-century Persia.

b. From Giovan Antonio Menavino's *Treatise on the Customs and Life of the Turks*
Italian • 1548 CE • Italy

Giovan Antonio Menavino, a well-informed Christian Italian who had been a captive in Ottoman lands in the early sixteenth century, offers a very different point of view on the Qalanders.

Dressed in sheepskins, the [Qalandars] are otherwise naked, with no headgear. Their scalps are always clean-shaven and well rubbed with oil as a precaution against the cold. They burn their temples with an old rag so that their faces will not be damaged by sweat. Illiterate and unable to do anything manly, they live like beasts, surviving on alms only. For this reason, they are to be found around taverns and public kitchens in cities. If, while roaming the countryside, they come across a well-dressed person, they try to make him one of their own, stripping him naked. Like Gypsies in Europe, they practice chiromancy,[4] especially for women who then provide them with bread, eggs, cheese, and other foods in return for their services. Amongst them there is usually an old man whom they revere and worship like God. When they enter a town, they gather around the best house of the town and listen in great humility to the words of this old man, who, after a spell of ecstasy, foretells the descent of a great evil upon the town. His disciples then implore him to fend off the disaster through his good services. The old man accepts the plea of his followers, though not without an initial show of reluctance, and prays to God, asking him to spare the town and imminent danger awaiting it. This time-honored trick earns them considerable sums of alms from the ignorant and credulous. [Qalandars] . . . chew hashish and sleep on the ground; they also openly practice sodomy like savage beasts.

c. From Hayyim Vital's *Eight Gates*
Hebrew • 16th century • Syria/Palestine

Hayyim Vital (1542–1620), a rabbi from Safed (what is now Tzfat, in the State of Israel), describes the way of life of perhaps the most famous early modern Kabbalistic teacher, Isaac Luria.

As regards the attribute of charitableness and generosity, I observed that my teacher, of blessed memory, was not concerned with his own vanity, as expressed [for example] in the wearing of especially fine clothes. In his eating, as well, he would consume very little. However, when it came to his wife's apparel, he was exceedingly careful to honor her, and to clothe her well. He used to satisfy her every desire, even if it was not within his means.

When it came to giving charity and fulfilling the commandments, he was in no way a miser. With respect to the ceremony of *Havdalah*[5] which is celebrated in the synagogue, he used to give four florins of gold to charity in order to personally provide for the wine to be used. Whenever he purchased something for the purpose of performing some religious

---

4. Palm reading.
5. The ceremony that marks the end of the Sabbath and the beginning of the new week.

obligation, such as buying phylacteries[6] . . . he would not be concerned with finding out how much he was supposed to pay. Rather, he used to pay the amount which they asked of him the first time. He would say to the vendor: "Here is my money, take as much as you wish."

My master, of blessed memory, also frequently used to request members of his household to bring him wild grass from the field or thorns and thistles which some men are accustomed to eating. He would consume these in order to personally take upon himself the curse given to Adam, "Thorns and thistles shall it bring forth to thee; and thou shalt eat the herb of the field" (Gen. 3:18).

To Consider

1. Are the Jewish and Muslim mystics and ascetics described here more different than alike? Or vice versa?

2. What do you conclude from these similarities and differences?

3. What do the more radical Qalanders share in common with the seemingly more moderate Isaac Luria?

Sources

a–b. Karamustafa, Ahmed T. *God's Unruly Friends: Dervish Groups in the Islamic Later Middle Period, 1200–1550.* Oxford: One World Publications, 2006. Pp. 6–7, 34. Reproduced with permission of The Licensor through PLSclear.
c. Fine, Lawrence. *Safed Spirituality: Rules of Mystical Piety, the Beginning of Wisdom.* Mahwah, NJ: Paulist Press, 1983. P. 67. Copyright © 1983 by Paulist Press, Inc. New York/Mahwah, NJ. www.paulistpress.com

13.2 A MORISCO PROPHECY OF TURKISH TRIUMPH

Predictions of saving messiahs and mahdis[7] flourished throughout the Mediterranean in the fifteenth through seventeenth century. Courtiers proclaimed the Ottoman sultan, Suleyman the Magnificent (1520–1566), as the messiah, while European prophets predicted that the Holy Roman Emperor, Frederick III (1452–1493), would be the Last World Emperor, who would establish a universal Christian order. Such prophecies circulated everywhere, not least among the Moriscos—the Iberian Muslims forcibly converted to Catholicism in the early sixteenth century, and their descendants. Not surprisingly, many Moriscos longed for some sort of deliverer to free them from the oppressive hand of the "Old Christians" of Spain. Since the thirteenth century, predictions of the arrival of a liberator called al-Fatimi had circulated in the western Mediterranean, as in the prophecy below. Intriguingly enough, however, though written in Aljamiado (Spanish in Arabic letters) by an anonymous Morisco, this prophecy is actually a translation and revision of a widely-read

---

6. Leather boxes containing verses of the Torah, which can be worn by Jews when praying.

7. The Arabic term *mahdi,* meaning "the rightly guided one," refers to a Muslim messianic figure who would come at the of time to defeat evil and injustice and establish Godly rule.

Latin-Christian prophecy composed in the fourteenth century by a French Franciscan priest named Jean de Roquetaillade, whose name—in its Aljamiado form, Juan de Rokasiya—remains attached to it.

a. The Prophecy of Friar Juan de Rokasiya
Aljamiado • 16th century • Spain

Bismillah al-rahman al-rahim.[8]

This is the prophecy of Fray Juan de Rokasiya. Twenty-four doctors in astrology concurred with him in the year fourteen-eighty-and-a-half [1485?]. The Emperor Azara'il[9] spoke in the ninth chapter of the book of revelation: "The Turks and Greeks will come to destroy the Christian people." They will harm Italy and Lombardy and all of Hungary and Cologne, and a large part of Germany. And the noble town of Rhodes, which trusts its walls and fortress, which is renowned; God forbid that it be burnt, for God's ruling has already been decreed, for she [Rhodes] had no mercy for the poor of the earth of the monastery of St. Francis. . . . You, Rome, will be reduced by the said Turk with great cruelty, and they will not pity you. The city of Pisa, and Florence, and the city of Siena will be given as vengeance on account of their evils. They will be destroyed by God's wrath. The city of Ibiza and Valencia will cry copiously and will no longer laugh at their neighbors. Cologne and the city of the philosophers and jurists[10] will be abandoned. Milan and Lombardy will be destroyed by their kings. . . . The kingdom of Naples will not be praised for her evils; which, because of [its] ignorance and arrogance, will be destroyed and subjugated by the Turks. On the year of fourteen-eighty-and-a-half of the Incarnation, princes and lords and the people will rise against the clergy, abhorring their great pomp and temporal vanity, who on account of their evils will be persecuted and they will find nowhere to go or take refuge. . . . Great plagues will come after the members of the religious orders; some will die of hunger and others in war, and others of the plague, and all their possessions will be taken away by others, and those of the dead, at the hands of infidels. Thus, be certain and do not doubt, for without rest, impetuously many and great tribulations will come on earth; that before the fifteenth of July, fourteen-hundred-eighty-and-a-half arrives, the cardinals of the Holy Father in Rome will flee from the great tribulation that will come. . . . for no one will escape those hands except for those who have the sign of *la ilaha illa Allah Muḥammad rasul Allah.*[11] . . .

---

8. "In the name of God, the merciful, the compassionate." Though written in Spanish in Arabic characters, Aljamiado documents frequently include well-known Islamic phrases, like this one, in pure Arabic. This is the first of three such examples in this document, and it is the phrase with which all but one Qur'anic surah begins and was widely used by Muslims in other written and oral contexts.

9. This appears to be an entirely invented personage.

10. I.e., Paris.

11. This is the *shahada,* the basic Muslim creed or declaration of faith in Arabic, meaning "There is no god but God; Muhammad is the prophet of God."

Many tribulations, and tempests, and earthquakes, and famines, and droughts, and deaths, and wars will come on earth. He who is raised with provision, but not of money, will be free. . . . And because of the great and terrible tribulations, ills, and tempests that will fall from the sky, the Turks will subjugate the Christian peoples. . . . There will be illnesses, and ailments, and pestilence, which will violently kill people. There will be more showers than during the time of Noah. . . . And Ibiza and Valencia will bewail, they will not laugh at their neighbors, who will be reduced by the Antichrist; they will see [him] from the sea, the one who will be worthy and of great sanctity; [he] will serve God barefoot through the barren hills. He will have two signs that all men who serve him will see. People will go after him like ants, and he will besiege you Valencia, and your prince who is said to be strong will flee to the city of the river, and there he will cease the pursuit, and will be seized by you. . . . This Antichrist will be called Fatimi. He will do justice [by] reconquering Spain in forty-two months, as Isaiah said in the fifth chapter of Revelations: [in] forty-two months will be the conquest of Spain, and of the Antichrist, who will gather at the sea shore, who will be the destroyer of the Holy Mother Church and of the Franciscans and friars, because of the great pomp, ignorance of their riches, they will have what God abhorred, which you deserve in your properties and persons, before the year fourteen-eighty-and-a-half arrives, with the will of God Almighty. This Antichrist will be the young man from Denia,[12] that they will see it *In sha' Allah*.[13]

To Consider

1. In the original Latin-Christian version of this prophecy, Jean de Roquetaillade was attacking what he saw as the worldly corrupt church on behalf of his radical Franciscan brethren. Why would such a text seem useful to Moriscos?

2. What interactions between Muslims and Christians in Iberia must have been necessary for this Christian text, originally written in Latin, to wind up in Aljamiado (bearing in mind that we have almost no evidence of Moriscos knowing any Latin)?

3. Why would the Morisco translator of the text continue to ascribe it to the Christian friar Jean de Roquetaillade, even though his version was to be read solely by Muslims?

Source

a. Reprinted from Mayte Green-Mercado, *Visions of Deliverance: Moriscos and the Politics of Prophecy in the Early Modern Mediterranean*, pp. 263–67. Copyright © 2019 by Cornell University. Used by permission of the publisher, Cornell University Press.

---

12. Town on the coast of Spain.
13. "If God wills" in Arabic.

13.3 CONVERSION IN PUBLIC

In modern America, conversion from one religion (or no religion) can happen in a way that is largely hidden from viewers other than the religious congregation that one joins. But in a period when one's religion made a great deal of social, legal, and political difference, such as in the medieval and early modern Mediterranean, it was often impossible to convert without a great deal of public fanfare. Converts from one religion to another in the fifteenth through seventeenth century were sometimes inspired by religious arguments, or at least interpreted their conversions as the result of such argumentation; in other cases mere convenience or the desire for the higher status conferred by embracing the dominant religion was the motivation. But whatever the reasons for conversion, doing so was nearly always a very public event in the Mediterranean lands, as the following two accounts make clear.

a. From Václav Vratislav of Mitrovice, *Adventures of Baron Wenceslaus Wratislaw of Mitrowice: What He Saw in the Turkish Metropolis, Constantinopole, Experienced in His Captivity, and After His Happy Return to His Country, Committed to Writing in the* Year of *Our Lord 1599*
Czech • 1599 CE • Bohemia

In 1591, an Italian Christian from Crete named Niccolo de Bello converted to Islam while traveling in Ottoman Hungary with the ambassador of the Holy Roman Empire. It is not clear why he converted, but another member of this embassy, the Bohemian nobleman Václav Vratislav of Mitrovice described Bello's conversion in some detail.

[We] saw the Italian renegade, who had turned Turk,[14] being conducted with a grand procession by the Turks into town, in the following manner. First went about 300 Turkish soldiers, or *azais*, with long muskets, who shouted for joy, and some of whom fired; after these rode some horse-soldiers, apparently their commanders; next, five banner-bearers with red banners; after these went some disagreeable gipsy music, consisting of shawms,[15] fiddles, and lutes; next rode the unhappy [i.e., ill-fated] Italian renegade, on a handsomely caparisoned horse, on each side of whom rode a Turk of rank, and he in the midst, wearing a scarlet pelisse lined with foxskins, and a Turkish cap with several cranes' feathers in it. In his hand he held an arrow, and had one finger directed upwards, thereby making profession of the Turkish religion. After him rode several trumpeters, blowing their trumpets without intermission, who were followed by about 300 Turkish hussars, ornamentally dressed in pelisses of spotted lynxskin, who sometimes shouted, sometimes sprang from their houses, and exhibited tokens of great exultation. When they rode in at the gate, they halted in the gateway, and all thrice made profession of their faith with great clamour, saying, "'Allaha, illasa,

---

14. In the late Middle Ages and early modern period, "to turn Turk" meant "to convert to Islam."

15. A double-reed wind instrument used in medieval and Renaissance music.

Muhamet resulach!"[16] i.e. "One true God, save him no other God, and Mahomet his chief prophet!" They also fired thrice. They then rode in the same order past our boats, shouting all the time, no doubt in despite of us.

b. From Thomas Warmstry's *The Baptized Turk*
English • 1658 CE • London

When a Turkish Muslim named Rigep Dandulo converted to Christianity in London in 1657, an English clergyman named Thomas Warmstry wrote a small book recounting his conversion (which was the result, Warmstry contends, of arguments that he and other Christian ministers put to Dandulo). Entitled The Baptized Turk, *Warmstry's account concludes with a description of Dandulo's baptism.*

When the day came, and the holy and solemn business of his Baptism was to be performed in Exeterhouse Chapel . . . a full and cheerful Congregation being there assembled, Mr. Gunning[17] officiated; and after the first part of the Service ended, the Convert came in in his Turkish Habit; and at his entrance into the Congregation desired several times that he might be admitted to the Baptism of the Christian Church, which being granted him, and these honorable and worthy persons, the young Countess of Dorse, the Lord George, and Mr. Philip Warwick, being Witnesses at his Baptism. He having made confession of the Christian faith in the Apostles' Creed; and having answered the questions concerning the Christian Covenant and Profession for himself, which have been usually answered by the Godfathers and Godmothers at the Baptism of Children, and being commended to God's Grace and Mercy in the prayers of the Congregation, with such alterations as were necessary for the extraordinary case, he being stripped of his Garment to his Waste, received his Baptism upon his knees with great humility, and was named Philip. . . . In the afternoon of the same day he came in another Habit, after the English fashion (which was charitably provided for him by reverend Doctor Bernard of Gray's Inn) and then Mr. Gunning preached a learned Sermon. . . . And so the comfortable solemnity of that happy day was ended. Our new Convert having since declared that he found extraordinary joy and solace in his soul at the time of his Baptism.

To Consider

1. Based on these two passages, what, besides simply assenting to the doctrines of Islam or Christianity, was required of a convert?

2. What explicit or implicit obstacles to conversion—other than simple lack of belief in the other religion—must have inhibited conversion?

3. What in these accounts might have made conversion seem attractive?

---

16. A garbled version of the Islamic profession of faith: "La ilah illa Alla wa-Muhammad rasu-luhu." (There is no god but God and Muhammad is his prophet.)

17. Another of the Christian clergymen involved in Dandulo's conversion.

Sources

a. Graf, Tobias P. *The Sultan's Renegades: Christian-European Converts to Islam and the Making of the Ottoman Elite, 1575–1610.* Oxford: Oxford University Press, 2017. Pp. 60–61. Reproduced with permission of The Licensor through PLSclear.

b. Warmstry, Thomas. *The baptized Turk, or, A narrative of the happy conversion of Signior Rigep Dandulo, the onely son of a silk merchant in the Isle of Tzio, from the delusions of that great impostor Mahomet, unto the Christian religion and of his admission unto baptism by Mr. Gunning at Excester-house Chappel the 8th of Novemb., 1657.* London: J. Willliams, T. Garthwait, and Henry Marsh, 1658. Pp. 138–41. Reproduced with permission of The Licensor through PLSclear.

13.4 SIXTEENTH-CENTURY LATIN-CHRISTIAN VIEWS OF ISLAMIC SCIENCE AND MEDICINE

The Scientific Revolution is usually thought to begin with the publication in 1543 of Nicolaus Copernicus's *On the Revolutions of the Heavenly Orbs,* which argued persuasively for a heliocentric ("sun-centered") cosmos as opposed to the ancient and medieval earth-centered view, and to have ended with Isaac Newton's 1687 publication of his *Mathematical Principles of Natural Philosophy,* which demonstrated the basic principles of motion of all kinds, whether the flight of a baseball or orbit of the moon. Both these works, and many other scientific breakthroughs, made utterly clear that when it came to physics, at least, Aristotle had been thoroughly wrong. There is no question, moreover, that this was an overwhelmingly Latin European movement (bearing in mind, of course, that the Tusi couple described by Nasir al-Din Al-Tusi[18] somehow wound up precisely in Copernicus's great work), and it certainly sent European science off in a very different direction than the rest of the Mediterranean largely continued on, and is responsible for Europe and so-called Western civilization's great leap forward in technological and scientific prowess in the ensuing centuries. It is usually also characterized as involving a quick abandonment of the Greek and Arabo-Islamic science that had predominated in the medieval Mediterranean. Contemporary Europeans, however, did not necessarily see it that way. For one thing there were important areas of science such as medicine to which the Scientific Revolution brought no meaningful changes. As a result, many Europeans continued to have a very high opinion indeed of Islamic medicine, as the following two passages make clear.

a. From Foresti da Bergamo's *Supplementum Chronicarum*
Latin • 1483 CE • Bergamo, Italy

Foresti da Bergamo (1434–1520) was a Christian monk and historian who must have had a notable interest in medicine, for in his Supplement of the Chronicles, *which was meant to update the*

---

18. Nasir al-Din al-Tusi (1201–1274) was a Persian polymath and perhaps the greatest astronomer of the thirteenth century. He developed the so-called Tusi couple to account for the periodic retrograde ("backward") motion of the planets, something that the medieval understanding of the cosmos considered them to have.

standard universal chronicles of his day, he included short biographies of eleven Arab-Muslims who happened to be physicians. In the following passage, for example, he treats Ibn Rushd (Averroes) and Ibn Sina (Avicenna).

Averroes the physician, entitled "the commentator," a most renowned philosopher, flourished in Córdoba, the Spanish city, in this period [i.e., around 1149], as can be inferred from his book *On the Heavens.* He wrote so excellently on all the books of Aristotle that he deserved the title "the commentator." Further, he composed the books *On the Substance of the Orb* and *On the Sects,* and he compiled a beautiful book on medicine and on theriac[19] and on floods and many other books. For he was the rival and utmost enemy of the physician Avicenna.

Avicenna of Seville, the most famous of all physicians, a man of the greatest prudence, about whose life there is almost nothing certain, was most famous in these times in the entire world. The physicians Mesue and Avenzoar call him "Aboalim," whereas the ordinary people say that he was the king of Bythinia [in Asia Minor], and they relate that Avicenna was poisoned by the physician Averroes, but killed Averroes before he died. Since Avicenna was most learned in all disciplines, he wrote a most excellent book [i.e., *The Cure*], in which he wanted to cover the entire logic and the entire natural philosophy in many volumes; he then most accurately discussed metaphysics. After he had seen the writings of other physicians in Arabic and of all physicians in general, he discussed—in a more perspicuous and clearer way than all other physicians—the entire medicine in five books [i.e., *The Canon of Medicine*]. . . . He also wrote *On the Powers of the Heart, On Theriac, On Floods,* and also produced a book of songs.[20] Also, one ascribes to him *On Alchemy* dedicated to Assem the philosopher, and a book on colics.

b. From Nicolas de Nicolay's *The Navigations, Peregrinations, and Voyages*
French • 1576 CE • France

Nicolas de Nicolay (1517–1583), the French adventurer and geographer, traveled to Istanbul in 1551 with the French ambassador to the Ottoman court, and then wrote extensively about his experiences in the land of the Turks. The following is his description of medicine at the Ottoman court.

In Turkey and principally at Constantinople, are found diverse physicians professing the art of physic,[21] and exercising the practice thereof, but a greater number of the Jews than Turks, amongst the which are many that are skilled in theorica,[22] and experimented[23] in practice, and the reason wherefore in this art they do commonly exceed all other nations is the

---

19. Theriac is a medical compound used from the ancient Greeks on to treat a variety of illnesses.

20. This seems to refer to Ibn Sina's *Poem on Medicine.* For an excerpt, see chapter 9 above.

21. I.e., medicine.

22. I.e., theoretical medicine.

23. I.e., experienced.

knowledge which they have in the language and letters, Greek, Arabian, Chaldee[24] and Hebrew, in which languages . . . have written the principal authors of physic and natural philosophy and astronomy, being the sciences meet and necessary for those that study physic. Besides the common physicians . . . the great lord[25] hath his own proper and ordinary [physicians], waged with great stipends . . . whereof part are Turks and part Jews. He which in the time I was in [the] Levant, had the first dignity and authority amongst the order of physicians was of nation an Hebrew called Amon,[26] of age about sixty years, a personage of great authority, and much esteemed as well for his goods, knowledge, and renown.

To Consider

1. Foresti da Bergamo was misinformed about certain aspects of Ibn Rushd's and Ibn Sina's lives—the latter was from Persia, not Spain; not being contemporaries, neither could have plotted to murder the other—but he knew a lot about them. What is his general estimation of them as thinkers?

2. Nicolas de Nicolay was working from direct observation. What are his views of medicine as practiced in the Ottoman capital?

3. What does all this suggest about what these Europeans thought about their own scientific tradition, even in the midst of the Scientific Revolution?

Sources

a. Hasse, Dag Nikolaus. *Success and Suppression: Arabic Sciences and Philosophy in the Renaissance.* I Tatti Studies in Italian Renaissance History. Cambridge, MA: Harvard University Press, 2016. Pp. 32, 35. Harvard University Press, Copyright © 2016 by the President and Fellows of Harvard College. Used by permission. All rights reserved.
b. Nicolas de Nicolay. *The Nauigations, Peregrinations and Voyages, Made into Turkie by Nicholas Nicholay Daulphinois, Lord of Arfeuile, Chamberlaine and Geographer Ordinarie to the King of Fraunce . . . Translated out of the French by T. Washington the younger.* London: Thomas Dawson for John Stell, 1585. Pp. 92–94. Reproduced with permission of The Licensor through PLSclear.

13.5 BUILDING AND FIRING THE BOMBARDS

No one in the Mediterranean invented gunpowder. Chinese scientists had done that earlier in the Middle Ages. Nor was the Mediterranean the first place that gunpowder weapons were used, since invading Mongols of the thirteenth century had used them well before they were embraced in regions around the Sea in the Middle. But the Mediterranean became an arena in which they were used especially ferociously in the late Middle Ages and early modern

---

24. I.e., Aramaic.
25. That is, the Ottoman sultan.
26. I.e., Moses Hamon (1490–1567), a Jewish physician born in Spain.

period, first by Christian Europeans, and soon after by the Ottomans. The development of gunpowder weapons introduced a decisive change to military tactics and strategy, one that ushered in the vastly destructive capacities of modern warfare. Though the Ottomans learned the technology of constructing such weapons from Latin Europe, they became the Mediterranean's leader in designing and building them, especially the enormous cannons called "Bombards," such as the so-called Dardanalles Gun built in 1464 and fully seventeen feet long and weighing almost seventeen tons. The following passages describe the construction and use of these monster guns.

a. From the *Book of Travels* by Evliya Çelebi
Turkish • 17ᵗʰ century • Istanbul

Evliya Çelebi (1611–1682), a well-educated Turk whose parents were attached to the Ottoman court, traveled throughout Ottoman lands and adjoining regions and wrote about much of what he saw in his vast (ten-volume) Book of Travels. *In this passage he describes the manufacture of a bombard.*

On the day when cannon are to be cast, the masters, foremen and founders, together with the Grand Master of the Artillery, the Chief Overseer, Imam, Muezzin and timekeeper, all assemble and to the cries of "Allah! Allah!" the wood is thrown into the furnaces. After these have been heated for twenty-four hours, the founders and stokers strip naked, wearing nothing but their slippers, an odd kind of cap which leaves nothing but their eyes visible, and thick sleeves to protect the arms; for, after the fire has been alight in the furnaces twenty-four hours, no person can approach on account of the heat, save he be attired in the above manner. Whoever wishes to see a good picture of the fires of Hell should witness this sight. . . .

The Vezirs, the Mufti and Sheiks are summoned; only forty persons, besides the personnel of the foundry, are admitted all told. The rest of the attendants are shut out, because the [copper and tin],[27] when in fusion, will not suffer to be looked at by evil eyes. The masters then desire the Vezirs and sheiks who are seated on sofas at a great distance to repeat unceasingly the words, shovels throw several hundredweight of tin into the sea of molten brass, and the head-founder says to the Grand Vizier, Veziers and Sheiks: "Throw some gold and silver coins into the brazen sea as alms, in the name of the True Faith!" Poles as long as the yard of ships are used for mixing the gold and silver with the metal and are replaced as fast as consumed.

b. Excerpts from Greek and Latin Eyewitness Accounts of the Siege of Constantinople in 1453
From Doukas's Turco-Byzantine History *• Greek • late 15ᵗʰ century*

He yoked sixty oxen . . . to thirty wagons and they pulled it [the bombard] behind them. Next to the bombard there were two hundred men, on each side, to pull and steady it so that it

---

27. The bombards were made of bronze, an alloy of copper and tin.

would not slip from its carriage. Fifty builders to construct bridges over uneven ground preceded the wagons. Two hundred laborers accompanied them.

From Michael Kritovoulos's History • *Greek • late 15th century*

Then they turned the [bombard] toward its target; they stabilized it by taking certain engineering measures and calculations. They then positioned it against the target and placed beams under it that were arranged carefully together and further added, to weigh it down, very large rocks. They secured it on top, bottom, behind, and from every side so that it would not slip from its spot and miss its target by the force of the explosion and the momentum of the projectile.

From Antonio Ivani da Sarzana's Assault of Constantinople •
Latin • late 15th century

The next biggest cannons, after that wonderfully large one, were thirty-six bronze bombards, which the [sultan] deployed to destroy the walls. They heavily bombarded the wall, without a respite, for ten days and turned it to ruins; in many places they razed it.

From Giacomo Tetaldi's Information . . . Regarding the Taking of
Constantinople by the Turkish Emperor . . . • *Latin • late 15th century [?]*

In addition . . . there were also in the same place ten or twelve cannon firing [missiles] weighing twelve hundred and eight pounds. Every day stone projectiles were readied for firing, eighty or one hundred. And this went on without respite for fifty days.

From a Letter from Cardinal Isidore to Cardinal Bessarion • Latin • July 6, 1453

Although the thickness and strength of the walls [of Constantinople] could resist all of the smaller [bombards], the walls proved unable to endure the might of those three [large bombards] that maintained incessant, constant bombardment: with the second strike a part of the walls collapsed and was destroyed together with the towers themselves. . . . At the dawn's early light of the twenty-ninth day of last May . . . the Turks launched their attack and assault, concentrating on the sector of Saint Romanos which had been practically demolished [by the bombards]. In those parts the assault against the walls was particularly easy, because, as I have stated, it was almost destroyed by the missiles of the bombards.

To Consider

1. What kinds of engineering and scientific expertise were necessary for forging and firing a bombard?

2. What medieval Mediterranean economic, social, and political developments were necessary to create such enormous weapons and use them accurately?

3.   What general impression do the Latin and Greek authors have of the engineering prowess of the Turks?

Sources

a. Crowley, Roger. *1453: The Holy War for Constantinople and the Clash of Islam and the West.* New York: Hyperion, 2005. P. 92.

b. Phillippides, Marios, and Walter K. Hanak. *The Siege of Constantinople in 1453: Historiography, Topography, and Military Studies.* Farnham: Ashgate, 2011. Pp. 476, 482–83, 486, 487, 490–91. Reproduced with permission of The Licensor through PLSclear.

FOURTEEN

Family, Gender, and Honor

The fundamental institution of the patriarchal Mediterranean family was marriage, which perpetuated prescribed gender roles at the same time as it was shaped by them. Neither the institution nor the norms it upheld remained static over the 650–1650 period, but there was considerable consistency. While Muslim, Christian, and Jewish marriage contracts differed in their specific provisions and in the legal and economic protections they afforded wives and daughters, within all three religious communities the honor of the family in local society hinged to a significant extent on the chastity of its female members and on the readiness of its men to defend family honor, sometimes violently. Social custom and law combined to limit the activities of women outside the home and without the supervision of male relatives. Women nonetheless carved out important roles in economic, political, and religious spheres dominated by men.

The readings in this chapter deal mostly with the activities of women in patriarchal societies and with the institutions that structured their lives. We explore Jewish, Muslim, and Christian marriage contracts and negotiations and the roles and responsibilities of women and men; the diverse economic pursuits of women of all three faiths both inside and outside the home; the exercise of political power by royal women in Byzantine, Muslim, and Latin-Christian realms; women expressing their intense spirituality as Islamic mystics, Catholic nuns, and participants in a Jewish messianic movement; and the penalties that Jewish, Christian, and Muslim authorities imposed on men and women for sexual transgressions, in the interests of preserving family honor and social stability.

14.1 CONTRACTING MARRIAGE

In all three religious communities, marriage was a complicated affair involving the material interests of the bride and groom and their families at least as much as the couple's emotions. Marriage contracts thus recorded the assets that each party brought to the marriage while looking toward the couple's future life together through the provision of legal safeguards, especially for the bride. The first reading is a fragmentary Jewish marriage contract written in Tyre (Lebanon) in 1079. The city housed a large Jewish community and the Palestinian (Talmudic) Academy, which had moved there after the Seljuqs captured Jerusalem in 1073. The second reading, from a ninth-century Egyptian marriage contract, consists of specific clauses inserted at a Muslim bride's request. The third reading, dating from thirteenth-century Egypt, is from the marriage contract of a Muslim widow. The fourth reading comes from the letters of a prominent Florentine widow, Alessandra Strozzi (1407–1471), written to her son Filippo regarding her ultimately unsuccessful efforts to arrange a marriage for him while he was in political exile in Naples.

a. Jewish Marriage Contract
Aramaic • 1079 CE • Tyre

Halfon b. [ben] Aaron . . . came and said, intentionally and willingly [that he would, by his own choice, take as his wife Ghaliya ("Precious"), daughter of Musafir] . . . in the manner of Jewish men, who nourish, sustain . . . and honor their wives faithfully. And this Ghaliya . . . listened to him and consented to be married to him and to esteem and honor him, to attend and to serve [him in the manner of] respectable women, the daughters of Israel, who esteem, honor, attend, and serve their husbands in purity and cleanness. This Ghaliya appointed her brother, Halfon b. [ben] Musafir, to be her agent for the receipt of her *qiddush* [betrothal gift] from the hands of this Halfon b. [ben] Aaron. And she willingly consented to all he [her brother] does concerning her match and what he stipulates in behalf of her and as an obligation upon her. . . . The *mohar* [bridewealth or dower] that this Halfon, the groom, set for this Ghaliya, the bride, is twelve dinars. Two dinars he gave as a first payment . . . and there remain incumbent upon him ten perfect, weighed dinars . . . delayed as a debt upon him. . . . She has no right to claim of them [the ten remaining dinars] . . . as long as he is alive and she is under his jurisdiction and he fulfills her three needs.[1] But if he hates her without any misconduct [on her part] and does not fulfill her three needs, he shall pay to her the balance of her *mohar*, of twelve dinars, and release her with a bill of divorce. And these are what she brought with her . . . from the house of her fathers [as her dowry; items of jewelry, clothing, and furniture are listed]. . . . The sum total is 16 dinars and 1/2 dinar and 1/4 dinar.[2] And they are for her and her son after her. And if she passes away without leaving sons or daughters by him, what remains will be divided into two equal portions. One portion will be acquired by her husband, and the other portion will return to the house of her fathers.

---

1. Food, clothing, and sexual intimacy.
2. The small bridewealth and dowry indicate that the couple was of modest means.

b. A Muslim Bride's Concerns
Arabic • 892 CE • Ashmun, Egypt

Ishaq b. [ibn] Sirri [the groom] stipulated that if he were to marry another woman, Muslim or non-Muslim, control of her [the new wife's] fate would be in the hands of his bride Hindiyya bint Ishaq: she [Hindiyya] can divorce [the new wife] from him any time she wished and he would have to abide by it . . . and he would not deter her from her family's [company] or stop her family from [visiting] her.

c. Marriage of a Muslim Widow
Arabic • 13ᵗʰ century • Cairo

The learned jurist [and Qur'an] reciter Najm al-Din . . ., son of the jurist Burhan al-Din . . ., married the woman al-Kamil, daughter of Nusayr, who was previously married to 'Ali b. [ibn] Ja'far, who consummated the marriage [and] then died over nine months ago; her *'idda* [waiting period] from him being completed four months and ten days ago and she did not marry after him. He [Najm al-Din] married her and dowered her . . . a total of 500 dirhams . . ., the *hal* [advanced amount] being 100 dirhams and 400 dirhams, delayed, is due her from him in yearly installments, 40 dirhams [per year]. . . . He has to fear God Almighty in her regard, treat her well, and live with her in kindness as God ordered in His Holy Book and according to the Sunna of our master Muhammad. . . . He has due to him from her an extra degree of the same [kindness and good treatment] as she has due to her from him. . . . Her full brother . . . was delegated to marry her and transact the marriage contract . . . as per her permission and consent in the presence of witnesses.

d. Failed Marriage Negotiations
Italian • 1464–1465 CE • Florence

[April 20, 1464] Concerning the matter of a wife [for Filippo], it appears that if Francesco di Messer Guglielmino Tanagli wishes to give his daughter, that it would be a fine marriage. . . . Now I will speak with Marco [Parenti, Alessandra's son-in-law], to see if there are other prospects that would be better, and if there are none, then we will learn if he wishes to give her [in marriage]. . . . Francesco Tanagli has a good reputation, and he has held office, not the highest, but he still has been in office. You may ask: "Why should he give her to someone in exile?" There are three reasons. First, there aren't many young men of good family who have both virtue and property. Secondly, she has only a small dowry, 1,000 florins, which is the dowry of an artisan. . . . Third, I believe that he will give her away, because he has a large family and he will need help to settle them. . . .

[July 26, 1465] He [Francesco Tanagli] invited Marco to his house and he called the girl down. . . . Marco said that she was attractive and that she appeared to be suitable. We have information that she is affable and competent. She is responsible for a large family (there are twelve children, six boys and six girls), and the mother is always pregnant and isn't very competent. . . .

[August 31] We [Alessandra and Marco Parenti] decided that he [Marco] should say something to the father and give him a little hope, but not so much that we couldn't withdraw, and find out from him the amount of the dowry. . . .

[September 13] Marco came to me and said he had met with Francesco Tanagli, who had spoken coldly, so that I understand that he had changed his mind. . . . And he [Francesco] says that it would be a serious matter to send his daughter so far away [to Naples], and to a house that might be described as a hotel. [Filippo eventually married another woman in 1466.]

To Consider

1. What legal and financial protections did the Jewish and Muslim marriage contracts afford brides, and what sort of contractual provisions would have left the widow Alessandra Strozzi in a position to maintain a household and confidently seek suitable brides for her son Filippo?

2. What social, economic, and political considerations shaped marriage negotiations between the Strozzi and Tanagli families?

3. Explain the roles and interests, both immediate and long-term, that fathers and brothers had in the marriages of their daughters and sisters.

Sources

a. Friedman, Mordechai A. *Jewish Marriage in Palestine: A Cairo Geniza Study.* 2 vols. Tel Aviv: Jewish Theological Seminary of America, 1981. Vol. 2, pp. 130–40.
b–c. El-Azhary Sonbol, Amira. "A History of Marriage Contracts in Egypt." In *The Islamic Marriage Contract: Case Studies in Islamic Family Law,* ed. Asifa Quraishi and Frank E. Vogel. Cambridge, MA: Harvard University Press, 2008. Pp. 94–96.
d. Brucker, Gene, ed. *The Society of Renaissance Florence: A Documentary Study.* New York: Harper and Row, 1971. Pp. 37–40.

14.2 WOMEN IN THE ECONOMY

Beyond their inestimable contribution through running households and raising children, women had varied economic roles. Women from poor families labored as domestics for wealthier ones, sometimes moving to cities at a young age for this work. Teresa, whose marriage contract is excerpted in the first reading, was sent at age twelve to Valencia. Women played key roles in Mediterranean textile industries, whether spinning and embroidering for wages at home, like Sitt al-'Arab, whose husband Abu Shama, a Syrian Muslim scholar, praises in verse in the second reading, or doing such work in artisan guilds in European cities, at least until the fifteenth century, when guilds began to exclude women. But women remained a source of low-skilled, cheap labor, as the third reading, a sixteenth-century description of women's functions in Venice's silk industry, suggests. In the Muslim world, Muslim wives, and Jewish ones influenced by local custom, used their earnings, or other assets, to lend money at interest, as shown in the fourth reading, a ruling of Rabbi David Abi Zimra from Ottoman Cairo. In Christian realms, however, Jewish women often had to wait until widowhood to enjoy this degree of economic agency, as seen in the fifth reading, a notarized contract from Catalonia. The last two readings, both Italian but indicative of widespread patterns, treat women's occupations that addressed the needs of other women: midwife, described by the physician Scipione Mercurio; and wet nurse, normally the work of poor women hired by affluent families to suckle their own infants, as a Florentine father recorded in his account book.

a. Domestic Service
Catalan • 1429 CE • Valencia

I Teresa, daughter of Joan Dalarit, shieldmaker of the town of Sogorb, with the will of my father and of Francesc Oviet, ropemaker of the city of Valencia, and his wife Maria, in contemplation of the marriage between myself and you, Tomas Dauder, barber of Valencia, I give and concede to you Tomas for my dowry 40 pounds of Valencian money. Namely, 20 pounds that was given to me by Francesc Oviet and his wife Maria as payment for my work as a domestic servant. And 10 pounds that was given to me by my father Joan which he promised for marriage. The remaining 10 pounds of these 40 pounds will be given by Francesc Oviet in his last will and testament.

b. Wage Labor of a Muslim Wife
Arabic • 1257–1258 CE • Damascus

She always attends to household chores
despite her youth she shies away from nothing
tiraz[3] embroidery, needlework with golden threads
cutting cloth, sewing and spinning
She moves from this to that and from that to this
not to mention the cleaning, the cooking and the washing.

c. Silk Industry
Italian • 1586 CE • Venice

The silk is extracted from the cocoons placed in a cauldron on top of a stove, and rolled up on a sort of scraper, and then is sent to the carder, who combs it with combs . . . and then to the mistresses, who double the strands and the twists, and the reels and spindles, and putting it on the reels, both double and wind it. Then it goes to . . . the male spinner . . . and once spun it returns to the women's hands, who double it again on the reels, and it returns to the spinner to be twisted. It then goes to the dyer, after the merchant has seen it . . . and the dyer . . . dyes it a particular color. It returns to the merchant, who puts it in the winding spools . . . with which they stretch it well, and make it appear lustrous and polished.

---

3. Luxury textiles embroidered with Arabic script and decorated with complex patterns.

And then it goes back to the mistresses, who treat it according to the instructions of the weaver.

d. Wage Labor and Lending of a Jewish Wife
Hebrew • ca. 1517–1557 CE • Cairo

Concerning the custom in Egypt, whereby the husband stipulates [in a marriage agreement] that the wife's handiwork[4] belongs to her, and that he is responsible to pay her a yearly clothing allowance: Let us suppose that the wife is a good worker, and does not use up all her clothing allowance, but puts money aside, and becomes a money-lender, lending money to gentiles [Muslims or Christians] for interest, can the husband claim the profits from the use of the money? [Answer:] The husband has no grounds for such a claim since . . . he has already waived any claim to her handiwork. . . . Moreover, since it is the custom here for a woman to use her earnings to help relatives or marry off daughters, or in any other way she sees fit, and since the marriage contract stipulates that her handiwork is hers, the husband, by marrying her, automatically endorses this custom.

e. Loan of a Jewish Widow
Latin • 1395 CE • Girona

I Astrugona, widow of Astruch Lobell, Jew of Girona, acknowledge that you, Pere de Puig, of the parish of Saint Leocadia, paid me and that I have received from you . . . 7 pounds and 10 solidos of the money of Barcelona from that debt of 16 pounds and 10 solidos for which you obligated yourself for a certain reason [to pay] me in an instrument [notarized contract] in the possession of Pere de Pont, notary of Girona.[5]

f. Midwife
Italian • 1596 CE • Lendinara, Duchy of Venice

The wise and prudent midwife is as necessary to pregnant women as the good physician, in fact more so, because, if he helps with advice, she helps both with advice and her hands. . . .

The good midwife must be very skilled and experienced, and have safely helped at many births. She should not, however, be so old as to have problems with her eyesight or with weak and trembling hands. If she is, great problems may ensue, since in difficult deliveries she will need great strength to extract the baby. . . .

She must also be aware and very careful to know when the birth is close, distinguishing the real labor pains from other pains, and be ready to place the pregnant woman on the bed or on the birthing chair. . . . She should never leave the pregnant woman either by day or

---

4. That is, her earnings from her spinning, sewing, or embroidery.

5. The reason for Pere de Puig's debt to Astrugona is purposely vague because the royal authorities increasingly frowned upon interest-bearing Jewish loans. Jewish lenders would have been especially cautious in the years following the anti-Jewish violence of 1391.

night, because labor pains may start while she is not there, the waters may break and the delivery begin, and precious time may be wasted while the midwife is sent for. . . .

The good midwife should always have an assistant, not only as an apprentice, to be well-instructed in this most important practice, but also because in all circumstances [the assistant] should be ready to help as necessary, for example handing over oils or warm grease, towels, scissors and thread to cut the umbilical cord . . . and other such things.

g. Wet Nurse
Italian • 1460–1461 CE • Florence

I record how . . . on 3 December I gave my daughter Giovanna to be breastfed with Monna Orsina, the wife of the shoemaker Michele de Domenico . . . at a salary of 5 *lire* per month, if she gives good and healthy milk and looks after her with all the care reasonably required, and in the event anything proves unsatisfactory or that Monna Orsina gets pregnant or anything else we must retain part of our money, following reasonable usage. . . .

On March 8 . . . 25 *lire* for a green dress with sleeves of purple cloth I bought for the said Monna Orsina.

To Consider

1. What factors limited the roles that women might play, and which ones gave them greater economic opportunities?

2. How did women's economic activities affect relations between women from different social and economic backgrounds?

3. In what ways did women's economic activities have the potential to subvert the prescribed patriarchal order?

Sources

a. Wessell Lightfoot, Dana. *Women, Dowries, and Agency: Marriage in Fifteenth-Century Valencia.* Manchester: Manchester University Press, 2013. P. 196. Reproduced with permission of The Licensor through PLSclear.

b. Rapoport, Yosef. *Marriage, Money, and Divorce in Medieval Islamic Society.* Cambridge: Cambridge University Press, 2005. P. 31. Reproduced with permission of The Licensor through PLSclear.

c, f–g. Rogers, Mary, and Paola Tinagli, eds. *Women in Italy, 1350–1650: Ideals and Realities; A Sourcebook.* Manchester: Manchester University Press, 2005. Pp. 176–77, 261–62, 269. Reproduced with permission of The Licensor through PLSclear.

d. Lamdan, Ruth. *A Separate People: Jewish Women in Palestine, Syria, and Egypt in the Sixteenth Century.* Leiden: Brill, 2000. P. 124. Reproduced with permission of The Licensor through PLSclear.

e. Arxiu Historic de Girona, G5: 4, folio 15v. The editors thank Alexandra Guerson and Dana Wessell Lightfoot for providing access to a copy of this document.

14.3 WOMEN IN POWER

The patriarchal societies of the premodern Mediterranean discouraged women from openly participating in politics, though royal women still exerted considerable political influence through the various roles they played in relation to the males of their family. Compared to Muslim lands, where female political power rarely acquired a formal, public dimension, in Christian domains the power of royal women was more overt. In the Latin West, some queens ruled in their own right. In the first source, the chronicler Theophanes, an opponent of iconoclasm, describes the Byzantine empress Irene's (797–802) initial assertion of authority as regent for her young son Constantine VI (780–797) following the death of her husband, Leo IV (775–780), and her later efforts in 786–787 to restore icon veneration. After having her son blinded in 797, Irene ruled independently until nobles deposed her in 802. The Shiʻi Fatimid princess Sitt al-Mulk, "Lady of the Kingdom" (1021–1023), was the sister of the caliph al-Hakim (996–1021) and regent for his son al-Zahir (1021–1036). The second and third readings, from the chronicles of the Sunni historians Ibn al-Qalanisi and Ibn al-Athir, focus on her alleged role in engineering her brother's assassination, a charge still disputed among modern historians. Until her death Sitt al-Mulk ruled the Fatimid realm, correcting the oppressive policies of her brother toward religious minorities and women, improving relations with the Byzantine Empire, and restoring order in Fatimid Syria. The final two readings, penned by an anonymous chronicler and by the official royal chronicler Hernando del Pulgar, concern Isabel I of Castile (1474–1504), whose marriage to Fernando of Aragon (1479–1516) laid the foundations for the modern state of Spain. Though the couple was reputed to have governed in harmony, legally and institutionally Castile was Isabel's kingdom just as Aragon was her husband's. The two readings address Isabel's role in the administration of justice. Pulgar's viewpoint is more ambiguous, for though his chronicle was propagandistic, it could also be critical. Here he presents a speech supposedly made by a bishop to the queen in 1477, advising her how best to judge lawbreakers in Seville.

a. Empress Irene
Greek • 810–815 CE • Western Anatolia

In this year [780] ... God unexpectedly entrusted the rule to the most pious Irene and her son Constantine, so He could work a miracle through a widow-woman and an orphan child. By this means He intended to destroy the boundless impiety against Him and His helpers, as well as His enemy Constantine's tyranny over all the churches.[6] ...

After Irene had ruled for forty days, some of the men in power formed a cabal. Because Irene's son was only ten years old, they wanted to summon the Caesar Nikephoros and make him Emperor.[7] When this plot was revealed ... many ... were arrested. Irene beat and tonsured them, then exiled them to various places. She tonsured her in-laws, the Caesars, ... and made them priests, then made them minister to the people at the festival of Christ's birth.[8] At that time she also regally went out in public with her son. ...

In this year [786] ... the Empress sent ... Staurakios [her eunuch general] to the thematic forces from the opposite shore which were then in Thrace. Staurakios persuaded them

---

6. Constantine V (741–775), who harshly enforced iconoclasm.
7. Nikephoros was the half brother of the deceased emperor Leo IV.
8. The clerical tonsure disqualified them from ruling.

to cooperate with her and oust from the city the impious army which the accursed Constantine had levied and trained.[9] . . . Irene sent the palace guards a message: "Give me your weapons, for I have no service for you." Since God had made them foolish, they gave them up. Then she loaded their families into ships and exiled them from the city, ordering each of them to return to his own native village.

Once she had officers loyal to her and her own army, in May [787] she again sent messages everywhere, summoning bishops to the Bithynian city of Nicaea for a synod there. Everyone assembled at Nicaea all through the summer; nor had Irene sent the men from Rome and the easterners away from the court, but rather kept them there by her.

b. Sitt al-Mulk: Ibn al-Qalanisi
Arabic • ca. 1160 CE • Damascus

They [political and military elites] complained to Sitt al-Mulk about the gross misconduct of al-Hakim's policies. She accepted what they said to her and rejected the dangerous policies of her brother. She promised and assured them that she would seek a way to stop his conduct and protect them. Sitt al-Mulk found no other way but to get rid of him by assassination. That was her only way to stop his harm.

c. Sitt al-Mulk Addresses Ibn Dawwas: Ibn al-Athir
Arabic • ca. 1231 CE • Mosul

"The Muslims have become intolerant of his [al-Hakim's] madness and deeds, and I fear their revolt, which will be the end of him and us as well. As a result, our dynasty will be uprooted. . . . "[10]

"We kill him to stop his evils, and install his son [her nephew al-Zahir], and distribute a large amount of money among the men and commanders for their loyalty. You will be his regent, and commander of the army. I'm only a woman who stays behind the curtain and seeks nothing but safe conduct."

d. Isabel I: Anonymous
Spanish • 1476 CE • Castile

The queen . . . had to implement these *Hermandades*, which she had created, and in a few days she made them so feared, as she desired, that justice then asserted its might in the realm, and bad men and robbers . . . began to flee or to live peacefully.[11] . . . Who could

---

9. These iconoclastic troops had frustrated Irene's attempt to convoke a church council in Constantinople earlier in 786 before she successfully gathered a council at Nicaea that restored icon veneration.

10. The addressee, Ibn Dawwas, was leader of the strongest Berber tribe in the Fatimid realm and an alleged conspirator. She reportedly later had him killed.

11. *Hermandades* were municipal brotherhoods that policed towns and upheld peace. Isabel, however, was not their creator; her brother, Enrique IV (1454–1474), had employed them.

believe such marvels? . . . For those who knew it never imagined that this remedy and redemption of Castile might take place in their lifetime.

e. Isabel I: Pulgar
Spanish • 1482–1492 CE • Castile (Toledo?)

With tears and cries that you see and hear, [the people] bow down before you and ask that you have the same pity for your subjects that our Lord has for all living beings, and that your royal heart have compassion for their pains, for their exiles, for their poverty, and for their anguish and travails, which they continually suffer, forsaking their homes for fear of your justice. Most excellent queen and lady: although your justice should be discharged upon those who transgress, it should not be with such great rigor as to close that praiseworthy dose of clemency that makes kings beloved—so beloved that they are of necessity feared— because no one loves his king who does not fear to annoy him. It is true, most excellent queen and lady, that our Lord uses justice as well as mercy, but he uses justice at times, and mercy always. . . . Most excellent queen, taking that gentle doctrine of our Savior and his good and holy kings upon yourself, you must temper your justice and spread your mercy throughout your land . . . and you will be merciful to the extent that you have compassion and pardon the poor people who call for and await your clemency with great anguish.

To Consider

1. Consider the various manifestations of women's political power. What religious and political traditions shaped them?

2. How did female rulers use their familial roles to acquire and legitimize their political power?

3. How did the male writers' biases shape their portrayal of women rulers, and what factors encouraged them to overcome their biases?

Sources

a. Theophanes the Confessor. *The Chronicle of Theophanes: An English Translation of Anni Mundi 6095–6305 (A.D. 602–813)*. Trans. Harry Turtledove. Philadelphia: University of Pennsylvania Press, 1982. Pp. 140, 146–47.

b–c. El-Azhari, Taef. *Queens, Eunuchs, and Concubines in Islamic History, 661–1257*. Edinburgh: Edinburgh University Press, 2019. Pp. 202–3. Reproduced with permission of The Licensor through PLSclear.

d–e. Boruchoff, David A. "Historiography with License: Isabel, the Catholic Monarch, and the Kingdom of God." In *Isabel la Católica, Queen of Castile: Critical Essays*, ed. David A. Boruchoff. New York: Palgrave Macmillan, 2003. Pp. 241–42, 247.

14.4 WOMEN'S SPIRITUALITY

The manner in which Mediterranean women expressed their spirituality and even the places in which they chose to do it were shaped by the institutions of their own religion, their social and economic circumstances, and patriarchy. The first reading comes from an account of the deeds of the Muslim mystic Rabi'a al-'Adawiyya of Basra (ca. 714–801). The daughter of a poor family who led a celibate, ascetic life, Rabi'a was renowned for her piety and inspired other mystics with her poetry stressing the absolute love of God. Farid al-Din 'Attar (1145- ca.1221/30), a Persian poet and hagiographer of Sufis, was the author. The second reading, taken from the necrology of Corpus Domini, a Dominican convent in Venice, was composed by Sister Bartolomea Riccoboni (1369–1440). It provides insight into why some women entered the convent. The third reading is the trial record of the family of the Converso Rodrigo Cifuentes, one of several Valencian Converso families whom papal inquisitors prosecuted for attempting to sail to Ottoman domains to await the coming of the Jewish messiah. The Ottoman conquest of Constantinople in 1453 had sparked a messianic movement among some Iberian Conversos and Jews. The passages below include the testimonies of anonymous female witnesses regarding their encounters with Cifuentes's daughters.

a. Rabi'a
Persian • early 13th century • Nishapur

Veiled with a special veil, hidden by the curtain of sincerity, burned up in love and longing, enamored of proximity [to God] and immolation, deputy of the virgin Mary, accepted among men, Rabi'a al-'Adawiyya. . . . If anyone asks why we [Farid al-Din] placed her memorial among the ranks of men, we reply that the Master of the Prophets . . . declares: *God does not regard your forms.* It is not a matter of form but of right intention. . . . When a woman is a man on the path of the Lord most high, she cannot be called a woman. . . .

It is related that Hasan[12] said to Rabi'a, "Do you long for a husband?"

She said, "The marriage knot can only tie one who exists. Where is existence here? I am not my own—I am his [God's] under the shadow of his command. You must ask permission from him."

"Rabi'a," he asked, "how did you attain this rank?"

"By losing in him everything I'd attained." . . .

She said, " . . . For thirty years now I have performed each prayer as though it would be my last. . . . I made myself independent of creatures, so cut off, that when day broke, for fear that the created world would distract me, I prayed, 'O Lord, so distract me that no one will distract me from you'." . . .

It is related that a great man came to visit her. He saw her clothes in tatters. He said, "There are many people who would look after you if you would just give the word."

Rabi'a said, "I am ashamed to ask for things of this world from someone who has them on loan."

The great man said, "Behold the lofty aspirations of this weak woman! He [God] has brought her to such a height that she refuses to spend her time making requests."

---

12. Hasan of Basra (642–728), renowned Qur'anic scholar, theologian, and Sufi mystic.

b. Venetian Nuns
Italian • 1436–1440 CE • Venice

Sister Franceschina da Noale entered the convent seven days after it was enclosed, as a widowed lady forty-nine years old. During her marriage she lived in the world in a holy fashion and always wore a hair shirt under her velvet. When she was left a widow she dressed humbly in coarse cloth; and when this convent was built, moved by desire for greater perfection she came to the order, bringing with her a seven-year-old daughter. This blessed woman never meddled with her daughter, who was entrusted to the care of the [novice] mistress. Her own life was a constant round of prayers, vigils, flagellation, fasts, and other holy deeds, such that she fell ill and consumed that body, which did not have the appearance of a living thing. . . .

On November 25 of that same year [1423] died Sister Piera, a widowed woman who entered the convent at the age of thirty-eight and lived there for twenty-nine years. What, then, should I say of this blessed woman? My tongue is not able to describe her virtues. She was from Citta di Castello. She said that even when she was just a little girl she had a good understanding of God; she was married against her will, and she lived with her husband in the fear of God. When she was left a widow, she donned the habit of a penitent of Saint Dominic, to whom she was especially devoted. Having heard of this convent, she came to Venice with our father's permission and encouragement, and with great devotion she entered the convent. This blessed woman was adorned with all the virtues. She was poor in spirit, and she was satisfied with the barest minimum of temporal goods. . . . She was very humble and obedient and respectful toward everyone. She had such charity for all that she would have exposed herself to every danger in order to serve them, and they all called her mother. She tended all the sick women and washed all their filth. . . . She prayed tearfully for humankind, and when she heard that there was strife in the holy church or other wars, she would not leave her prayers except to eat or sleep. . . . She also prophesied the truth on many subjects. She saw many lovely visions, which were not written down on account of our negligence.

c. Converso Women
Catalan • 1464 CE • Valencia

The witness [also a Conversa] saw that Aldonça [daughter of Cifuentes] was cutting her finger and toenails and cleaning her body. The witness asked, "Why are you doing that?" Aldonça answered that since she had to fast and so that our Lord God would take and accept her fast, she cut her nails and purified her body. . . .

The witness was discussing with Angelina and [her sister] Aldonça certain Converso women who had left the present city [Valencia] to go to the Levant to become Jews. . . . [The sisters] said that the [women] went to those parts to become Jews, . . . that they were shown much honor [by the Ottomans] and that they were on beds covered in silk and that the husbands of those women served them; and the husbands wore outer garments of black silk . . . which signified that they were mourning those [Conversos] who did not go to those parts to become Jews . . . and save their souls. . . . And the said Angelina and Aldonça [tried to] persuade the said witness to go to those parts and become a Jew. . . .

Sperança [daughter of Cifuentes] told the witness [probably an Old Christian maidservant] that letters came from Constantinople, from which it was certain and true that the messiah was born. The witness asked, "What is this messiah?" Sperança answered that the messiah was a youth . . . who was on a mountain near Constantinople, like that mountain on which our Lord God gave the Law to Moses, and that no person could see him if he was not already a Jew and circumcised. . . .

Sperança [later] said to the witness, "The Gentiles [Christians] do not see us, for they are blind. They don't know that our Lord God has allowed us for some time to be subject to them, but now we will dominate them, for God has promised us that since we are going to those parts [the Levant], we will ride over them. Haven't you heard it said that Antichrist has to come (saying that the Turk is that one). For he will destroy the Christians' churches and make them stables for animals, and he will do much honor to the Jews and their synagogues and show reverence to all those who go to those parts and return to the good side [Judaism]."

To Consider

1. To what extent were the spiritual expressions of these women manifestations of their desire to escape their current circumstances?

2. Why were chastity and poverty so important for Rabi'a and the Venetian nuns, and why might they have been luxuries that the Converso women felt that they could not afford?

3. How did normative gender roles shape the spiritual life and hopes of these women?

Sources

a. 'Attar, Farid al-Din. *Farid ad-Din 'Attar's Memorial of God's Friends: Lives and Sayings of Sufis.* Trans. Paul Losensky. New York: Paulist Press, 2008. Pp. 97, 104, 108–9. Used with permission of Paulist Press. www.paulistpress.com.
b. Bornstein, Daniel, ed. and trans.. *Life and Death in a Venetian Convent: The Chronicle and Necrology of Corpus Domini, 1395–1436.* Chicago: University of Chicago Press, 2000. Pp. 72, 91–92. Republished with permission of University of Chicago Press. Permission conveyed through Copyright Clearance Center, Inc.
c. Meyerson, Mark D. *A Jewish Renaissance in Fifteenth-Century Spain.* Archivo Historico Nacional: Inquisition: legajo 545, no. 7: folio 15r-v. Princeton: Princeton University Press, 2004. Republished with permission of Princeton University Press. Permission conveyed through Copyright Clearance Center, Inc.

14.5 SEXUAL TRANSGRESSIONS AND THE LAW

In Mediterranean societies and families, anxieties about the sexual purity of wives, daughters, and sisters were pervasive and persistent, such that governments thought it imperative to limit and punish a wide range of sexual transgressions. In effect, authorities, both secular and religious, became key players in the local politics of honor and shame. The first reading is from the highly influential code of Talmudic law, the *Mishneh Torah*, composed by the great Jewish scholar Moses ben Maimon, or Maimonides (1138–1204). The next two readings come from laws issued by Emperor Frederick II of Sicily (1198–1250) in the *Constitutions of Melfi* and by King Alfonso X of Castile (1252–1284) in the *Siete Partidas*. The final reading consists of criminal laws from the secular code (*kanunname*) first compiled on the command of Sultan Bayezid II (1481–1512) at the end of the fifteenth century, but reaching its final form around 1540. However, the extent to which any of these laws was strictly enforced is unclear. Not all Jewish communities relied on Maimonides's code, and the ability of Jewish authorities to administer penalties varied from one realm to the next. Also, there were limits to the reach and consistency of the judicial systems of premodern Christian and Muslim rulers. The laws nonetheless reflect widespread social views that rulers and their people shared.

a. *Mishneh Torah*
Hebrew • 1170–1180 CE • Cairo

When a man seduces a virgin, he is fined 50 pieces of pure silver. . . . The same law applies if he rapes her. Payment of this fine is one of the Torah's positive commandments, as [Deuteronomy 22:29] states: "The man who raped her must give the maiden's father 50 silver pieces. . . .

The fine of 50 silver pieces represents merely the payment for the pleasure of sexual relations. In addition, a seducer is obligated to pay for the embarrassment and damages. . . .

A rapist, moreover, also pays for the pain [he caused the girl]. [A seducer is not required to make this payment,] because a girl who willingly engages in relations does not [suffer] pain. A girl who is raped does, as reflected by [Deuteronomy 22:29]: "because he violated her." . . .

The amount paid for embarrassment, damages and pain is not uniform. . . . How is the evaluation made? With regard to embarrassment, everything is dependent on the identity of the person who is embarrassed. . . . The embarrassment suffered by a girl of high repute from a family of known lineage cannot be compared to the embarrassment suffered by a poor, ignoble maiden. . . .

The three payments made because of seduction, and the four payments made because of rape are made to the girl's father, for all the monetary benefit that accrues during a girl's youth belongs to her father.

If her father is no longer alive . . . [these payments are made] to her.

b. *Constitutions of Melfi*
Latin • 1231 CE • Melfi

We order that the capital punishment which the statutes of the divine Augustuses sanctioned against those who rape virgins, widows, wives, or even engaged girls and against their accomplices and supporters should be observed inviolably. Those customs, which obtained in some parts of the Kingdom of Sicily until the present, by which those who raped a woman escape capital punishment by marrying her or by arranging for another to marry her, should not be permitted at all. . . .

We curtail the very evil and abhorrent ground for an accusation, which has prevailed until now to the serious expense of our subjects, whereby a woman who had not suffered the violence or injury of rape made accusations about some persons untruthfully. And thus the accused, for fear of the accusation which would be brought, . . . insofar as they were afraid of the contest of the law courts and the outcome of the affair, chose unequal marriages [to escape the rape charge by marrying the accusing woman]. . . . If any woman should in the future be convicted of such false calumny, she should know that she has been caught in the trap of death [capital punishment]. . . .

The penalty against adulterers who attack the wives of others must no longer be the sword. Rather we introduce the penalty of confiscation of their property if they have no legitimate children from the violated marriage or another. . . . But a woman must not be handed over to her husband who would rage against her until he killed her. Instead, the slitting of her nose . . . should pursue the vengeance of the violated marriage. But if her husband is unwilling to give her a punishment, we will not allow such a crime to go unpunished but will order her to be publicly flogged. . . .

If a husband catches his wife in the very act of adultery, he may kill both the adulterer and his wife, but without any further delay.

c. *Siete Partidas*
Spanish • ca. 1256–early 14th century • Castile

Adultery is an offense which a man knowingly commits by lying with a married woman, or one betrothed to another. . . . Wherefore the learned men of the ancients declared that, although a married man might lie with another woman who had a husband, his own wife could not accuse him before the secular judges on this account. . . . They consider this just for several reasons. First, because no injury or dishonor results to his own wife from adultery committed by a man with some other woman. Second, because from the adultery which his wife commits with another man her husband becomes dishonored through her receiving another into her bed, and, moreover, because through adultery committed by her great injury may result to her husband. For, if she should become pregnant by the man with whom she committed adultery, the child of another would become an heir along with his own children, which could not happen to a wife from the adultery which her husband commits with another woman; and, therefore, since the injury and dishonor are unequal, it is proper that the husband should have this advantage . . . and that she should not have the right to accuse him; and this was established by the ancient laws, although, according to the decrees of the Holy Church, it is not so.

d. Ottoman Law
Turkish • ca. 1499–1540 CE • Istanbul

If it is a married woman who commits fornication [*zina*, unlawful sexual intercourse], her husband shall pay the fine. If . . . her husband does not repudiate [her but] accepts [her] and he is rich, he shall pay 100 *akçe* [Ottoman coins] by way of a fine [imposed] on a [consenting] cuckold . . . ; if he is in average circumstances . . . 50 *akçe*; if he is poor, 40 or 30. . . .

A person who abducts a girl [or] boy or enters [another] person's house with malice, and a person who joins him [as an accomplice] for the purpose of abducting a woman or girl shall be castrated by way of punishment. . . .

If a person finds his wife somewhere committing fornication with [another] person [and] kills both of them together—provided he immediately calls people into his house and takes them to witness—the claims of the heirs of those killed shall not be heard in court. . . .

[A person] who abducts a girl or woman and forcibly marries her shall be forced to divorce [her] and shall be punished. . . .

If a woman is spoken ill of [as having secret and illicit relations] with a certain man and her husband divorces her, that ill-reputed woman shall not be married to that man. If a marriage has [nevertheless] been contracted [between them], the cadi [judge] shall immediately separate them by force and compulsion. . . .

If a woman or girl says to a person, "You have committed fornication with me," and the man denies [it], her words shall not be relied upon without [corroboration by] a witness. [The cadi] shall administer an oath to the man and [after the latter has sworn that he is innocent] shall chastise the woman or girl and a fine of one *akçe* shall be collected for every two strokes. . . .

Furthermore, if a person says to another, "You have committed fornication with my wife or my female slave" [and] he cannot prove [it], [the cadi] shall chastise [him], [but] no fine shall be collected. . . .

If a person falsely accuses [another] person of fornication, [the accused thereby] becoming liable to *hadd* [divinely sanctioned] punishment . . . if *hadd* is [inflicted], a fine of one *akçe* shall be collected for [every] three strokes.

To Consider

1. Why were governments so concerned to curtail and to penalize the sexual transgressions of their subjects? Would such penalties have been effective at preventing families from administering "private justice" to offenders?

2. To what extent do these laws take into account the emotions of the men and women involved in acts of illicit sexuality, and do they give modern historians a useful perspective on the emotional life of premodern people?

3. Though laws such as these were geared toward upholding a patriarchal social order, did they offer women effective protection or provide them with a means of escaping the designs of their families?

Sources

a. Maimonides, Moses. *Mishneh Torah: The Laws of a Virgin Maiden.* Trans. Rabbi Eliyahu Touger. New York: Moznaim Publishing, 1995. Pp. 154, 162–64, 170. Reproduced with permission of The Licensor through PLSclear.

b. *The Liber Augustalis, or Constitutions of Melfi, Promulgated by the Emperor Frederick II for the Kingdom of Sicily in 1231.* Trans. James M. Powell. Syracuse: Syracuse University Press, 1971. Pp. 24, 26, 145, 147. Reproduced with permission of The Licensor through PLSclear.
c. *Las Siete Partidas.* Trans. Samuel Parsons Scott. Chicago: Commerce Clearing House, 1931. Reprint. Philadelphia: University of Pennsylvania Press, 2001. Vol. 5, p. 1411. Reproduced with permission of The Licensor through PLSclear.
d. Heyd, Uriel. *Studies in Old Ottoman Criminal Law.* Oxford: Clarendon Press, 1973. Pp. 96–99, 101, 109. Reproduced with permission of The Licensor through PLSclear.

FIFTEEN

Mediterranean Economies and Societies in a Widening World

Patterns of economic and social change in the era 1350 –1650 were shaped in many ways by natural catastrophes. The huge death toll of the Black Death of 1346–1353 impacted local economies and worsened relations between peasants and lords and urban workers and their elite employers. Lower-class rebellion was widespread. Demographic recovery in the sixteenth century heightened productivity and profits for some but also increased poverty and hunger. Although governments responded by developing institutions of social welfare, they proved inadequate, especially in the face of the droughts and famines of the "little ice age" that began in the late sixteenth century. Through all this, Mediterranean commerce persisted and sometimes flourished, though imperial conquests altered some trade routes. Most consequential was the emergence after 1492 of a booming Atlantic economy, which gradually changed the place of the Mediterranean in the global economy and made northern European merchants the dominant players in the Middle Sea.

The readings for this chapter explore the response of Muslim and Christian cities to plague epidemics; the outbreaks of rural and urban rebellion in the decades following the Black Death; the efforts of private individuals and urban governments to meet the needs of the poor, the sick, and the hungry who migrated to cities in growing numbers; and the great unrest caused by the climatic changes of the "little ice age" and heavy royal taxation in the Ottoman and Spanish empires. Trade is also addressed through an examination of commercial agreements between the Mamluks and the Florentines in 1497 and the Ottomans and the Dutch in 1612, when northern European merchants began exercising their economic might.

15.1 RESPONSES TO THE PLAGUE

For nearly 400 years following the Black Death of 1346–1353, plague epidemics periodically decimated communities and created horrifying scenes, such as the one in Constantinople in 1467, described by the Greek chronicler Kritovoulos in the first reading. Governments responded with a variety of measures to limit the devastation of a disease the causes of which they did not properly understand. Some thought that the pestilence was carried in corrupted air—a "miasma"—and acted to limit the exposure of people to the infection. The second reading records quarantines imposed by the government of Ragusa (Dubrovnik) in 1377—perhaps the first of the kind—and 1527. Other authorities took steps to prevent the advent and spread of a disease that they believed was ultimately a matter of divine will. The third and fourth readings include measures of a more "spiritual" nature taken by Valencia's city council in 1383 and 1395 and by the Mamluk rulers of Cairo in 1438.

a. Constantinople
Greek • 1460s CE • Imbros

More than six hundred deaths a day occurred, a multitude greater than men could bury, for there were not men enough. For some, fearing the plague, fled and never came back, not even to care for their nearest relatives, but even turned away from them, although they appealed to them with pitiful lamentation, yet they abandoned the sick uncared for and the dead unburied. . . .

And the terrible fact was that each day the disease grew worse, spreading among all ages. . . . The City was emptied of its inhabitants, both citizens and foreigners. It had the appearance of a town devoid of all human beings. . . . And there was great hopelessness and unbearable grief, wailing and lamentation everywhere. Despair and hopelessness dominated the spirits of all. Belief in Providence vanished altogether.

b. Ragusa
Latin • 1377 CE • Ragusa

Gathered in the Major Council, . . . thirty-four Councillors voted in favor of the proposed measure, which stipulates that those who came from plague-infested areas shall not enter Dubrovnik [Ragusa] or its district unless they previously spend a month on the islet of Mrkan (St Mark) or in the town of Cavtat, for the purpose of disinfection.

Furthermore . . . the residents of Dubrovnik are strictly forbidden to visit those who arrive from plague-infested areas. . . . Those who dare bring food or any other necessities to the interned, without the permission of the officials designated for that function, will have to stay there in isolation for a month.

Latin • 1527 CE • Ragusa

If any person of whatever means and whichever social class, healthy or recovered, should enter someone's house, in which he or she did not stay before, without the permission of the gentlemen health officials, that person should be publicly lashed while being led through the whole city. . . .

Any person who should possess or keep items on consignment, anywhere and in any place, especially infected goods or items which had not been disinfected, should these items not be reported to the Health Office within two days, the accused who is in the city should be punished with three jerks of the rope and the items should be immediately burned. If such items cause someone's death, the owner of these items should be punished by hanging.

c. Valencia
Catalan • 1383 CE • Valencia

Considering that . . . already in the past few days some in the city have died from the illness of the plague and pestilential fever, according to the opinion and assertion of physicians, and that in such a case there may be nothing so suitable as seeking divine mercy and aid, the council . . . orders that for this reason devout processions and prayers, celebrations of masses and other meritorious works should be carried out. And that the aldermen and treasurer of the city's common fund should make a charitable distribution of 10,000 sous for the celebration of masses and for the shamefaced poor and beggars and other pious things.

Catalan • 1395 CE • Valencia

And, since it was proposed and discussed by some on the council who understand and believe that, among the other sins for which divine wrath sent the plague of general mortality that is currently in the city, was the continuing presence of pimps, loose women, proprietors of gambling dens and gamblers . . . as well as the foul swearing that the uncouth common people do by the unmentionable, diverse parts of the precious body of Jesus Christ and of the sacred Virgin, his mother, and of other saints . . . all the said inconvenient [persons and actions] were and should be prohibited by the strong, penal measures and statutes of the council . . . to be diligently and vigorously enforced by the criminal justice and his lieutenant.

d. Cairo
Arabic • early 15th century • Cairo

The Sultan asked the qadis [judges] and legal scholars if there were sins that God would punish by sending the plague. Some of the scholars answered that when fornication becomes usual among the people, they are hit by the plague and now the women were adorning themselves and were walking the streets day and night. Another scholar said that it would be best for the community to forbid women to go to the market places. . . . The Sultan favored the opinion that would not allow women to go out at all. He believed that this prohibition would put an end to the plague.

To Consider
    1.   For Mediterranean port cities, would the enforcement of quarantine laws such as those passed by the government of Ragusa in 1377 and 1527 have been an

effective means of preventing the entry or spread of the plague? Considering what we now know about the causes of the plague, what more effective measures could premodern cities have taken?

2. How did widely accepted notions of proper social and gender hierarchies shape ruling authorities' responses to the plague, and how did these responses serve to uphold the social and gender order?

3. If premodern people often viewed plague and other natural disasters as expressions of divine wrath, then how might the periodic outbreak of epidemics for centuries have affected their belief in God?

Sources

a. Kritovoulos, Michael. *History of Mehmed the Conqueror by Kritovoulos.* Trans. Charles T. Riggs. Princeton: Princeton University Press, 1954. Pp. 220–21.

b. Blazina Tomic, Zlata, and Vesna Blazina. *Expelling the Plague: The Health Office and the Implementation of Quarantine in Dubrovnik, 1377–1533.* Montreal: MQUP, 2015. Pp. 106–7, 200–201.

c. Rubio, Agustin. *Peste Negra, crisis y comportamientos sociales en la España del siglo XIV: La ciudad de Valencia (1348–1401).* Granada: Universidad de Granada, 1979. Pp. 122–23, 129.

d. Perho, Irmeli. "The Sultan and the Common People." *Studia Orientalia* 82 (1997): 150.

15.2 SOCIAL REBELLION

Repeated epidemics of plague caused economic turmoil, increased hardship, and intensified the discontent of the lower classes, moving some to take up arms to better their circumstances or even to overturn the social order. Such rebellions rarely effected lasting change. The first two readings concern revolts that Shaykh Bedreddin (1358–1416), a mystical revolutionary of mixed Muslim-Christian parentage, inspired against the Ottoman government. Both readings, written by the Muslim chronicler Şukrullah and his Greek-Christian counterpart Doukas, describe the activities of one of Bedreddin's disciples, Borkluçe Mustafa (d. 1416), in southwestern Anatolia. The third reading is an anonymous contemporary record of the initially successful uprising of the Ciompi in Florence in 1378. Artisans and laborers who had been excluded from the guild system and thus denied a political voice, the Ciompi had a role in government for only a few years. The fourth reading includes excerpts from the Sentence of Guadalupe of 1486, in which Fernando II of Aragon abolished serfdom in Catalonia after more than a century of peasant unrest.

a. Şukrullah
Persian • ca. 1460 CE • Constantinople

In the province of Aydin . . . an antinomian[1] [Borkluçe] rose up among the people. He called himself a sufi. Taking charge of the sufis, he gathered many around him. . . . He per-

---

1. An antinomian is someone who believes that moral laws need not be obeyed.

petrated some actions that were overtly against the *shari'a* of Muhammad. The sultan Mehmed sent . . . troops against him. . . . The sufis were crushed. Among the 4,000 sufis who regarded their chief [Borklüçe] as a prophet . . . were those who, although they recognized that one must worship only God, denied that Muhammad was the Messenger of God. Those who recognized Muhammad as the Messenger of God were not executed but granted freedom.

b. Doukas
Greek • ca. 1462 CE • Lesbos

There rose up among the Turks an ignorant peasant [Borklüçe]. . . . This man preached poverty to the Turks, and he urged them to hold everything, except women, in common: food, clothing, herds, and land. . . . Deceiving the peasants with this doctrine, he displayed a misleading friendship toward the Christians: he asserted that if a Turk says that Christians are impious, it is he himself who is showing his impiety. And all those who followed his way of thinking, when they met a Christian, they received him with friendship and honored him as if he were sent by God.

c. The Ciompi
Italian • 1378 CE • Florence

When the *popolo* [people] and the guildsmen had seized the [government] palace, they . . . said that, for the peace and repose of the city, they wanted certain things: . . . that the combers, carders, trimmers, washers, and other cloth workers would have their own [guild] consuls, and would no longer be subject to the Lana [Wool] guild [of affluent master artisans]; . . . that all outlaws and those who had been condemned by the Commune [government] . . . except rebels and traitors would be pardoned. Moreover, all penalties involving a loss of limb would be cancelled, and those who were condemned would pay a money fine. . . . Furthermore, for two years none of the poor people could be prosecuted for debts of 50 florins or less. . . .

The next morning the *popolo* brought the standard of justice from the palace and they marched, all armed, to the Plaza of the *Signoria* [Government], shouting: "Long live the *popolo minuto* [lower classes]!" . . . Then the *popolo* ordered the priors [city officials] to abandon the palace. . . . Then they decided to do everything necessary to fortify themselves and to liberate the *popolo minuto*. . . . Then [the *popolo*] decided to call other priors who would be good comrades and who would fill up the office of those priors who had been expelled. . . .

And this was done to give a part to more people, and so that each would be content, and each would have a share of the offices, and so that all of the citizens would be united. Thus poor men would have their due, for they have always borne the expenses [of government], and only the rich have profited.

d. Sentence of Guadalupe
Latin and Spanish • 1486 CE • Monastery of Santa María de Guadalupe

Since on behalf of the said [Catalan] peasants a great complaint has been made to Us [Fernando II] regarding the so-called six "bad customs" ["redemption" fees for being freed from the land, taxes on inheritance and marriage, fines for adultery], which, they say, the said [noble] lords unduly and unjustly . . . exact from them, forcing them through the sworn act of homage that they have made to them [to the lords, for possession of the lands they farm] . . . [and] considering that the said bad customs, because of the many and diverse abuses that stem from them, involve evident iniquity, which cannot be tolerated by Us without great sin and heavy conscience. . . . We therefore sentence, judge, and declare that the said six bad customs . . . can neither be demanded nor exacted from the said peasants or their descendants or their property; rather, through this our sentence we abolish them. . . . But . . . we declare that the said peasants are held and obligated to give and pay for each property [they hold and farm] 60 solidos in the currency of Barcelona. . . .

. . . We end and abolish the right and ability that the lords pretend to have to mistreat the said peasants, and if they [the lords] use it [the "right" to mistreat], the peasants can have recourse to Us and our officials, before whom the said lords may be obliged to appear, respond, and make compensation [to the peasants], but through this we do not intend to remove from the lords the civil jurisdiction they may have over the said peasants [that is, lords adjudicating law suits involving peasants in their own courts]. . . .

. . . We declare that the said peasants should have to make a sworn act of homage to their lords for their property as many times as the latter want, acknowledging that they hold from their lords their farmhouses and buildings with their lands . . . but without the burden of personal redemption and the other five bad customs. . . . And the peasants and their heirs, notwithstanding their act of homage, can leave . . . and abandon their farmhouses . . . and lands whenever they want and they can go freely wherever they want . . . nevertheless paying all that they owe to their lords [for rent or any debts incurred] until the day that they depart, and in this case the full, direct ownership [of the property] should be reaffirmed such that it is in the power of the lord to do with the farmhouse, buildings, or lands [what he or she wants]. . . .

. . . Since it is known to Us . . . and is notorious how . . . the peasants . . . putting aside all fear of God and of Us and our officials . . . have risen up in great number with arms [and] have made a public war in our Principality [Catalonia], entering royal towns and villages by force, killing and slitting the throats of many persons . . . of noble and of other social status, usurping our royal banner and, what is worse, in our royal name, occupying many [noble] fortresses and robbing them and holding them violently . . . [and] considering that there are among the said delinquents and criminals some who did not fear to be leaders [and] others who actually had a hand in the killing [and] robbing, . . . we condemn each one of the aforesaid to death . . . wherever they are found. . . . We condemn all the other peasants . . . for giving counsel, assistance, and support to the perpetration of the said crimes . . . [to pay collectively] the quantity of 50,000 pounds in the currency of Barcelona.

To Consider

1. What common concerns and objectives tie the three rebellions together? What makes each one distinctive?

2. What were the social, political, and religious forces that defeated the aims of most lower-class rebels?

3. How much would the social and economic status of Catalan peasants have really changed after the Sentence of Guadalupe?

Sources

a–b. Balivet, Michel. *Islam mystique et revolution armée dans les Balkans ottomans: Vie du chiekh Bedreddin, le "Hallaj des Turcs," 1358/59–1416*. Istanbul: Editions Isis, 1995. Pp. 70–72.
c. Brucker, Gene, ed. *The Society of Renaissance Florence: A Documentary Study*. New York: Harper and Row, 1971. Pp. 236–39.
d. Vicens Vives, Jaume. *Historia de los Remensas (en el siglo XV)*. Barcelona: Vicens Bolsillo, 1978. Pp. 339–49. © Editorial Vicens Vives, S.A., (Barcelona, 1978) Jaume Vicens Vives, Historic de los Remensas (en el siglo XV).

15.3 MUSLIM-CHRISTIAN COMMERCIAL AGREEMENTS

The upheaval associated with the Black Death did not loosen either Western Christian dominance of major maritime trade routes or Muslim control over access to the commodities Western merchants sought. As the following readings reflect, however, the cast of characters did change between 1350 and 1650. The first reading includes some of the commercial privileges that the Mamluk sultan Qaytbay granted to the Republic of Florence in a treaty of 1497. The privileges are often phrased as Florentine requests to which the sultan acceded. The precedent of similar agreements with the Venetians, who continued to be the Mamluks' major Christian trading partner, guided both parties. The second reading is from the trade agreement reached between the Ottoman sultan Ahmed I and the Dutch Republic in 1612. Murad III had extended commercial privileges to another northern European Protestant power—England—in 1580.

a. Mamluk-Florentine Agreement
Arabic • 1497 CE • Cairo

[That] anyone be prohibited from interfering with the Florentine nation in respect of their goods, their merchandise, and their money, their ships and their mariners in a hostile manner, and that they [Florentines] not be held to pay duty on their goods except in accordance with that attested by the established administrative dues in the flourishing treasuries from the days of former rulers. . . .

That when a sale by Muslim merchants of goods such as spices to the Florentine nation takes place the contract between them shall be in the presence of notaries. . . .

The Muslim merchants buy from the aforesaid Florentine merchants articles of their merchandise such as cloth and wool and other things, the purchaser accepting the goods and depositing them in his care— . . . that when a sale takes place . . . [let] it be witnessed by notaries. . . .

It has been mentioned among the privileges of the Venetians that when they have an adjudication, litigation or claim for money or other things, such as a Muslim against one of the Florentine Franks or a Frank against a Muslim, the adjudication should be brought before the noble presence [the sultan] if they are at the noble portals, or to the viceroy or chamberlain or officials of that province, and that none-other than the above-mentioned should adjudicate between them. . . .

That corvettes [small warships], in which there are Turcomans and others lying in wait to commit robbery, emerge from the ports to rob them [Florentines] at sea [The sultan prohibits this]. . . .

That it is among the earlier privileges of the Venetians that from the Frankish nations are some who . . . commit piracy and robbery at sea, capturing Muslims and bringing them to the coasts near Ramla and Acre and attempting to sell them. And the Muslims interfere and compel the community of Venetian merchants to ransom the prisoners, but the offenders are not of their nation. And the noble decrees of former rulers have been issued . . . that when the offender is of the Venetian nation they shall be liable for him, but when the offender is not of their number they shall not be liable for him. [The same for the Florentines]. . . .

The Frankish merchants, such as the Venetians and others, travel continually from land to land and from province to province, and must have provisions, victuals, and drink; but there are some who interfere with them and extort bribes from them. [This is prohibited]. . . .

It is among the privileges of the Venetians that a number of their nation has business in the land of Syria, going from village to village for the purchase of cotton and Ba'albaki cloth,[2] and that they fear for their persons and property from tribesmen and robbers. And they have asked that they be permitted to wear the clothes of Muslims, Mamluk and Bedouin on their journeys, so that there be no temptation to rob them. [Permission granted to the Florentines].

b. Ottoman-Dutch Agreement
Turkish • 1612 CE • Istanbul

The community of merchants of the countries and places belonging to the Dutch Provinces may come and go, buy and sell in our well-guarded dominions. . . .

So long as the Dutch merchants board ships of the enemy of Islam to exercise their own trade they may not be detained on the pretext of being on enemy ships nor their goods be

---

2. Cloth from Ba'albak, in the Biqa' Valley of modern Lebanon.

taken, since they have been doing their own trade and not behaving in a hostile manner on corsair ships. . . .

Cotton, cotton-thread, Morocco leather, beeswax and coarse leather will be sold [to Dutch merchants] for money, as they are sold to the French. . . .

When any persons enter upon a law suit against the [Dutch] consuls appointed for the merchants' affairs . . . their law suits must be heard at our threshold of felicity [sultan's government]. . . .

Their ambassadors and consuls may employ the consular guards they desire and those persons whom they wish to procure . . . as dragomans [interpreters]. . . .

No one may interfere when they [the Dutch] are . . . making wine for their own use in their residences. . . .

When corsairs of Algiers reach Dutch harbors, they must be treated with respect and sold powder, lead, other arms and sail, but when corsairs meet merchants [who are] subjects of the Dutch Republic they may not make prisoners nor rob their possessions. . . .

If merchants, consuls and dragomans of places subject to the Dutch Provinces are engaged in our well-guarded dominions with selling and buying, trade and standing surety and other legal business, they must go to the *cadi* [Islamic magistrate] and have registration or a document made. If a dispute arises later the registration or the document will be taken into consideration and acted upon accordingly. . . .

The Dutch importing into our well-guarded dominions lead, tin, iron, steel and other scrap metal merchandise may not be hindered. According to what is written in the imperial capitulation, 3% . . . may be taken as customs duties and no more may be demanded. . . .

No one may hinder those from the Dutch Provinces . . . who are travelling under safe conduct to Holy Jerusalem. The priests and other persons who are in the Church [of the Holy Sepulchre] . . . may not molest nor interfere. They may not seek a pretext, saying: "you belong to the Lutheran community." They must let him visit the necessary places.

To Consider

1. In what ways were Western Christian merchants operating in Mamluk and Ottoman domains vulnerable, and how did the commercial agreements address these vulnerabilities? Would such protections have been effective?

2. In these trade agreements, did one party, the Muslim or the Christian, have the upper hand?

3. How did sectarian strife among European Christians facilitate and shape the Ottomans' commercial treaty with the Dutch?

Sources

a. Wansbrough, John. "Venice and Florence in the Mamluk Commercial Privileges." *Bulletin of the School of Oriental and African Studies* 28:3 (1965): 509–18. Reproduced with permission.
b. De Groot, A. H. *The Ottoman Empire and the Dutch Republic.* Leiden: Nederlands Historich-Archaeologisch Institut, 1978. Pp. 247–58.

15.4 PRIVATE AND PUBLIC CHARITY

During the sixteenth century, royal and urban governments expanded their efforts to meet the needs of the poor whose distress natural disasters and rapid population growth compounded. Governmental initiatives, however, did not always win universal approval because they threatened to supersede or obscure the charitable acts and intentions of pious individuals. The first reading, a *fatwa* (legal ruling) from the vast collection of *fatwas* compiled by al-Wansharisi (1430–1508), a jurist in Fez, addresses the question of the legitimacy of changing the uses of revenue from private pious endowments (*waqf*). In the second reading, the Ottoman historian Mustafa 'Ali (1541–1600) considers whether the charitable foundations of sultans are publicly or privately funded. In the third reading, the aldermen of Toledo, in a letter to their king, the Holy Roman Emperor Charles V, describe the actions of individual citizens in 1546 to assist starving peasants driven into the city by the floods that had destroyed their crops, while in the fourth, Juan Martínez Siliceo (1486–1547), cardinal and archbishop of Toledo, reflects on the benefits of almsgiving in a letter to a village priest. The final two readings concern the controversy aroused by municipal programs to consolidate small, privately endowed hospitals into larger, publicly managed institutions. The fifth reading includes the justification for the foundation of Toledo's new public begging hospital, which held 330 beds, in 1587—at the same time the city outlawed public begging—while in the sixth, urban representatives in Castile's Cortes (parliament) explain, in 1598, why Madrid's General Hospital was having difficulty attracting donations.

a. Al-Wansharisi
Arabic • late 15ᵗʰ century • Fez

He was asked about some pious endowments donated quite a long time ago in favour of whoever recited the Qur'an by their founders' tombs.[3] . . . And also about some land donated [as a pious endowment] in favour of the poor whose rent was used to purchase clothes which were later distributed among them on the occasion of the Feast of Sacrifice. Now, some people have tampered with the said endowments and want to transfer their revenues to the fortress of Zalía, may God protect it, due to its precarious situation.[4] Is this licit according to the law [*shari'a*] so that both they [the original donors] and those who perpetrated such an act can be worthy of God's favours and rewards?

He replied: The said endowments must not be devoted but to the two aims mentioned above as a donation made in their favour is legal, and God said: "if any man changes it after hearing it the sin shall rest upon those who change it" [Qur'an 2:181].

---

3. "He" is al-Saraqusti (1382–1461), a notable legal scholar from the Nasrid sultanate of Granada.

4. The fortress of Zalía was located near the city of Málaga in the sultanate of Granada.

b. Mustafa 'Ali
Turkish • 1581 CE • Baghdad

As long as the glorious sultans, the Alexander-like kings, had not enriched themselves with the spoils of the Holy War and have not become owners of lands through the gains of campaigns of the Faith, it is not appropriate that they undertake to build soup kitchens for the poor and hospitals ... or, in general, to construct establishments of charity. ... For the Divine Laws do not permit the building of charitable establishments with the means of the public treasury, neither do they allow the foundation of mosques and religious schools that are not needed. Unless a sultan, after conducting a victorious campaign, decides to spend the booty he has acquired on pious deeds rather than on his personal pleasures, and engages to prove this by the erection of [public] buildings.

c. Aldermen of Toledo
Spanish • 1547 CE • Toledo

In the past year of great hardship and sterility, many lords, nobles, clerics and citizens, all in complete conformity and with great humanity and charity, devoted themselves to visiting the beggars and the parish poor, to taking in poor peasants who came to the city, to curing the sick and making hospitals in their own homes, and to giving money to succour all those in need.

d. Archbishop Siliceo
Spanish • 1546 CE • Toledo

You know that the wealth I possess can be called a deposit of the poor vested in me ... [for] in times of such extreme need all that we possess belongs to the poor. ... And do not close the door to strangers who will come by chance, knowing that there are alms, because God gave us the large rents we have for everyone. ... If you knew the spiritual gain we receive from the many paupers who come to us, you would make all haste to receive and welcome them. We do not know, nor begin to know, the mercy that God gives to the rich in offering them an opportunity to use their wealth so well. And I have ordered that my wheat, in all the places I have it, not be sold so that if all of it is necessary to remedy this calamity, I will use all of it.

e. Founders of Toledo's New Beggars' Hospital
Spanish • 1587 CE • Toledo

[The hospital will] free the republic [Toledo] from a great number of dissolute and licentious persons who disturb and infect it, ... a seminary of robbers and dishonest young men and women who deceive and carry after them the children of good and poor parents by their evil words and even more evil deeds, ... and remove the present danger of contagious diseases which are spread and transmitted by these poor people.

f. Representatives in the Cortes
Spanish • 1598 CE • Madrid

When there were many hospitals, persons were moved to leave their fortune for something so holy and necessary, seeing that their spiritual obligations were conserved. . . . By fusing all the hospitals into one, the spiritual obligations of the founders are obscured, which is the reason why those persons who ought to leave their worldly possessions to hospitals leave them for other pious works that do conserve these obligations.

To Consider

1. Were private donors more concerned with the fate of their own souls, or with the needs of the poor?

2. Were the founders of public institutions moved by the same charitable spirit as private donors, or did they have other concerns?

3. What social and economic conditions limited the impact of charity, whether public or private?

Sources

a. García Sanjuán, Alejandro. *Till God Inherits the Earth: Islamic Pious Endowments in al-Andalus (9th-15th Centuries)*. Leiden: Brill, 2007. P. 522. Reproduced with permission of The Licensor through PLSclear.
b. 'Ali, Mustafa. *Mustafa 'Ali's Counsel for Sultans of 1581*. Ed. and trans. Andreas Tietze. Vienna: Osterreichische Akademie der Wissenschaften, 1979. P. 146.
c-f. Martz, Linda. *Poverty and Welfare in Habsburg Spain: The Example of Toledo*. Cambridge: Cambridge University Press, 1983. Pp. 85, 130-31, 142. Reproduced with permission of The Licensor through PLSclear.

15.5 CLIMATE CHANGE, WAR, AND DISCONTENT

For subjects of the Ottoman and Spanish Habsburg empires living during the "little ice age" of the late sixteenth and seventeenth centuries, the stress of having to support their monarchs' military endeavors while dealing with the effects of catastrophic climate events was too much to bear. The readings here testify to the resulting unrest in the very hearts of these empires. The first reading includes the contemporary chronicler Mustafa Selaniki's observations on the impact of drought and military provisioning in Ottoman Anatolia in 1596, at an early stage of the long war the sultans waged against the Austrian Habsburgs in Hungary (1593–1606). One result was the long-lasting Celali Rebellion (1596–1610) of bandit bands composed of soldiers, desperate peasants and townspeople, and *madrasa* graduates. Kayarazıcı, a mercenary commander, formed an entire army of bandits in 1598. He is mentioned in the second reading, the report of the Venetian ambassador in Istanbul, Girolamo Capello. The final three readings concern natural catastrophes in Castile in 1647 and bread riots in Seville in 1652. Of all the realms comprising the Spanish empire, the kingdom of Castile paid the most taxes to a monarchy that had been almost perpetually at war. Like the other revolts erupting in Andalucía from 1648 to 1652, the one in Seville was suppressed.

a. Selaniki
Turkish • 1596 CE • Istanbul

This blessed year, by the wisdom of God . . . there was a shortage of rain. The waters drew back, the wells dried up, and the signs of famine appeared. . . . The cursed speculators of Istanbul began to hide provisions first in one place then another. In this way, food grew scarce and there was nothing left to sow. Once the royal campaign began, fodder and barley became dear. Everyone fell into a panic that winter provisions would go short once the army returned from campaign. . . .

His Majesty the Sultan took it upon himself to . . . embark upon a campaign. When men were sent around to procure sheep from the provinces of Anadolu and Karman [in Anatolia] for the campaign provisions of the men of state, some disgraceful profaner . . . stirred up the rabble and the traitors to his cause. . . . Claiming, "the house of Osman [Ottoman dynasty] has gone the way of injustice and oppression, and I shall bring truth and justice," he took the sheep back from the hands of those gathering them for the campaign.

b. Venetian Ambassador
Italian • 1599 CE • Istanbul

The uprisings and rebellions of Karaman and Anadolu make themselves felt more every day, to judge by the continuous lamentations of the many people who have come from those parts, who cry out in the Divan[5] over the cruelty done them by that Huseyin,[6] who appears to have no other aim but to destroy those provinces altogether; putting all the country to fire and sword and wiping out those who fail to show themselves ready to obey him, and principally the powerful . . . and the literate. . . . To that destruction and suffering is added the uprising of . . . the Scribe [Kayarazıcı], who, accompanied by two thousand arche-busiers [musketeers] and one thousand five hundred horsemen, . . . searches for a way to acquire the spirit of the people, affording them every kindness and granting them liberty to take the goods and treat as they please the great and powerful who depend upon the Sultan.

c. A Madrid Newspaper
Spanish • 1647 CE • Madrid

In Spain, and even they say in all Europe, the era of Noah's flood came again with a venge-ance, because the rains that fell were so heavy and so continuous, and the rivers rose so excessively, that commerce and communication ceased between the cities, towns and vil-lages. Many lives were at risk; many buildings collapsed.

---

5. The Ottoman Imperial Council.
6. A corrupt provincial governor with a private bandit army.

d. Royal Minister to Felipe IV
Spanish • 1647 CE• Madrid

God has chosen to wear out these realms with every calamity—war, famine and plague—each one of which normally suffices to raise great anguish and a sense of panic. . . . The population is very volatile and every day becomes more insolent, which leads to fears of some violence. . . . Hunger respects no one, and so it is necessary to do all we can to help, and to avoid any decision which the people might regard as a burden. . . . There is no shortage of people who blame Your Majesty, saying that he does nothing and that the council is at fault—as if we had any control over the weather!

e. Royal Judge to Felipe IV
Spanish • 1652 CE • Seville

I send this dispatch urgently to inform you of the unfortunate state Seville has been in since half past eight this morning. Because of the bread shortage, the people have rioted, and there are no forces capable of calming them. They have seized the arms that the city had, . . . dividing themselves up into squads throughout the city; it is estimated that there must be as many as ten thousand men who are going around rioting in this way. . . .

And the worst of it is that it [wheat] is lacking throughout the entire district, though all that can be found is being brought in. Until today it had not run out, and when the uprising began there was bread, with much more coming, but when the uproar broke out the bakers became terrorized and did not dare come into work. . . . As I have said, the riot did not occur because of the lack of bread but rather because of the excessive price. Still, I fear that as a result of the tumult there will be neither bread nor wheat, because those who do not live here will flee Seville, and with bread lacking the riot will only get worse, and even greater excesses will be committed. So far no one has been murdered or injured and no houses sacked because we officials have always been in view, scattered among the troops, seeking to calm people.

[The next day] The problems here have been growing excessively, as the number of people in rebellion is now greater and the excesses they are committing are worse, as they are losing all respect. When a large amount of bread was brought in and offered to them at four *cuartos* [copper coins] per pound, the commotion that the bakers had to endure was so great that almost all of it was taken violently . . . and without paying for it, accomplishing all of this and everything else while bearing arms. . . . Not content with this, they violently forced the cardinal and me, as well as some other officials, town governors, and other gentlemen to mount our horses, and they led us throughout the city to hear the announcements, and they had the cancellation of the *millones* [sales tax] and the pardon of any crimes they had committed included in the announcements.

To Consider

I.   In the late sixteenth- and seventeenth-century Mediterranean, what were the economic and social conditions that made it so hard for people to recover from periods of unusually bad weather?

2. Why did people respond to climatic disaster by challenging social superiors and questioning the fitness of their rulers?

3. What could the Ottoman and Spanish imperial governments have done to help their subjects to endure the "little ice age" more easily?

Sources

a–c. White, Sam. *The Climate of Rebellion in the Early Modern Ottoman Empire*. Cambridge: Cambridge University Press, 2012. Pp. 155, 163–64, 173–74. Reproduced with permission of The Licensor through PLSclear.

d. Parker, Geoffrey. *Global Crisis: War, Climate Change, and Catastrophe in the Seventeenth Century.* New Haven: Yale University Press, 2013. Pp. 279–80. Reproduced with permission of The Licensor through PLSclear.

e. Cowans, Jon, ed. *Early Modern Spain: A Documentary History.* Philadelphia: University of Pennsylvania Press, 2003. Pp. 172–74.

BIBLIOGRAPHY

'Ali, Maulana Muhammad. *A Manual of Hadith*. Lahore: Ahmadiyya anjuman ishaati-Islam, 1944.

'Ali, Mustafa. *Mustafa 'Ali's Counsel for Sultans of 1581*. Edited and translated by Andreas Tietze. Vienna: Osterreichische Akademie der Wissenschaften, 1979.

The Alphabet of Galen: Pharmacy from Antiquity to the Middle Ages. Edited and translated by Nicholas Everett. Toronto: University of Toronto Press, 2012.

Anooshahr, Ali. *The Ghazi Sultans and the Frontiers of Islam: A Comparative Study of the Late Medieval and Early Modern Periods*. London: Routledge, 2009.

Aquinas, Thomas. *Summa theologiae*. Translated by the Fathers of the English Dominican Province. https://www.newadvent.org/summa/1002.htm.

Atiya, Aziz Suryal. *Some Egyptian Monasteries According to the Unpublished Ms. Of Al-Shābushtī's "Kitāb Al-Diyārāt."* Cairo: Institut Français d'Archéologie Orientale, 1939.

'Attar, Farid al-Din. *Farid ad-Din 'Attar's Memorial of God's Friends: Lives and Sayings of Sufis*. Translated by Paul Losensky. New York: Paulist Press, 2008.

Ayalon, David. "Mamlukiyyat." *Jerusalem Studies in Arabic and Islam* 2 (1980): 340–49.

El-Azhari, Taef. *Queens, Eunuchs, and Concubines in Islamic History, 661–1257*. Edinburgh: Edinburgh University Press, 2019.

El-Azhary Sonbol, Amira. "A History of Marriage Contracts in Egypt." In *The Islamic Marriage Contract: Case Studies in Islamic Family Law*, edited by Asifa Quraishi and Frank E. Vogel, 87–122. Cambridge, MA: Harvard University Press, 2008.

The Balavariani (Barlaam and Josaphat): A Tale from the Christian East Translated from the Old Georgian. Translated by David Marshall Lang. Berkeley: University of California Press, 1966.

Balivet, Michel. *Islam mystique et revolution armée dans les Balkans ottomans: Vie du chiekh Bedreddin, le "Hallaj des Turcs," 1358/59–1416*. Istanbul: Editions Isis, 1995.

Barber, Malcolm, and A. K. Bate. *Letters from the East: Crusaders, Pilgrims, and Settlers in the 12th–13th Centuries*. Burlington, VT: Ashgate, 2010.

Bede. *Commentary on the Acts of the Apostles*. Translated by Lawrence T. Martin. Kalamazoo, MI: Cistercian Publications, 1989.

Beinart, Haim. *Records of the Trials of the Spanish Inquisition in Ciudad Real*. Vol. 1. Jerusalem: Israel National Academy of Sciences and Humanities, 1974.

Bennison, Amira K. "Almohad Tawḥīd and Its Implications for Religious Difference." *Journal of Medieval Iberian Studies* 2 (2010): 195–216.

Bhayro, Siam. "The Judaeo-Syriac Medical Fragment from the Cairo Genizah: A New Edition and Analysis." In *Collecting Recipes: Byzantine and Jewish Pharmacology in Dialogue,* edited by Lennart Lehmhaus and Matteo Martelli, 225–94. Boston: Walter de Gruyter, 2017.

Blazina Tomic, Zlata, and Vesna Blazina. *Expelling the Plague: The Health Office and the Implementation of Quarantine in Dubrovnik, 1377–1533.* Montreal: MQUP, 2015.

Blöndal, Sigfús. *The Varangians of Byzantium.* Cambridge: Cambridge University Press, 2007.

Blumenthal, Debra. *Enemies and Familiars: Slavery and Mastery in Fifteenth-Century Valencia.* Ithaca: Cornell University Press, 2009.

Bornstein, Daniel. *Life and Death in a Venetian Convent: The Chronicle and Necrology of Corpus Domini, 1395–1436.* Chicago: University of Chicago Press, 2000.

Boruchoff, David A. "Historiography with License: Isabel, the Catholic Monarch, and the Kingdom of God." In *Isabel la Católica, Queen of Castile: Critical Essays,* ed. David A. Boruchoff. New York: Palgrave Macmillan, 2003.

Brucker, Gene, ed. *The Society of Renaissance Florence: A Documentary Study.* New York: Harper and Row, 1971.

Le Calendrier de Cordoue. Edited and translated by Charles Pellat and Reinhart Dozy. Leiden: Brill, 1961.

Cantor, Norman, ed. *The Medieval World, 300–1300.* 2nd ed. New York: Macmillan, 1963.

Catlos, Brian A. "To Catch a Spy: The Case of Zayn Al-Dîn and Ibn Dukhân." *Medieval Encounters* 2 (1996): 99–113.

———. "Who Was Philip of Mahdia and Why Did He Have to Die?" *Mediterranean Chronicle* 1 (2011): 73–103.

Cave, Roy C., and Herbert H. Coulson. *A Source Book for Medieval Economic History.* Milwaukee: Bruce, 1936.

Cervantes Saavedra, Miguel de. *Don Quixote.* Translated by Edith Grossman. New York: Ecco, 2003.

Çelebi, Evliya. *Evliya Çelebi in Albania and Adjacent Regions: Kossovo, Montenegro, Ohrid; The Relevant Sections of the Seyahatname.* Edited and translated by Robert Dankoff and Robert Elsie. Leiden: Brill, 1998.

Chaucer, Geoffrey. *A Treatise on the Astrolabe.* Edited and translated by James E. Morrison in "Chaucer's Astrolabe Treatise." www.chirurgeon.org/files/Chaucer.pdf.

Cobb, Paul M. *The Book of Contemplation: Islam and the Crusades.* New York: Penguin Books, 2008.

Cohen, Jeremy. *Living Letters of the Law: Ideas of the Jew in Medieval Christianity.* Berkeley: University of California Press, 1999.

Colbert, Edward P. *The Martyrs of Córdoba, 850–859: A Study of the Sources.* Washington, DC: Catholic University of America Press, 1961.

Constable, Olivia Remie. *Medieval Iberia: Readings from Christian, Muslim, and Jewish Sources.* 1st ed. Philadelphia: University of Pennsylvania Press, 1997.

———. *Medieval Iberia: Readings from Christian, Muslim, and Jewish Sources.* 2nd ed. Philadelphia: University of Pennsylvania Press, 2012.

Corcos, David. "The Nature of the Almohad Rulers' Treatment of the Jews." *Journal of Medieval Iberian Studies* 2 (2010): 264–65.

Cortes del reinado de Fernando el Católico. Edited by Ernest Belenguer Cebrià. Valencia: Universidad de Valencia, 1972.

Cory, Stephen. *Reviving the Islamic Caliphate in Early Modern Morocco.* Surrey: Ashgate, 2013.

Cowans, Jon, ed. *Early Modern Spain: A Documentary History.* Philadelphia: University of Pennsylvania Press, 2003.

Crowley, Roger. *1453: The Holy War for Constantinople and the Clash of Islam and the West.* New York: Hyperion, 2005.

De Groot, A. H. *The Ottoman Empire and the Dutch Republic.* Leiden: Nederlands Historich-Archaeologisch Institut, 1978.

De Sosa, Antonio. *An Early Modern Dialogue with Islam: Antonio de Sosa's "Topography of Algiers" (1612).* Translated by Diana de Armas Wilson. Notre Dame: University of Notre Dame Press, 2011.

Devereux, Andrew W. "Empire in the Old World: Ferdinand the Catholic and His Aspiration to Universal Empire, 1479–1516." In *In and Out of the Mediterranean: Medieval and Early Modern Iberian Studies,* edited by Michelle M. Hamilton and Nuria Silleras-Fernandez, 119–41. Nashville: Vanderbilt University Press, 2015.

Digenis Akritas, The Two-Blood Border Lord: The Grottaferrata Version. Translated by Denison B. Hull. Athens: Ohio University Press, 1972.

Doussinagüe, José M. *La política internacional de Fernando el Católico.* Madrid: Espasa-Calpe, 1944.

Einhard and Notker the Stammerer. *Two Lives of Charlemagne.* Translated by David Ganz. London: Penguin, 2008.

Fine, Lawrence. *Safed Spirituality: Rules of Mystical Piety, the Beginning of Wisdom.* Mahwah, NJ: Paulist Press, 1983.

Friedman, John, Jean Connell Hoff, and Robert Chazan. *The Trial of the Talmud, Paris, 1240.* Toronto: Pontifical Institute of Mediaeval Studies, 2012.

Friedman, Mordechai A. *Jewish Marriage in Palestine: A Cairo Geniza Study.* 2 vols. Tel Aviv: Jewish Theological Seminary of America, 1981.

Fulcher of Chartres. *Fulcheri Carnotensis Historia Hierosolymitana: 1095–1127.* Edited by Heinrich Hagenmeyer. Heidelberg: C. Winter, 1913.

García Sanjuán, Alejandro. *Till God Inherits the Earth: Islamic Pious Endowments in al-Andalus (9th-15th Centuries).* Leiden: Brill, 2007.

Gardiner, Noah. "Esotericism in a Manuscript Culture: Al-Buni and His Readers through the Mamluk Period." PhD diss., University of Michigan, 2014.

Geanakoplos, Deno John. *Greek Scholars in Venice: Studies in the Dissemination of Greek Learning from Byzantium to Western Europe.* Cambridge, MA: Harvard University Press, 1962.

Geary, Patrick. *Readings in Medieval History.* 5th ed. Toronto: University of Toronto Press, 2015.

Gibbon, Edward. *The History of the Decline and Fall of the Roman Empire.* 6 vols. 1796. London: Peter Fenelon Collier & Sons, 1901.

George-Tvrtković, Rita. *A Christian Pilgrim in Medieval Iraq: Riccoldo da Montecroce's Encounter with Islam.* Turnhout: Brepols Publishers N.V. 2012.

Goitein, S. D. *Letters of Medieval Jewish Traders.* Princeton: Princeton University Press, 1972.

Graf, Tobias P. *The Sultan's Renegades: Christian-European Converts to Islam and the Making of the Ottoman Elite, 1575–1610.* Oxford: Oxford University Press, 2017.

Grant, Edward, ed. *A Sourcebook of Medieval Science.* Cambridge, MA: Harvard University Press, 1974.

Green-Mercado, Mayte. *Visions of Deliverance: Moriscos and the Politics of Prophecy in the Early Modern Mediterranean.* Ithaca: Cornell University Press, 2019.

Griffith, Sidney. "The *Kitab Misbah al-'Aql* of Severus ibn al-Muqaffa: A Profile of the Christian Creed in Arabic in Tenth-Century Egypt." *Medieval Encounters* 2 (1995): 15–41.

Hagler, Aaron M. "The Echoes of Fitna: Developing Historiographical Interpretations of the Battle of Siffin." PhD diss., University of Pennsylvania, 2011.

Halevi, Abraham ben David Ibn Daud. *A Critical Edition With a Translation and Notes of the Book of Tradition: (Sefer ha-Qabbalah).* Edited and translated by Gerson D. Cohen. London: Routledge & K. Paul, 1969.

Al-Harawi, 'Ali ibn Abi Bakr. *A Lonely Wayfarer's Guide to Pilgrimage: 'Alī ibn Abī Bakr Al-Harawī's "Kitāb Al-Ishārāt Ilā Ma'rifat Al-Ziyārāt."* Translated by Josef W. Meri. Princeton, NJ: Darwin Press, 2004.

Hasse, Dag Nikolaus. *Success and Suppression: Arabic Sciences and Philosophy in the Renaissance.* Cambridge, MA: Harvard University Press, 2016.

Heyd, Uriel. *Studies in Old Ottoman Criminal Law.* Oxford: Clarendon Press, 1973.

Hillenbrand, Carole. *The Crusades: Islamic Perspectives.* New York: Routledge, 2000.

Homza, Lu Ann. *The Spanish Inquisition, 1478–1614: An Anthology of Sources.* Indianapolis: Hackett Publishing Company, 2006.

Hunwick, John. "Islamic Law and Polemics over Race and Slavery in North and West Africa (16th-19th Century)." In *Slavery in the Islamic Middle East,* edited by Shaun Marmon, 43–68. Princeton: Markus Wiener Publishers, 1999.

Ibn Buluggin, 'Abd Allah. *The Tibyān: The Memoirs of 'Abd Allah B. Buluggīn, Last Zīrid Amīr of Granada.* Translated by Amin T. Tibi. Leiden: E. J. Brill, 1986.

Ibn Fadlan, Ahmad. *Ibn Fadlan and the Land of Darkness.* Translated by P. Lunde and C. Stone. London: Penguin, 2012.

Ibn Hayyan. *Crónica del califa Abderramán III an-Násir entre los años 912 y 942 = (Al-Muqtabis V).* Translated into Spanish by Maria Jesús Viguera y Federico Corriente. Zaragoza: Anubar, 1981.

Ibn Hazm. *Ring of the Dove: A Treatise on the Art and Practice of Arab Love.* Translated by A. J. Arberry. London: Luzac and Company, 1953. www.muslimphilosophy.com/hazm/dove/ringdove.html#ch8.

Ibn Jubayr. *The Travels of Ibn Jubayr, Being the Chronicles of a Mediaeval Spanish Moor Concerning His Journey to the Egypt of Saladin, the Holy Cities of Arabia, Baghdad the City of the Caliphs, the Latin Kingdom of Jerusalem, and the Norman Kingdom of Sicily.* Translated by Ronald J. C. Broadhurst. London: J. Cape, 1952.

Ibn Munquidh, Usamah. *The Book of Contemplation: Islam and the Crusades.* Translated by Paul M. Cobb. New York: Penguin Books, 2008.

Ibn al-Muqaffa', Sawirus. *History of the Patriarchs of the Egyptian Church: Known as the History of the Holy Church, Volume 2, Part 2, Khaël III–Šenouti II (A.D. 880–1066).* Edited and translated by Aziz Atiyah and Yassa 'Abd al-Masih. Cairo: Institut Français d'Archéologie Orientale, 1948.

Ibn Shaddad, Baha al-Din. *The Rare and Excellent History of Saladin.* Translated by D. S. Richards. Aldershot: Ashgate, 2002.

Ibn Sina. *Poema de la medicina = 'Urǧuza fī 't-tibb.* Edited and translated by Najaty S. Jabary and Pilar Salamanca. Salamanca: Junta de Castilla y León, 1999.

Ibn Taymiyya. *A Muslim Theologian's Response to Christianity: Ibn Taymiyya's al-Jawab al-Sahih.* Edited and translated by Thomas F. Michel, SJ. Delmar, NY: Caravan Books, 1984.

James I of Aragon. *The Book of Deeds of James I of Aragon: A Translation of the Medieval Catalan Llibre Dels Fets.* Translated by Damian J. Smith. Burlington, VT: Ashgate, 2003.

Karamustafa, Ahmed T. *God's Unruly Friends: Dervish Groups in the Islamic Later Middle Period, 1200–1550.* Oxford: One World Publications, 2006.

Khalidi, Tarif, ed. and trans. *The Muslim Jesus: Sayings and Stories in Islamic Literature.* Cambridge, MA: Harvard University Press, 2001.

———, trans. *The Qur'an: A New Translation.* New York: Viking Penguin, 2008.

Khusraw, Nasir-i. *Nāṣer-e Khosraw's Book of Travels (Safarnāma)*. Translated by W. M. Thackston. Albany: Bibliotheca Persica, 1986.

Kimhi, Joseph. *The Book of the Covenant of Joseph Kimḥi*. Translated by Frank Talmage. Toronto: Pontifical Institute of Mediaeval Studies, 1972.

Kinnamos, Ioannes. *Deeds of John and Manuel Comnenus*. Translated by Charles Macy Brand. New York: Columbia University Press, 1976.

Kritovoulos, Michael. *History of Mehmed the Conqueror by Kritovoulos*. Translated by Charles T. Riggs. Princeton: Princeton University Press, 1954.

Krochalis, Jeanne, and Alison Stones. *The Pilgrim's Guide to Santiago de Compostela: A Critical Edition*. London: Harvey Miller Publishers, 1997.

Lamdan, Ruth. *A Separate People: Jewish Women in Palestine, Syria, and Egypt in the Sixteenth Century*. Leiden: Brill, 2000.

Leclercq, Jean, OSB. *The Love of Learning and the Desire for God: A Study of Monastic Culture*. Translated by Catherine Misrahi. New York: Fordham University Press, 1981.

Lewis, Bernard. "An Anti-Jewish Ode: The Qasida of Abu Ishaq against Joseph ibn Nagrella." In *Salo Wittmeier Baron Jubilee Volume on the Occasion of His Eightieth Birthday*, edited by Saul Lieberman, 657–68. Jerusalem: American Academy for Jewish Research, 1975.

The Liber Augustalis, or Constitutions of Melfi, Promulgated by the Emperor Frederick II for the Kingdom of Sicily in 1231. Translated by James M. Powell. Syracuse: Syracuse University Press, 1971.

Little, Donald P. "Coptic Conversion to Islam under the Baḥrī Mamlūks, 692–755/1293–1354." *Bulletin of the School of Oriental and African Studies* 39 (1976): 552–69.

Lopez, Robert S., and Irwin W. Raymond. *Medieval Trade in the Mediterranean World*. New York: Columbia University Press, 2001.

Loyn, Henry R., and John Percival, ed. and trans. *The Reign of Charlemagne: Documents on Carolingian Government and Administration*. New York: St. Martin's Press, 1976.

Machiavelli, Niccolo. *The Prince*. Translated by Robert M Adams. 2nd ed. New York: Norton, 1977.

Maimonides, Moses. *Mishneh Torah: The Laws of a Virgin Maiden*. Translated by Rabbi Eliyahu Touger. New York: Moznaim Publishing, 1995.

Makdisi, George. *The Rise of Colleges: Institutions of Learning in Islam and the West*. Edinburgh: Edinburgh University Press, 1981.

Marco Polo. *Marco Polo. The Description of the World*. Translated by Sharon Kinoshita. Indianapolis: Hackett, 2016.

Martz, Linda. *Poverty and Welfare in Habsburg Spain: The Example of Toledo*. Cambridge: Cambridge University Press, 1983.

Mas Latrie, Louis de. *Traités de paix et de commerce et documents divers concernant les relations des Chrétiens avec les Arabes de l'Afrique septentrionale au moyen-âge*. Paris: Plon, 1866.

Massip i Fonollosa, Jesús, ed. *Costums de Tortosa*. Barcelona: Fundació Noguera, 1996.

McNeill, William H., and Marilyn Robinson Waldman, eds. *The Islamic World*. Chicago: University of Chicago Press, 1973.

Melville, Charles, and Ahmad Ubaydli. *Christians and Moors in Spain*. Vol. 3, *Arabic Sources*. Warminster, Eng.: Aris & Phillips, 1988.

Meyerson, Mark D. *A Jewish Renaissance in Fifteenth-Century Spain*. Princeton: Princeton University Press, 2004.

———. "Slavery and Solidarity: Mudejars and Foreign Muslim Captives in the Kingdom of Valencia." *Medieval Encounters* 2:3 (1996): 286–343.

Modena, Leon. *The Autobiography of a Seventeenth-Century Venetian Rabbi: Leon Modena's Life of Judah*. Translated by Mark R. Cohen. Princeton: Princeton University Press, 1987.

Monroe, James T. *The Shu'ubiyya in Al-Andalus: The Risala of Ibn Garcia and Five Refutations.* Berkeley: University of California Press, 1970.

Morkinskinna: The Earliest Icelandic Chronicle of the Norwegian Kings (1030–1157). Translated by M. Andersson and Kari Ellen Gade. Ithaca: Cornell University Press, 2012.

Muldoon, James. *The Expansion of Europe: The First Phase.* Philadelphia: University of Pennsylvania Press, 1977.

Muntaner, Ramon. *Crònica de Ramon Muntaner.* Edited by Ferran Soldevila and Maria Teresa Ferrer i Mallol. Barcelona: Institut d'Estudis Catalans, 2011.

Mutgé i Vives, Josefina. "Les ordinacions del municipi de Barcelona sobre els esclaus." In *De l'escalvitud a la llibertat: Esclaus i lliberts a l'Edat Mitjana,* edited by Maria Teresa Ferrer i Mallol and Josefina Mutgé i Vives, 245–64. Barcelona: CSIC, 2000.

New Revised Standard Version of the Bible. New York: Oxford University Press, 1989.

Nicolas de Nicolay. *The Nauigations, Peregrinations and Voyages, Made into Turkie by Nicholas Nicholay Daulphinois, Lord of Arfeuile, Chamberlaine and Geographer Ordinarie to the King of Fraunce . . . Translated out of the French by T. Washington the younger.* London: Thomas Dawson for John Stell, 1585.

Nizam al-Mulk. *The Book of Government: Or, Rules for Kings: The Siyar al-muluk or Siyasat-Nama of Nizam Al-Mulk.* Translated by Hubert Darke. Boston: Routledge & Keegan Paul, 1978.

Núñez Muley, Francisco, and Vincent Barletta. *A Memorandum for the President of the Royal Audiencia and Chancery Court of the City and Kingdom of Granada.* Edited and translated by Vincent Barletta. Chicago: University of Chicago Press, 2006.

Odo de Deuil. *De profectione Ludovici VII in Orientem.* Edited and translated by Virginia Gingerick Berry. New York: Columbia University Press, 1948.

Origo, Iris. "The Domestic Enemy: The Eastern Slaves in Tuscany in the Fourteenth and Fifteenth Centuries." *Speculum* 30:3 (1955): 321–66.

Özdemir, Lale. *Ottoman History through the Eyes of Aşıkpaşazade.* Istanbul: The Isis Press, 2013.

Pactum Hlotharii I. In *Monumenta Germanica Historica: Legum sectio II. Capitularia regum Francorum,* vol. 2, ed. Alfred Boretius. Hanover: Bibliopilii Hahniani, 1883.

Palamas, Saint Gregory. *The Triads.* Translated by John Meyendorff. New York: Paulist Press, 1981.

Parker, Geoffrey. *Global Crisis: War, Climate Change, and Catastrophe in the Seventeenth Century.* New Haven: Yale University Press, 2013.

Perho, Irmeli. "The Sultan and the Common People." *Studia Orientalia* 82 (1997): 145–57.

Peter of Les-Vaux-de-Cernay. *The History of the Albigensian Crusade: Peter of Les-Vaux-de-Cernay's Historia Albigensis.* Translated by W. A. Sibley and M. D. Sibley. Woodbridge, UK: Boydell, 1998.

Peters, Edward. *The First Crusade: The Chronicle of Fulcher of Chartres and Other Source Materials.* Philadelphia: University of Pennsylvania Press, 1998.

Petrus Alfonsi. *The Scholar's Guide: A Translation of the Twelfth-Century "Disciplina Clericalis" of Pedro Alfonso.* Translated by Joseph Ramon Jones and John Esten Keller. Toronto: Pontifical Institute of Mediaeval Studies, 1969.

Philippides, Marios, ed. *Mehmed II the Conqueror and the Fall of the Franco-Byzantine Levant to the Ottoman Turks: Some Western Views and Testimonies.* Tempe: Arizona Center for Medieval and Renaissance Studies, 2007.

Phillippides, Marios, and Walter K. Hanak. *The Siege of Constantinople in 1453: Historiography, Topography, and Military Studies.* Farnham: Ashgate, 2011.

Rapoport, Yosef. *Marriage, Money, and Divorce in Medieval Islamic Society.* Cambridge: Cambridge University Press, 2005.

The Rare and Excellent History of Saladin, or, al-Nawādir al-Sulṭāniyya waʾl-Maḥāsin al-Yūsufiyya. Translated by D.S. Richards. Burlington, VT: Ashgate, 2001.

Rehatsek, B., trans. "Book of the King's Son and the Ascetic." *Journal of the Royal Asiatic Society of Great Britain and Ireland,* 1890, 119–55.

Riddle, John M. *Byzantine Commentaries on Dioscorides.* Dumbarton Oaks Papers 38 [Symposium on Byzantine Medicine, ed. John Scarborough]. Washington, DC: Dumbarton Oaks Research Library and Collection, 1985.

Rogers, Mary, and Paola Tinagli. *Women in Italy, 1350–1650: Ideals and Realities; A Sourcebook.* Manchester: Manchester University Press, 2005.

Rubio, Agustin. *Pest Negra, crisis y comportamientos sociales en la España del siglo XIV: La ciudad de Valencia (1348–1401).* Granada: Universidad de Granada, 1979.

Rycaut, Paul. *The Present State of the Greek and Armenian Churches, anno Christi 1678.* London: Printed for John Starkey, 1679.

Sahas, Daniel J. *Icon and Logos: Sources in Eighth-Century Iconoclasm.* Toronto: University of Toronto Press, 1986.

Scholz, Bernhard Walther, and Barbara Rogers, eds. *Carolingian Chronicles: Royal Frankish Annals and Nithard's Histories.* Ann Arbor: University of Michigan Press, 1970.

Shaw, Margaret R.B. *Chronicles of the Crusades.* New York: Penguin, 1963.

Las Siete Partidas. Translated by Samuel Parsons Scott and edited by Robert I. Burns. 5 vols. Chicago: Commerce Clearing House, 1931. Reprint. Philadelphia: University of Pennsylvania Press, 2001.

Skylitzes, John. *A Synopsis of Byzantine History, 811–1057.* Translated by John Wortley. Cambridge: Cambridge University Press, 2011.

The Song of the Cathar Wars: A History of the Albigensian Crusade. Translated by Janet Shirley. Brookfield, VT: Scolar Press, 2001.

Stillman, Norman A. *The Jews of Arab Lands: A History and Source Book.* Philadelphia: Jewish Publication Society of America, 1979.

Stow, Kenneth R. *Alienated Minority: The Jews of Medieval Latin Europe.* Cambridge, MA: Harvard University Press, 1992.

———. *Catholic Thought and Papal Jewry Policy.* New York: Jewish Theological Seminary of America, 1977.

Sturluson. Snorri. *King Harald's Saga: Harald Hardradi of Norway; From Snorri Sturluson's Heimskringla.* Translated by M. Magnusson and H. Pálsson. London: Penguin, 1966.

al-Tabari, Muhammad ibn Jarir. *The Commentary on the Qurʾan.* Translated by J. Cooper, Wilferd Madelung, and Alan Jones. Vol. 1. New York: Oxford University Press 1987–.

al-Tamimi al-Saraqusti Ibn al-Ashtarkuwi, Abu al-Tahir Muhammad Ibn Yusuf. *Al-Maqamat al-luzumiyah by Abū l-Tāhir Muhammad Ibn Yūsuf al-Tamīmī al-Saraqustī Ibn al-Aštarkūwī.* Translated by James T. Monroe. Leiden: Brill, 2002.

Tanner, Norman P., ed. *Decrees of the Ecumenical Councils.* 2 vols. Washington, DC: Georgetown University Press, 1990.

Theophanes the Confessor. *The Chronicle of Theophanes: An English Translation of Anni Mundi 6095–6305 (A.D. 602–813).* Translated by Harry Turtledove. Philadelphia: University of Pennsylvania Press, 1982.

Usque, Samuel. *Consolation for the Tribulations of Israel.* Translated by Martin Cohen. Philadelphia: Jewish Publication Society of America, 1965.

Uzdavinys, Algis. *The Heart of Plotinus.* Bloomington, IN: World Wisdom, 2006.

Verlinden, Charles. *L'esclavage dans l'Europe medievale.* 2 vols. Ghent: University of Ghent, 1955, 1977.

Une version Byzantine du traité sur l'astrolabe du Pseudo-Messahalla. Edited and translated by Anne Tihon, Régine Leurquin, and Claudy Scheuren. Louvain-la-Neuve, Belgium: Bruylant-Academia, 2001.

Vicens Vives, Jaume. *Historia de los Remensas (en el siglo XV).* Barcelona: Vicens Bolsillo, 1978.

Vitry, Jacques de. *Iacobi de Vitriaco . . . Libri duo, quorum prior orientalis, siue Hierosolymitanae.* Douai: Balthazaris Belleri, 1597.

Wakefield, Walter L., and Austin P. Evans. *Heresies of the High Middle Ages: Selected Sources, Translated and Annotated.* New York: Columbia University Press, 1991.

Wansbrough, John. "Venice and Florence in the Mamluk Commercial Privileges." *Bulletin of the School of Oriental and African Studies* 28:3 (1965): 483–523.

Warmstry, Thomas. *The baptized Turk, or, A narrative of the happy conversion of Signior Rigep Dandulo, the onely son of a silk merchant in the Isle of Tzio, from the delusions of that great impostor Mahomet, unto the Christian religion and of his admission unto baptism by Mr. Gunning at Excester-house Chappel the 8th of Novemb., 1657.* London: J. Willliams, T. Garthwait, and Henry Marsh, 1658.

Wasserstein, Abraham, and David Wasserstein. *The Legend of the Septuagint from Classical Antiquity to Today.* Cambridge: Cambridge University Press, 2006.

Watson, Warren. E. *Tricolor and Crescent: France and the Islamic World.* Westport, CT: Praeger, 2002.

Weinberger, Leon J. "Moses Dar'ī, Karaite Poet and Physician." *Jewish Quarterly Review* 84 (1994): 445–83.

Wessell Lightfoot, Dana. *Women, Dowries, and Agency: Marriage in Fifteenth-Century Valencia.* Manchester: Manchester University Press, 2013.

White, Sam. *The Climate of Rebellion in the Early Modern Ottoman Empire.* Cambridge: Cambridge University Press, 2012.

Wickens, G. M. "Al-Jarsifi on Hisba." *Islamic Quarterly* 3 (1956): 176–87.

William of Tyre. *A History of Deeds Done beyond the Sea.* Edited and translated by Emily Atwater Babcock and August C. Krey. New York: Columbia University Press, 1943.

Wolf, Kenneth Baxter. *Conquerors and Chroniclers of Early Medieval Spain.* Liverpool: Liverpool University Press, 1999.

Yarbrough, Luke B. *The Sword of Ambition: Bureaucratic Rivalry in Medieval Egypt.* New York: NYU Press, 2016.

INDEX

Aaron, Halfon: marriage contracts of, 205

Abarca, Pedro: on Fernando II, 155, 156

'Abbasid caliphate: Arabic language in, 113–14; establishment of, 7; Mongol conquest of, 177n1; Persian elite of, 113

Abbey of Longchamp, Louis IX's founding of, 109

'Abd Allah, *amir*, 15

'Abd al-Rahman al-Ghafiqi: Charles Martel's defeat of, 9–12; death of, 10; line of march, 11; spoils taken by, 11

'Abd al-Rahman III al Nasir (Umayyad caliph of al-Andalus): Isma'il ibn Badr's panegyric to, 16; killing of Count Amat, 14; rebellions against, 14; subjugation of Calatayud, 16; Toda of Navarre and, 14–17

abduction, punishment for, 219

Abendu, Mahomet: rights as slave, 181

Abu al-Tufayl, at Battle of Siffin, 8

Abu Bakr Muhammad al-Turtushi, *The Book of New Things*, 104

Abu Hurayrah, *hadiths* of, 54–55

Abu Ishaq ("Mirabussac"), *amir*, 84–85

Abu Ja'far, at Battle of Siffin, 8

Abul Abaz (elephant): death of, 19; gift to Charlemagne, 17–19

Abu Shurayh al-Judhami, at Battle of Siffin, 8

Abu Yaqub Yusuf, Caliph: Almohad Creed of, 80

Abu Zakariyya Yahya (sultan of Tunis): Innocent IV's request to, 78

Acre: fall of (1291), 87–88; Ibn Jubayr's embarkation from, 91, 92; Spring of the Ox, 89

Acts of the Apostles, Bede on, 56

adultery: fines for, 218–19; murder for, 219; in Ottoman law, 218–19

Aeneas Silvius Piccolomini, *A Brief Treatise on the Capture of Constantinople*, 152, 153

Africa, sub-Saharan: enslaved Blacks from, 176, 187–88

Africans, Black: in early modern Mediterranean, 186–88. *See also* Blacks, enslaved

Agli, Aglio degli: letter on his slave, 182

Agobard of Lyon, address to Louis the Pious, 43, 44

Agramun, Garcia d', will of, 182–83

agronomoi (market inspectors), 98

Ahmad ibn Yusuf al-Akhal (Kalbid *amir*), 23n3

Ahmed I (Ottoman sultan), trade agreement with Dutch Republic, 227, 228–29

A'isha (wife of the Prophet), *hadith* on *hajj*, 55

akritai (Byzantine border lords), 123

Albigensians. *See* Cathars

Alexander III, Pope, 77

Alexander VI, Pope: Bull of, 156; on conquest of North Africa, 155, 156

Alexandria: Ibn Jubayr at, 91; library of, 50–51

Alfonsi, Petrus (Moses Sephardi): clerical audience of, 119; conversion to Christianity, 119; *Disciplina Clericalis*, 118–20; on fear, 120; parable of the poet and the hunchback, 119–20

Alfonso III (the Great, ruler of Asturias, Galicia, and León): sovereignty over Iberia, 13

Fortun (Count Amat), al-Nasir's killing of, 16
France, education in, 51–53
Franciscan order, preaching against heresy, 110
Franks: bathing by, 104; Charles Martel's control of, 10; in Crusade-Era Palestine and Syria, 72–74; cultural/economic sphere of, 22; diplomacy with Muslims, 72; Ibn Munqidh on, 73–74; intolerance of Islam, 73–74; Muslims' dining with, 74; pilgrimage to Jerusalem, 92; trade with Muslims, 228
Frederick Barbarossa (Holy Roman Emperor): anti-papal propaganda of, 86
Frederick II (king of Sicily), *Constitutions of Melfi*, 217–18
Frederick III (Holy Roman Emperor), as Last World Emperor, 193
Friars Minor, protection for, 78
Fuentes, Bernat, 96
Fulcher of Chartres: *Chronicle* of, 72–73; on Frankish settlers, 72–73

Gaffarel, Giacomo (Jacques), 170
Galen, tomb of, 90. See also *The Alphabet of Galen*
galleys: of Knights of Malta, 184; slaves on, 186
García Sánchez I (king of Pamplona), 15, 16
gender roles, in marriage, 204
Geniza of Cairo: documents from, 45–46; Jewish communities of, 45–46; Jewish traders' letters from, 31–33; Muslim authorities and, 45–46
Genoa, *societatas maris* of, 95
George (emissary to Charlemagne), 18
Gerard of Cremona, 29; *Life* of, 136–37; scientific translations of, 136–37
ghazis (warriors), Muslim: Osman princes as, 150
ghettos (Renaissance Italy), 163; of Rome, 168, 169; of Venice, 168, 169–70
Gibbon, Edward: on Battle of Tours, 11–12; *History of the Decline and Fall of the Roman Empire*, 11
Giraud de Pipieux, betrayal of Crusaders, 111–12
God: Cathar belief in, 112; dealings with Satan, 57; judgment of Christians, 88; nature of, 49; proof of existence, 140–41; unity of, 141
Gondolphus, Dom, 53
Granada: decree of expulsion (1492), 165; Fernando and Isabel's conquest of, 149;

forced conversion of Muslims in, 155; Moriscos of, 166–67
Granada, *taifa* kingdom of: Jewish administrators of, 66–69; Zirid rule over, 66
Great Khaqan (king of Khazars): capital of, 35; prostration before, 34; tomb of, 34
Greek Orthodox Church, rise of Islam and, 36
Gregorian Reform, 77, 110
Gregory III, Pope, 10
Gregory VII, Pope: trade embargo of, 78
Gregory Palamas, Saint: on the dangers of philosophy, 142–43; defense of Hesychasm, 142; *Triads*, 142–43
Grilion, Benedict, 78
Grillo, Joseph, 170
Gui, Bernardo: *The Techniques of Inquisition into Heretical Depravity*, 112
Guimera, Bernat, 164
Guimera, Violant: inquisitorial prosecution of, 164
gunpowder, 190; Chinese invention of, 200; use in Mediterranean, 200–201

Habsburg empire: challenge of Tudor England to, 159–60; conflict with Ottoman empire, 159, 232–33
hadiths: on charity, 54–55; circulation of, 54; on fasting, 54; *isnads* of, 54
Hadrian, Pope: letter to Charlemagne, 179–80
Hagar (Old Testament), 114
Hagia Sophia, 90, 172; at fall of Constantinople, 153
hagiographies, 120–21
hajj (pilgrimage): *hadith* on, 55; Ibn Jubayr's, 91, 92–93; memoirs of, 88–91
al-Hakim (Fatimid caliph): assassination of, 211, 212; Jews under, 28; as Mahdi, 27; persecution of religious minorities, 45; repression of Christians, 27–28
al-Hakim bi-Amr Allah, divinity for, 131
Hamon, Moses, 200
Harald Hardradi (king of Norway), 23–25; as *Manglavites* to Michael VI, 25; pilgrimage to Jerusalem, 23; in Sarkland, 23–24; Sicilian campaign of, 23, 24; in Varangian guard, 23, 24; verse on, 25
al-Harawi, Ali ibn Abi Bakr: *Lonely Wayfarer's Guide to Pilgrimage*, 89–90
Harold Godwinson (Anglo-Saxon king), 23

Machiavelli, Niccolo: diplomatic missions of, 157; on Fernando II of Aragon, 156–57; on love and fear, 158; on Ottoman government, 158; on the papacy, 158–59; on political pragmatism, 149, 157–59. Works: *Discourses on Livy*, 158–59; *The Prince*, 155, 156–58

madrasas, origins of, 52

madrasa students, in Celali Rebellion, 232

mahdis, predictions of, 193

Maimonides, Moses: *Mishneh Torah*, 217; on rape, 217

Malamati (mystics), 191

al-Malik, Maslama ibn 'Abd: Congregational Mosque of, 90

Maliki school (Islamic jurisprudence), 104

Malik Shah, Sultan, 101

Mamluks: commercial agreements with Florence, 221, 227–28; Coptic Christians under, 163, 171; trade with Venice, 227, 228. *See also* Cairo; Egypt

mandrake, medical use of, 139

Maniakes, George (Byzantine general), 23n3

Manicheism, 110

al-Mansur, Ahmad (Sa'did sultan): Ibn al-Qadi's panegyric of, 150, 151–52; justification of slavery, 187, 188; just rule of, 151–52; as *mujahid*, 150; righteous nature of, 152

Manzil al-Amir (Sicily), tomb of Galen at, 90

al-Maqrizi, on Coptic Christians, 171

Mar Hanna monastery, bathing at, 104

Maria of Antioch (widow of Manuel Komnenos), regency for Alexios, 75

marketplace: *hisba* manuals for, 98–100; morality in, 98–100

marriage: following rape, 218; gender roles in, 204; norms of, 204; Rabi'a al-'Adawiyya on, 214

marriage contracts: assets in, 205; Egyptian, 205, 206

marriage contracts, Christian: failed negotiations for, 206–7

marriage contracts, Jewish: dowries in, 205; *qiddush* (betrothal gift) in, 205; wage labor in, 209

marriage contracts, Muslim: brides' concerns in, 205, 206; domestic service in, 208; widows', 205, 206

Mary, Virgin: intercession for Pelagius, 14

Mary I (queen of England), Catholic restoration under, 160

meala (coin), 106n12

medical fragment, Judeo-Syriac (ca. 1000–1200 CE), 139

medicine, 138–40; Greek basis for, 138; humoral, 138–39

medicine, Islamic: Latin-Christian views of, 198–200; at Ottoman court, 199–200; theoretical/experimental, 199

Mediterranean: foreigners' role in, 22; ordinary peoples' voices, 2; role of women in, 2; textual record of, 1

Mediterranean, 7th–11th centuries: commonalities of, 22, 48; decline of imperial powers, 65; educational institutions of, 48, 51–53; movement within, 22; Viking raids in, 23; women rulers of, 14–17

Mediterranean, 11th–14th centuries: Christian-Muslim relationships in, 74–76, 82, 83; climate change in, 65; collaboration in, 82, 94–96; conflict/competition in, 65, 82; credit in, 94–96; diversity in, 97; ethnicities of, 65; ethno-religious relations of, 82; expansion of Latin Europe into, 85–86; Frank/Muslim coexistence in, 72–74; heresy during, 110–12; hinterlands of, 65; identity in, 113–16; integration of, 97–98; Latin-Byzantine relations in, 74–76; marginalized peoples of, 82; medicine of, 138–40; mercantile powers of, 65; migration in, 65; multiconfessionalism of, 97; negotiation in, 83–85; nonrationalism of, 143–45; porous borders of, 123; religio-cultural spheres of, 97; sectarian violence in, 74–76, 97; social/political integration in, 74, 82

Mediterranean, 14th–17th centuries: climate change in, 232–34; cross-religious boundaries of, 149; gunpowder use in, 200–201; imperial expansion in, 149; natural catastrophes in, 221; northern European commerce during, 221–22; philosophy in, 190; rebellion in, 232, 233; slavery in, 176; social rebellion in, 221, 224–27; warfare in, 232

Mediterranean, Islamic: Crown of Aragon in, 83; women's power in, 211

Mediterranean, Latin: relations with Byzantine Empire, 74–76; slavery in, 181–83

al-Mu'tasim ('Abbasid caliph), slave soldiers of, 177

al-Muzaffar, Badis ibn Habus (king of Granada): slaves of, 66–67

mysticism, 190; Jewish, 191–93; Kabbalah, 191; letter, 144–45; Muslim, 191–93; women's, 204. *See also* spirituality, women's

al-Nabulusi, 'Uthman: *The Sword of Ambition*, 102–3

Nar al-Babunaj synagogue (Khazar Kingdom), 35

al-Nasafi, Umar ibn Muhammad: translation of Qur'an into Persian, 127

Nasir Khusraw, on Fatimid Cairo, 27

Neoplatonism, 48; beauty in, 58–59; unity in, 59

New Testament, Greek, 50

Newton, Isaac: *Mathematical Principles of Natural Philosophy*, 198

Nicolay, Nicolas de: *The Navigations, Peregrinations, and Voyages*, 199–200

Nikephoros Phokas, Emperor: Basil Lakapenos and, 20; cabal against Irene, 211–12

Noale, Franceschina da, 215

nonrationalism, 143–45; medical, 143; in use of Qur'an, 144

Normans, Viking origin of, 23n1

Núñez Muley, Francisco: *Memorandum* of, 166–67

nuns, Venetian: spirituality of, 215

Nusayris (Alawis), 131

Odo of Chateauroux (bishop of Tusculum), letter to Pope Innocent IV, 127–29

Odo of Deuil: chaplaincy to Louis VII, 115; *Journey of Louis VII to the East*, 115

Olaf II (king of Norway), 23

Onneca (mother of Queen Toda), 15

On the Operation and Use of the Astrolabe (Arabic manual), 134

Oppa (bishop of Seville), 14

Order of Saint Claire, Louis IX's founding of, 109

ostrich eggs, trade in, 30n16

Ottoman empire: Christians of, 171–72; commercial agreements with Dutch, 221, 227, 228–29; conflict with Habsburgs, 159, 232–33; conquest of Constantinople, 149, 152–54, 173, 202, 214; defeat of Safavids, 160; expansion of, 149; gunpowder use in, 201; practice of Judaism in, 173; prophecies of triumph, 193–95; Protestant allies of, 149; religious propaganda of, 149; Safavid challenge to, 159; sectarian enemies of, 159–60; Sheykh Bedreddin's rebellion against, 224; taxation in, 221; threat to Italian Peninsula, 157

Ottonians, German, 7

Oviet, Francesc and Maria, 208

Pact of Umar, 27

Palestine, Frankish settlers of, 72–73

papacy: conflict with Eastern Churches, 41; conflict with Latin kings, 77; embargo on trade, 77–78; Gregorian reforms to, 77, 110; on icon veneration, 41; Jewish policy of, 43; Machiavelli on, 158–59; relationship with Carolingian Empire, 41; relations with Byzantine Empire, 36, 41, 77; role in Italian politics, 158–59; temporal power of, 65, 77–79, 102, 159

Papal States, Carolingian Empire and, 36

Parenti, Marco and Alessandra: marriage contract negotiations of, 206–7

patriarchy, women under, 204, 210–11

Paul, Saint, 161

Paulicianism, Armenian, 110

Paul IV, Pope: *Cum nimis absurdum*, 168, 169; institution of Roman ghetto, 168, 170

peasants, Anatolian: in Celali Rebellion, 232

peasants, Spanish: acts of homage, 226; assistance to, 230, 231; tax obligations of, 226–27; uprising in Catalonia, 226–27

Pelagius (Pelayo, ruler of Asturias): divine intercession for, 14; escape from Tariq, 14; rape of sister, 12, 13–14

Peoples of the Book: diversity facing, 82; eligibility for *dhimma*, 104n8; reading of translations, 118; women, 104

Pepin the Short, 10

Peppin III (Carolingian ruler), defeat of Lombards, 41

Pere the Great (ruler of Aragon), 83; on death of al-Mustansir, 84; intervention in Tunis, 84–85

Perfecti (Cathar leaders), 110

Perri, Benedict de, 181–82

Persia, travel memoirs, 88–89
Persian Empire, fall of, 7
Petahyah of Regensburg, travelogue of, 88
Peter, Saint: in *Donation of Constantine*, 41
Peter des Vaux de Cernay, *Albigensian History*, 111–12
Philip Augustus (king of France), 184
Philip of Mahdia: collusion with *'ulama'*, 71; conquest of 'Annaba, 69–70, 71; execution of, 69, 71; feigned Christianity of, 70, 72; Ibn al-Athir on, 71–72; Roger II's anger at, 70–71; trial of, 69–72
philosophy: in 14th–17th century Mediterranean, 190; rationalist, 133
philosophy, Greek: Aristotelian, 142; translations of, 118
phylacteries, 193
physicians, Arab-Muslim, 199
physicians, Jewish, 199; learning of, 200
physics, Aristotelian, 198
Piera, Sister, 215
piety, rulers', 107–10
pilgrimage: bathing during, 104–5; Dutch-Ottoman agreement on, 229; guides to, 88–91; sea travel in, 91–93; Syrian guide to, 89–90
piracy, 176; Jewish traders' losses to, 31; Mamluk-Florentine agreement on, 228
piracy, Muslim: Christian participation in, 77
Pirenne, Henri: "Pirenne Thesis" of, 22
plague: causes of, 222; as divine retribution, 223; economic turmoil during, 224; responses to, 222–24; spiritual measures combatting, 222, 223. *See also* Black Death
Plato, 55n7
Plato of Tivoli, 136
Plotinus: on beauty, 58–59; *Enneads* of, 58; on the One, 59
The Poem of the Cid, 123
Polo, Marco, 89; description of Suzhou, 86–87
polychronia (Byzantine gestures of honor), 115
Pont, Pere de, 209
Porphyrogenita, Zöe, Empress, 23
Portugal: Black slaves of, 176; expansion into West Africa, 186
poverty: amelioration of, 221, 230; Borkluçe's preaching of, 225
Prester John, kingdom of, 86

primary sources, historical, 1–2; reading of, 2
prophecies: crypto-Muslim, 190; of Turkish triumphs, 193–95
Psalm 8 (Hebrew Bible), 48
Pseudo-Justin, *Cohortatio ad Graecos*, 50–51
Ptolemy (king of Egypt), Alexandrian library of, 50–51
Ptolemy, Claudius: *Almagest*, 137; *Tegni*, 136
Puig, Pere de: loan to, 209
Pulgar, Hernando del: on Isabel I, 211, 213
Pullani (Frankish-indigenous people), 106
pyramids, pilgrim narratives of, 90

qadis, Copts, 171
Qalandars: customs of, 191–92; dervishes among, 191
al-Qalanisi, Ibn: on Sitt al-Mulk, 211, 212
Qaytbay (Mamluk sultan): Fernando II's response to, 155; treaty with Republic of Florence (1497), 227–28
qintar (currency), value of, 95n27
qirad, Islamic (trade agreement), 94
qirat (measurement), 138
Qur'an: Arabic language of, 50; first sura of, 49–50; invocation at Battle of Siffin, 8–9; nonrational uses of, 144; recitation at tombs, 230; similities to Hebrew Bible, 49–50; translations of, 127

ra (letter), mystical belief in, 145
Rabi'a al-'Adawiyya: on marriage, 214; mysticism of, 214
Radbert (emissary of Charlemagne), 18
Ragusa (Dubrovnik), plague quarantine in, 222–23
al-Rahman (merchant), 95
Ramadan, 191n1
ransoming, 176; of Muslim captives, 183, 184; slave trade and, 184. *See also* piracy
rape: Maimonides on, 217; marriage following, 218; punishment for, 217–18; untruthful allegations of, 218
rationalism: of Arab science, 133; philosophical, 133
rationalism, European: influence of Almohadism on, 79
rationalism, medieval, 133, 141, 143; in religious truth, 142

shawm (double-reed instrument), 196

al-Shirazi, Abu Ishaq (scholar), 52

shu'ubiyya (anti-Arab literature), 113–14

Sicily, under Ahmad ibn Yusuf al-Akhal, 23n3. *See also* Roger II (king of Sicily)

Siddhartha Gautama, Arabic account of, 121

Siffin, Battle of (657 CE), 8–9; invocation of Qur'an at, 8–9

Sigimund (emissary of Charlemagne), 18

Siliceo, Juan Martínez (archbishop of Toledo): on almsgiving, 230, 231

silk industry: of Suzhou, 87; women in, 207, 208–9

Simhah, Rachel, 169

Simon de Montfort, Cathar Crusade of, 110, 111

Sitt al-'Arab, embroidery of, 207

Sitt al-Mulk: address to Ibn Dawwas, 212; and al-Hakim's assassination, 211, 212; regency for al-Zahir, 27, 211

Skylitzes, John: *Synopsis of Histories*, 20–21, 38–39, 40

slave merchants: Christian, 176; trade in Europe, 179–80

slavery: Barcelona legislation on, 182; Carolingian prohibition of, 176, 179–80; justification for, 187–88; in Latin Mediterranean, 181–83

slaves: children, 177, 178, 187; Christian, 176; of corsairs, 185–86; galley, 186; leasing of, 181–82; legal protections for, 181, 182; life experiences of, 181–83; literacy among, 1; manumission of, 182–83; runaway, 188; women, 182, 187. *See also* Blacks, enslaved

slave soldiers, 176; guarding of jihadist fortresses, 188; janissaries, 178; of Mamluk regime, 177–78; in Morocco, 187, 188; origin of practice, 177

slave trade: Byzantine, 179–80; early medieval Europe and, 179–80; profitability of, 179; ransoming and, 184

social welfare, developing institutions of, 221

societates maris (sea societies): Genoese, 95; for investment, 94

society, Mediterranean: bathing in, 103–7; integration of, 74, 82; literacy in, 1; sexual purity in, 216–19

Solomon (king of Israel), 151

Song Dynasty (China), 87n8

Sosa, Antonio de: *Topography of Algiers*, 184, 185–86

Soul, recognition of beauty, 58

Spain: Arabic learning in, 136; dominance in Italy, 149; expulsion of Jews from, 163–65; resistance to Muslims in, 7

Spanish empire: expansion of, 149, 154–57; natural catastrophes in, 232, 233–34; rebellion in, 234; religious propaganda of, 149; taxation in, 221, 226–27, 234

spirituality, women's, 204, 213–16; nuns', 215. *See also* mysticism

Stamford Bridge, Battle of (1066), 23

Staurakio (eunuch general), 211–12

St. Martin (Tours), Muslim raid on, 9–10

Straery, Guillem, 181

Straery, Jaume, 181

Strozzi, Alexandra, 205

Strozzi, Filippo, 205

Sturlson, Snorri: *King Harald's Saga*, 23–24

Sudan, slavery in, 187–88

Sufis, Muslim: orders of, 191

al-Suhrawardi, Hafs 'Umar: description of the Qalandars, 191

Suhrawardiyya (dervishes), 191

Şukrullah: *Joy of Histories*, 150–51; on Shaykh Bedreddin, 224–25

Suleyman the Magnificent (Ottoman sultan): as messiah, 193; slave soldiers of, 178

Suzhou (China): Marco Polo on, 86–87; silk industry of, 87

Sylvester I, Pope: in *Donation of Constantine*, 41–42

Syr, Sigurd, 23

Syria: Frankish settlers of, 72–74; trade with Venice, 228

Syria-Palestine, Muslim-Christian relations in, 105

al-Tabari, Abu Jaf'ar Muhammad ibn Jarir: *Commentary on the Qur'an*, 57

Tabriz, Shi'i massacres in, 160n9

Taherti clan (Kairouan), correspondence with Tustari clan, 32–33

Talmud: Christian condemnation of, 127–28; French Dominican translators of, 127; Latin-Christian encounters with, 127–30; "Trial of," 107

Tamim ibn Hudhaym, at Battle of Siffin, 8
Tamir, *amir*, 104
Tanagli, Francesco: marriage contract negotiations of, 206–7
al-Tanukhi, Sahnun ibn Sa'id ibn Habib: *Al-Mudawwana*, 188
Tariq ibn Ziyad, 12, 13, 14
tawhid doctrine, of divine unity, 79–80
taxation: in Jerusalem, 46; Ottoman, 221; in Spanish empire, 221, 226–27
taxation, Fatimid: poll tax (*jizya*), 45, 46
tax collectors, corrupt, 101
technology: medieval, 133; military, 190, 201
Templars, respect for Islam, 73–74
Temple Mount (Jerusalem), 56n12; al-Aqsa Mosque, 73
Tetaldi, Giacomo: *Information . . . Regarding the Taking of Constantinople by the Turkish Emperor*, 202
textile industry and trade, 32; women in, 207
texts, Mediterranean: production of, 3; translation of, 3
texts, sacred: authority of, 48; commentaries on, 48, 55–57; commonalities in, 49; education in, 51–53; hagiographies, 120–21; interreligious debates over, 118, 128; levels of meaning in, 51; memorization of, 51; translations of, 48, 118. *See also* Bible; scriptures
Theodora, Empress: resistance to icons, 39
Theokiste (mother of Theodora), icon veneration of, 39
Theophanes (monk): *Chronicle*, 38, 39; at court of Leo IV, 38; on Empress Irene, 211
Theophilus, Emperor: iconoclasm of, 39, 40
theriac (medical compound), 199
Thjódólfr Arnórsson, 25
Three Indies (kingdom of Prester John), 86
Timothy (patriarch of Jerusalem), embassy to Charlemagne, 18
Timur-Lenk (Tamurlane), Safavid resistance to, 159
Toda (queen of Navarre): and 'Abd al-Rahman III, 14–17; hostages of, 15
Toledo: beggars' hospital, 230, 231; school of translation at, 68
Toledo, aldermen of: on assistance to peasants, 230, 231
Torah, Arabic translation of, 127

Torres, Juan de: testimony at Inquisition, 164–65
Tortosa, baths of, 106
Tours, Battle of (732 CE), 9–12; Chronicle of 754 on, 10–11; Gibbon on, 11–12; Muslim account of, 11
trade, maritime: Western Christian dominance of, 227
trade, Mediterranean: challenges of, 22; *commende* (commercial contracts) in, 94, 95–96; credit in, 94–96; following fall of Roman Empire, 22; with "Lands Beyond the Sea," 96n30; oaths in, 94–95; papal embargo on, 77–78; *societates maris* (sea societies) for, 94
traders, Jewish: letters from Cairo Geniza, 31–33; losses to pirates, 31. *See also* commerce; merchants
translations: into Arabic, 118, 121; from Greek, 118; by missionaries, 127; of sacred texts, 48, 50, 51, 118
travel, Mediterranean: across borders, 123. *See also* pilgrimage; sea travel
travelogues, Jewish, 88
Treves family (Venice), 169
Trinity: Jewish objections to, 129; Muslim objections to, 131
al-Tujibi, Muhammad ibn Hisham (governor of Zaragoza), 15
Tunis: Pere the Great's intervention in, 84–85; tribute to Crown of Aragon, 84
al-Tusi, al-Hasan (Nizam al-Mulk): *The Manner of Kings*, 101
al-Tusi, Nasir al-Din: Tusi couples of, 198
al-Tustari, Abu Nasr Fadl: Rabbanites' petition to, 45, 46
al-Tustari, Sa'd Ibrahim, 45
Tustari clan (Fustat), correspondence with Taherti clan, 32–33
Tyre (Lebanon), Jewish community of, 205
Tzimiskes, John: assassination of Nikephoros, 20; Basil Lakapenos and, 20–21; campaign against Hagarenese, 20; poisoning of, 19, 21

'ulamas' (learned men): Copts, 171; *fatwas* of, 160
Umayyad Caliphates, establishment of, 7. *See also* Córdoba, Umayyad

unity: of God, 141; in Neoplatonism, 59

Usque, Samuel: *Consolation for the Tribulations of Israel*, 173, 174

'Uthman ibn 'Affan, Caliph, murder of, 8

Valencia: Conversos of, 214, 215–16; expulsion of Moriscos from, 167–68; Inquisition at, 164; Morisco population of, 166; response to plague in, 222, 223

Valla, Lorenzo: on *Donation of Constantine*, 41

Varangian guard, Harald Hardradi in, 23, 24

Venetians, expulsion from Constantinople, 75

Venice: anti-slavery treaty of, 179, 180; Jewish ghetto of, 168, 169–70; silk industry of, 207; trade with Mamluks, 227, 228; trade with Muslims, 77–78; trade with Syria, 228

viarii (urban officials), 98

Vikings, raids on Mediterranean, 23

violence: anti-Jewish (1391), 209n5; anti-Latin, 74–75

Virgil: commentaries on, 55; teaching of, 53

Vital, Hayyim: *Eight Gates*, 192–93

Vladislav I (king of Hungary), Murad's defeat of, 150n3

Vratislav, Václav, of Mitrovice: *Adventures of Baron Wenceslaus Wratislaw of Mitrowice*, 196–97

Vulgate, Latin, 51, 129. *See also* Bible; scriptures; texts, sacred

al-Wansharisi: *fatwa* on private charity, 230

waqf (pious endowments), 230

warfare: effect of climate change on, 232; technology of, 190, 201. *See also* slave soldiers

Warmstry, Thomas: *The Baptized Turk*, 197

Warwick, Philip, 197

al-Wathiq, Yahya: control of Tunis, 85n4

wazirs, duties of, 101

the West, Latin: barbarian kingdoms of, 7; clerical administrators of, 19; *compangnie* (trade companies) of, 94; expansion into Mediterranean, 85–86; papal/royal power in, 41; royal women of, 211

wet nurses, 208, 210

Wickens, G. M., 100n3

widows, Jewish: money-lenders, 209

widows, Muslim: marriage contracts of, 205, 206

William III (king of Sicily), aid to shipwreck victims, 93

William of Ockham, 142

William of Tudela, *Song of the Crusade*, 110–11

William of Tyre, *Deeds Done beyond the Sea*, 75–76

wine, Jewish: Christian prohibition on, 44

wives: economic protections for, 204; sexual purity of, 216–19. *See also* widows; women

wives, Jewish: money-lenders, 207–8; wage labor by, 209

wives, Muslim: money-lenders, 207–8; wage labor of, 208

women, 2; adulterous, 218–19; and conquest of al-Andalus, 12–14; Conversos, 215–16; in domestic service, 207, 208; in the economy, 207–10; institutions structuring, 204; mysticism of, 204; in patriarchal society, 204; during plague, 223; political power of, 210–13; rulers, 14–17; sexual purity of, 216–19; in silk industry, 207, 208–9; spirituality of, 204, 213–16. *See also* widows; wives

women, Byzantine: political power of, 204

women, Greek: marriage to Muslims, 171–72

women, Morisco: face coverings of, 167

women, royal: of Latin West, 211; political influence of, 204, 210–11. *See also* Irene, Empress

women, slave, 187; manumission for sex, 182

Yaqub b. Killis (Fatimid wazir), satiric verse on, 26

Yazid II, 39

Yuhanna (Christian merchant), correspondence of, 31

al-Zahir (Fatimid caliph), Christians under, 27–28

Zahirite school (Islamic jurisprudence), 60

Zalía, fortress of: endowments held at, 230

Zimra, David Abi, 208

Zirids, rule over *taifa* kingdom of Granada, 66

Zlatitsa, Battle of (1443), 150n2

Founded in 1893,
UNIVERSITY OF CALIFORNIA PRESS
publishes bold, progressive books and journals
on topics in the arts, humanities, social sciences,
and natural sciences—with a focus on social
justice issues—that inspire thought and action
among readers worldwide.

The UC PRESS FOUNDATION
raises funds to uphold the press's vital role
as an independent, nonprofit publisher, and
receives philanthropic support from a wide
range of individuals and institutions—and from
committed readers like you. To learn more, visit
ucpress.edu/supportus.